To: TOM

1-17-19

IN THE LAND OF THE BEAR

DANGER AND ADVENTURE HUNTING BROWN BEARS IN RUSSIA'S FORBIDDING SIBERIA

by Denny Geurink

TARGET COMMUNICATIONS OUTDOOR BOOKS LLC
10459 N. Wauwatosa Rd.
Mequon, WI 53097
www.targetcommbooks.com

ISBN: 978-0-913305-17-1
Library of Congress Control Number: 2017930584

Illustrator: A. N. Hitarman

DEDICATION

This book is dedicated to the men and women who were brave enough to accompany me on my journeys to the far ends of Russia. It was their spirit of adventure and penchant for exploration that made these trips and, in turn, this book, possible.

This book also is dedicated to the hardworking outfitters, guides, interpreters, and cooks who helped make our wilderness camps warm and comfortable in many inhospitable places.

CONTENTS

ACKNOWLEDGEMENTS

Putting together a book like this is an enormous project and takes the help of many people.

First, I thank my friend and outfitter, Dmitri Sikorski, who helped gather much of the historical data about the former Soviet Union and Russia that appears in this book. Dmitri also contributed a number of photos and added his recollections and perspective of my early years in Russia.

I thank Bob Coker for allowing me to use the story he wrote about the harrowing trip he took to Russia on his own in 1996. It reveals what can sometimes happen if you deal directly with the Russians.

I also thank Tom Huggler, Tom Thompson, Noel Hilty, and my wife Connie for sharing their stories and letting the stories be used in this book.

I'm grateful to all the hunters who provided photos from their trips, such as Jim McDivitt, Terry Geurink, David Moore, Ken Horm, Michael Silin, Michael Shutt, and others.

I thank Connie for her help with typing, editing, and research, and my daughter Kelli for her editing help.

Most of all, I'd like to thank the many hunters, friends and family who encouraged me to write this book. Every time I told them a story about what happened on a trip they would say, "You've got to be kidding! That's incredible! Denny, you need to write a book."

So I did. Here it is. Hope you enjoy it.

FOREWARD

ONE OF THE FEW things I remember about the Soviet Union from my childhood is Nikita Khrushchev pounding his shoe on a table at a United Nations General Assembly meeting in 1960.

I don't remember why he was beating the table, but I do remember the former Soviet leader as being something short of a real charmer. He's the same guy who told the world his country would bury ours ... not exactly an open invitation to Americans to stop by for a visit. Throw in the fear of Russia generated on our side of the pond when President Reagan referred to the Soviet Union as the "Evil Empire" and you can understand my reaction to an invitation I received in August, 1991, to be part of an exploratory safari to the Land of the Bear and then write a story or stories about it.

So began one of the most exciting chapters in my life. This country boy from Allendale, Michigan, was about to have his world changed. That pioneering visit took place between the coup and the collapse. It was still the Soviet Union when we arrived in Moscow in 1991, and I was one of the first Americans to get up-close-and-personal with this vast, secretive country. This was a land that Americans had heard only scary stories about, a nation and a people judged to be enemies.

After returning from that journey, I wrote a number of stories for various newspapers and magazines. Many of my friends and colleagues from throughout the United States interviewed me for stories they wanted to write for their newspapers and magazines. As far as we knew, I was the first outdoor writer invited to the Soviet Union. There was high interest in what I did, what I thought, and how easy -- or how difficult -- the trip was. Endless questions.

It was a special time in history. The world as we knew it was changing. Even the Berlin Wall came tumbling down.

Stories of my historical trip were highlighted by my colleagues in articles written for the Denver Post, the Chicago Tribune, the Detroit News, the Cleveland Plain Dealer, the Grand Rapids Press, and many other daily newspapers. Those stories spawned a huge interest in Russia, so much interest my phone began ringing off the hook! I received more than 400 calls in one week. My wife finally took the phone off the hook so we could get some sleep.

In the ensuing years, I had a chance to explore new lands, learn new customs and traditions, and study a culture few people knew anything about. I've met many wonderful people, including a number of dignitaries, such as the President of Kalmykia, the Vice President of Crimea, the ministers of various conservation and forestry departments, and even a colonel in the Russian army.

I also met everyday people from all walks of life -- guides, cooks, hotel clerks, taxi drivers, teachers, professors, outfitters, and interpreters. I've had the great privilege of sharing many a wilderness campfire with the Eveny, an Inuit-like people inhabiting the wild regions of Siberia.

I learned from my new Russian friends what the Soviet Union was like before the collapse. I'll never forget when one of them told me his wife would get up at 6 a.m. to stand in line at the store, which opened at 8 a.m., to buy bread. We heard a lot about the bread shortages in the Soviet Union, but this put it in perspective.

"Denny, if you ever go back, I'd love to go with you," was what I often heard. I did want to go back, because I enjoyed myself and liked the Russian people.

After a few more trips and with interest still growing, I decided there might be some money to be made from this burgeoning desire to visit Russia. I contacted Dmitri Sikorski, the outfitter who set up my first trip, and asked him if he wanted to get into the tourism business.

"Yes, I do," he said.

I started a company called Denny Geurink's Outdoor Adventures and began taking people to Russia regularly.

Over those years, I shared campfires with wonderful people from the United States and Canada. Among them, prominent people such as Apollo 9 astronaut Jim McDivitt and his friend Earl O'Loughlin, a four-star Air Force general who flew spy plane missions over the Soviet Union during the Cold War. Jim and Earl took two trips with me.

During the 20-plus years I outfitted, I made more than 50 trips to Russia. I took hundreds of clients with me, many of them more than once. One has been there nine times. Most trips have been more than a month long, and some have been almost three months long. (For me, not my clients. I stayed in Russia while my clients shuttled in and out.) This means I've spent a lot of time in small trapper's cabins and tents in the middle of Siberia, miles away from civilization, showers, electricity, and flush toilets.

This book is about those many journeys to the Land of the Bear. It's not a book about just hunting or fishing; it's as much about the people, the food, the land, the impressions, adventures, and excitement of trekking through the Siberian wilderness. Many of the stories were written shortly after they happened, so they give you my impressions of that particular time in Russia politically.

A number of stories were written with the help of friends and clients. They give you an insight into their impressions when they visited this wild land.

Some stories come from the Russian people themselves. They reveal the harsh reality of living in this wilderness called Siberia. One of the most touching is about a teenage girl who calls her mother on a cell phone to say good bye ... as she is being killed and eaten by a bear.

So pull up a log, sit close to the warmth of a Siberian

campfire and, as one of my Eveny guides once told me, "listen to what the flames tell you about the great adventures that lurk in the wilderness around you."

CHAPTER 1

JOURNEY TO THE EVIL EMPIRE

WHAT'S THE WILDEST, MOST OUTRAGEOUS adventure you can imagine? Really wild! Can you top road hunting from a Russian army tank in Siberia? How about stalking red stag with the KGB on a Soviet naval base a few miles from where Gorbachev had been placed under house arrest a few months earlier? How about sharing vodka toasts with the Vice President of Crimea?

That's what I did. If you have trouble believing it, you know how I felt while it was happening. It began in August, 1991, when I received a call from Bob Knoop, a booking agent in Dearborn, Michigan. He wanted to know if I would be interested in joining him and a few other guys on a trip in September to the Soviet Union to go big game hunting. I thought he was pulling my leg.

"Sure, and then you can come along with me on an exploratory trip to the moon," I said, chuckling.

"No, I'm serious," Knoop said.

"A hunting trip to the Soviet Union?"

"Yes," he answered. "Are you interested?"

Does a bear...?

Upon further questioning, I learned that Knoop was working with the Russians to set up this trip via a company called CMI International. The people at CMI had been collaborating with the Russians on a mining project when talk of big game hunting came up. The Russians were interested in tourism. This was the era of Glasnost (open discussion of political and social issues) and Perestroika (restructuring of the economic and political system). They wanted to set up a hunt and have an American writer see what they had to offer.

Knoop had read my work in *Field & Stream* (I was a regional editor) and thought I'd be a good fit. Thus the call. The clincher was when Knoop said the trip would not cost me anything. They were planning to give me the trip in hopes of generating publicity for this new hunting frontier. The price certainly was right.

Preparations for the trip ran smoothly until August 19, 1991, when my wife came into the bedroom at 7 a.m. and said, "You'd better get up and turn on the TV. I just heard on the radio there was a coup in Russia."

"A COUP?" I vaulted from the bed. "I get a chance to go to Russia and they decide to have a coup! You're kidding?"

Unfortunately, she wasn't kidding. The early news reports were saying that Gorbachev was "too ill" to continue in his post as president of the Soviet Union. A group of new leaders was taking over.

It wasn't long before the truth came out. The Communist Party hierarchy didn't like the direction Gorbachev was taking the country. All this talk of Glasnost and Perestroika -- and exploratory hunting trips -- wasn't sitting well with them. In reality, Gorbachev had been placed under house arrest in a resort area near the Black Sea.

When we inquired about the status of the trip, we were told we were still welcome, but we weren't feeling that welcome. We didn't want to jump into the middle of a political crisis. If Mr. Glasnost wasn't going to be around, we weren't sure we were interested.

We felt much better about the situation several days

later when the coup failed. The hunt was on.

Unfortunately, the instability knocked our departure date back to September 27. This meant the brown bears we hoped to hunt might already be denned by the time we got to camp in early October. Also, wild boar would be more difficult to hunt with crops out of the fields. We would still have moose, red stag, roe deer, and plenty of birds to chase. Plus, plans allowed for a day in Moscow and Leningrad (now St. Petersburg). That was good enough for me.

The big day finally arrived. After a short connecting flight from Grand Rapids, Michigan, to New York, we found ourselves aboard a 747 heading for Moscow. This was my first trip overseas. We were about half way across the Atlantic before reality began to sink in. I was on my way to Russia! Unbelievable!

Making the trip with me, along with Knoop, were Ed Stone, a booking agent from Grand Rapids, Michigan, and Terry Geurink, a cousin from Wyoming, Michigan. I had worked out an arrangement with CMI for Terry to come along as a photography and videography aide to document this historic trip.

We met Phil Belsito, a vice president with CMI, at the airport in New York. On board the plane we met John Hodge, Executive Vice President at CMI, and Lance Parker, a client of CMI. Everyone was pumped. We chattered excitedly the entire flight.

What had started out as a hunting expedition in the U.S. quickly turned into an outright adventure the minute the wheels of Pan Am Flight 30 hit the runway in Moscow. It took a minute for reality to sink in as we taxied down the runway to the terminal. We were surprised by the dark and dreary appearance of the terminal compared to airport terminals in the United States. Not much lighting, no little shops, eateries or stands. The terminal's interior reminded me of the inside of a storage shed.

We arrived in Moscow at 9:30 a.m. Saturday, the 28th.

Dmitri Sikorski, a tall man in his late twenties and a CMI contact in Russia, met us at the airport. I was surprised by how well he spoke English. Many people who learn English as a second language have quite an accent, but he had very little. He spoke American English, not British English, as most of our interpreters later on did. He had learned the language on his own, not in a formal program at a school. Dmitri said he would be our interpreter and tour guide for the next two weeks. He had made all the arrangements for our in-country travel, hotels, and stays at the hunting camps.

One thing I learned immediately was that Dmitri was from the Ukraine. "I'm not a Russian," he corrected when I introduced him to the rest of our crew, "I'm Ukrainian."

It's a distinction people from the Ukraine and other Soviet Bloc countries repeatedly pointed out. If they were from a Soviet Bloc country like Romania, Czechoslovakia or the Ukraine, and not from Russia, they didn't want to be called Russians. In fact, they even seemed a bit offended by it.

I asked Dmitri why the big fuss? "In the U.S. we are from different states but refer to ourselves as Americans. Why do people from the countries who joined the Soviet Union not want to be called Russians?"

"There's a big difference in the way the states in America joined the union and the way the states of the Soviet Union joined," Dmitri pointed out. "In the U.S., the states all petitioned to become part of the union. We didn't petition to become part of the Soviet Union. We were annexed."

Yes, you could say that is a big difference. Just one of the many things we all learned about the former Soviet Union and Russia on this trip.

Before leaving for Russia, I had asked Belsito if there was anything special I should take on the trip to make things easier and more comfortable. I was told to take toilet paper and a carton of Marlboro cigarettes.

"Toilet paper and cigarettes? Why?"

"The toilet paper there is like recycled sandpaper," Belsito told me. "You might want to take your own. All Russians smoke, but their cigarettes are really bad. They love our Marlboros, but they can't buy Marlboros over the counter in Russia. They buy them on the black market, where they are really expensive. A pack of Marlboros will grease a lot of wheels in Russia."

He was spot on. After retrieving our baggage and meeting Dmitri, we got in line to go through customs.

While in line, I overheard the customs agent ask the guy in front of me -- somebody from England or Germany, I believe -- if he had any cigarettes. He said he didn't.

The customs agent took his passport, visa and customs declaration and scrutinized them thoroughly. He asked a lot of questions in broken English and scribbled and checked and putzed for five minutes before finally clearing the guy.

By the time I shuffled up to the window, I had already fished a pack of Marlboros from my carry-on bag. I could see what was happening here.

"Do you have any cigarettes?," the agent asked as I stepped to the booth.

"Yes, I do," I said with a big smile, handing him a fresh, crisp pack of Marlboros. He took the cigarettes, stashed them in a corner of the booth, promptly stamped all my papers and handed them back to me. Then he said, with a wide grin, "Welcome to Russia."

Belsito was right; a pack of Marlboros will grease a lot of wheels in Russia. Cigarettes in hand, we hustled through customs and headed for a big van Dmitri had waiting for us outside the terminal.

The ride through downtown Moscow to the hotel was like traveling through a time warp. The buildings seemed

100 years old and were run-down and dirty. The hotel was old and run-down as well. Everything was dull, dreary and colorless; the check-in process was long and tedious. The clerks in the hotel spoke no English; Dmitri had to translate everything. An American on his own here would quickly be snarled in paperwork and misunderstandings.

After checking into a hotel and getting something to eat (an adventure in itself, which will be detailed in a later chapter), we caught a cab and headed to Red Square.

A visit to this iconic Russian landmark was high on everyone's priority list. Unlike the rest of the city, Red Square is ornate and steeped in tradition. It was by far the most colorful place we visited in Moscow. One of the highlights of our visit was watching the changing of the guard at Lenin's tomb.

Never dreamed I'd ever walk around Red Square! I saw it on TV as a kid, with all its pomp and pageantry during the country's May Day celebrations. Long lines of soldiers, tanks, anti-aircraft missiles, and other military hardware passed in front of Khrushchev as he briskly saluted them. Now I was standing where the missiles went through.

The square seemed to be filled with people. Policemen were everywhere. So were army personnel and tanks, a definite holdover from the recent coup. Wreaths of flowers were stacked on the corners where people had been killed during demonstrations against the communist-led coup. We were standing in the middle of a titanic chapter in history!

We encountered hustlers trying to sell us everything from Soviet military watches and uniforms to "Gorby" dolls. We also soon discovered the American dollar is highly coveted. We were offered 35 rubles for one dollar, the black market price.

The next morning we caught a flight out of Moscow to Sverdlovsk in western Siberia. The flight was an adventure in itself. First, the airplane we flew on wasn't exactly the latest model off the Aeroflot assembly line. Second, the tires on the plane were showing wear and tear. I don't know how many plies an airplane tire is supposed to have, but at least two were showing. This made us a little nervous.

• *Our travels through the Soviet Union were done on very old, small prop planes with nearly-bald tires. (Denny Geurink photo)*

The flight attendants were curt and cold. Not much smiling or "How can we make your flight more comfortable?" attitude. When the plane touched down at Koltsovo airport, all the Russians began clapping. We wondered if this meant we were lucky to have made it. Looking out the windows of the plane and seeing nearly a dozen wrecked airplanes bulldozed off the runway didn't do anything to allay this suspicion.

Later we learned the Russians and people in many other European countries like to give the flight crew a round of applause upon landing as thanks for a good trip. That was a new one on us.

When we asked about the wrecked airplanes lining the runway, we were told that when a flight comes into this part of Siberia it sometimes encounters bad weather, with big snow drifts and ice on the runway. Because the airport is in such an isolated part of the world, there is nowhere else to divert the flight to, so they just land and hit the snowdrifts or skid off the runway. If the repairs are more than the plane is worth, they simply bulldoze it to the side and use it for spare parts.

When we tried to take pictures of the wrecks, we were told to put our cameras away.

Dmitri told us that Sverdlovsk is the unofficial capital of Siberia, which starts east of the Ural Mountains. Boris Yeltsin got his start here as a big shot in the Communist Party. Yeltsin was the communist boss of the Sverdlovsk region until 1985. This place was hard-core pro-Soviet, so it is ironical that Yeltsin had been the leader of the resistance movement against the communist coup, just a few weeks earlier in Moscow.

Dmitri also told us that President Franklin D. Roosevelt had reportedly stopped here on his way home from the 1943 Tehran Conference, where he met with Churchill and Stalin to discuss the reconstruction of post-war Europe. We were once again smack in the middle of an area of historical significance. That fact was not lost on any of us.

After deplaning and gathering our gear, we jumped into a couple of waiting army jeeps and took a long, bumpy ride through the forest to camp. We were amazed to see that most of the people here were living in log cabins. It was like stumbling onto a set of the Little House on the Prairie TV show. We wouldn't have been surprised to see Laura Ingalls Wilder walk around the corner of one of these log homes.

We arrived at our hunting lodge late that night and fell exhausted into bed. The following morning, after a breakfast of bear meat and noodles, the guides told us to load up and get ready to go hunting.

They didn't have to tell us twice. We were pumped and ready for the hunt to begin. We grabbed our gear and headed outside to where the jeeps we had traveled to camp in the previous evening were parked. As I opened the door to one of the jeeps to climb in, Dmitri said, "No, no. Over there. Load up over there." He was pointing to an old, stripped down army personnel carrier parked in front of the lodge.

"That?," I asked. "We're going hunting in that thing? You're kidding!"

"Yes, that thing," Dmitri said, chuckling.

Must be they are going to take us out in the tank and drop us off somewhere, I thought to myself as we climbed aboard. I soon found that wasn't the plan.

"They're taking us to the hunting area in this thing?," I asked Dmitri, as the tank rumbled out of the yard.

"No, you are going to hunt from the tank," Dmitri grinned. "What do you think of that?"

Hunt from a tank? That's when it struck me. We were heading out to do some road hunting Russian style.

"Hunt what?," I asked, still a bit in shock. "If something runs across the trail, shoot it," Dmitri instructed.

"You're kidding?," I shot back, again in disbelief. "You're saying the deal is ... if it's brown, it's down, and if it flies, it dies."

"Yes. Real Russian hunting," Dmitri chuckled.

I sure hope there aren't any skunks or opossums around here, I mumbled to myself as we rumbled out of the yard and into the woods. 'Cause I know whatever we shoot, we're going to eat. And what about road kill?

"I can't believe I am actually riding a Russian tank," I shouted to Terry over the roar of the engine as we clunked through the forest. "I figured the only time I'd ever see one would be in a Vietnamese rice paddy."

• *Road hunting Russian style! This is the decommissioned tank the Russians wanted us to hunt from. (Denny Geurink photo)*

We soon learned why the tank was used; the roads were rutted and extremely muddy, not negotiable by truck or jeep. The tank even got stuck a couple of times.

The ride proved to be a thrill. Everyone should try it ... once. It makes the Demon Drop at Cedar Point look like a kiddy car ride. Going 25-30 miles an hour down muddy trails and through the woods, knocking down trees and careening off old stumps, was an experience. We hung on for dear life.

We didn't shoot anything from the tank. No surprise. It made so much noise roaring through the woods it scared everything away long before we could get close to it. I thought the Russians were just taking us on a joy ride to see the countryside on our first day in camp, and, just maybe, to see if they could scare us a bit. I have to admit, it was exciting and I will never forget it.

That evening, Boris Shiryaiev, one of our guides, asked me if I wanted to hunt moose. I explained to him, through Dmitri, that while I had enjoyed the tank ride a bit earlier, as an editor for a large outdoor magazine, I'd have difficulty selling a hunting story that involved shooting game from the front of a tank. Could we hunt on foot? No problem, Boris told Dmitri.

An hour later, we left the lodge. On foot. Dmitri, however, stayed behind. This ought to be interesting, I thought as we headed for the woods. No interpreter. I don't speak Russian and Boris doesn't speak English. Now we're talking adventure.

It turned out to be one of the most exciting hunts I've ever been on.

As soon as we hit the woods, we came across a fresh set of moose tracks. Boris studied the tracks a few seconds, then stood up and began a game of charades. He spread his arms wide over his head and shook his head. He cupped his hands over his chest and nodded.

As he did this a second time, I understood and smiled. He was telling me this moose was not a bull. It had no rack. It was a cow. It had, well . . . it was a cow. I nodded in understanding.

Ten minutes or so later, we came across another set of fresh moose tracks. This time Boris put his arms up and spread them wide, nodding. This was a bull. I figured these were a bull's tracks; they were much larger than the first set. Boris jumped on the tracks.

After following the trail several hundred yards, Boris knelt and pointed to the tracks. He showed me how they were spaced farther apart now, and mud was kicked up in front of the toes. He then pointed to his nose to tell me the bull had winded us. He pumped his arms and hands at his sides quickly, to show me that the bull was running.

After following the tracks several hundred more yards, Boris stopped to show me the tracks were closer together again. He pumped his arms slowly; the bull was walking. He pointed to willow leaves that had just been nibbled on. The bull wasn't spooked any more and was feeding. I understood what he was showing me. We were in sync.

Then, suddenly, Boris grabbed my arm, brought one finger to his lips and signaled to walk very quietly. The moose was close. We slowly moved along the trail. Boris froze, motioning for me to get my rifle ready. He motioned that the bull was right around the next bend in the trail. I had no idea how he knew this, but I believed everything he was telling me via hand signals. I brought up my rifle as we eased around the bend.

There, about 75 yards away in the woods, stood a large bull moose. I eased my rifle to my shoulder, aimed and squeezed the trigger. A solid "whump" told me the bullet had found its mark. The moose ran into the brush.

Boris turned with a questioning look and shrugged his shoulders. He was asking me if I thought I made a good shot. I smacked my right fist into my left hand, nodding my head. Yes, I had made a good shot.

Boris grinned from ear to ear, and we went to look for the bull. We found it piled up in the brush less than 100 yards away. After a round of back slapping and hugging, we went to work field dressing the bull. Day One and I had my moose. What a great hunt!

It wasn't a record book bull, but it was a trophy to me. Besides, I sensed that if I hadn't shot this bull, Boris would have shot me. Siberian winters are long and cold; a moose in the freezer gives these people a warm, fuzzy feeling. They live on what they harvest, as was evidenced by every meal. We ate bear, moose, rabbits, fish, game birds, and some 'mystery' meat.

The next morning we learned there was only one moose tag in camp. This was a major oversight. The guys from CMI explained to the Russians that there must be one tag in camp for each hunter. We were promised that more tags would be in camp the following morning. Unfortunately, they didn't arrive until Thursday, our last day in Siberia, too late for us to shoot another moose.

While waiting for the moose tags to arrive, we hunted birds and bear. There were a few fresh bear tracks around, but we soon realized most of the bruins were denned for the winter. As we had feared, because of the coup we had missed the best time for bear.

"You come back next year in August and you will get bear, and moose, too," Boris told us. "I guarantee it."

The birds we hunted were called wood grouse or capercaillie. They are odd-looking critters if you are unaccustomed to them. The males, about the size of a big chicken, have heads like a duck, a feathery beard under their chin, sharp beaks and claws like a hawk, bluish-green metallic-like feathers, and they fan their tails like a turkey gobbler. They look like something a taxidermist might concoct after an all-nighter at the Dead Reindeer Saloon. Females resemble our sharp-tailed grouse. They are an odd couple.

We later learned the capercaillie is a much-sought-after species of grouse by European hunters. The bird is the largest species of grouse in the world and is rare, even close to extirpation in some countries. They were all over this part of Siberia, however. We shot and ate them for lunch.

Late one afternoon, as we lounged in the cabin, I looked out the window and saw a big, black Mercedes pull into the driveway. Three men in suits and ties stepped out.

"Who are these guys?," I asked Dmitri.

"It's the head of the Department of Hunting for this part of Siberia, and a couple of his associates," Dmitri replied. "They are here to greet you and welcome you to this region. You are the first Americans ever to hunt in this area. They want to meet you."

"I wish we had known they were coming, we could have dressed up a little," I said. "They're dressed in suits and ties, while we're sitting here in T-shirts, with three days' worth of whiskers. I'm a little embarrassed."

"Oh, don't worry about it. They know you guys are here hunting and not at a birthday party," Dmitri replied.

As we gathered around the dinner table a few minutes later, Anatoli Kiselev, the head of the hunting department, welcomed us and made several vodka toasts to celebrate the occasion. This was our introduction to Russia's national drink. (More on this ceremonial Russian custom a bit later ... several times.)

After a toast welcoming us to this part of Siberia, and another to our health, and a third wishing us a good hunt, an awkward silence filled the room. Kiselov looked at all of us questioningly.

Dmitri leaned over and whispered, "They are waiting for one of you to make a toast. It's Russian tradition. The host makes a toast or two, then the guest makes a toast."

"What kind of toast should I make?," I whispered. "It doesn't really matter," Dmitri whispered back. "Just make up something."

That put me on a spot. I wished I had known they were coming, and that I could make a toast to an intern or political science student, not to the chief of the Hunting Department of Sverdlovsk. I also wished I had more time to think about it. This could be an important advance in Russian/American detente, as I saw it. We were the first Americans they had ever seen. They had heard a lot about us, probably most of it bad. I didn't want to confirm this with an improper toast.

After thinking about it for a minute, all the time I had because the silence in the room was deafening, I stood up and gave it my best shot. "I'd like to propose a toast," I said, mustering all the courage I could.

"We thank Mr. Kiselev for coming here to greet us tonight. This is a proud and momentous occasion. We are proud to be the first Americans to visit this area. We are enjoying our stay. You have made us feel very welcome. Your hospitality is much appreciated. All the Russian people we have met have been very kind and helpful. On this trip we have learned that Russians and Americans are really not all that different. We are a lot alike, especially those of us who love the outdoors and like to hunt. We share a kindred spirit."

Everyone stood, touched shot glasses and chugged the poison ... er, ah, vodka. Kiselev looked pleased, as did my comrades.

"Good toast, Denny," they said. "Good toast."

• *Anatoli Kiselev, head of the Sverdlovsk Regional Hunting Department, presents Denny with a Capercaillie Medal making him an honorary member of the Sverdlovsk Urals Hunting Society.*

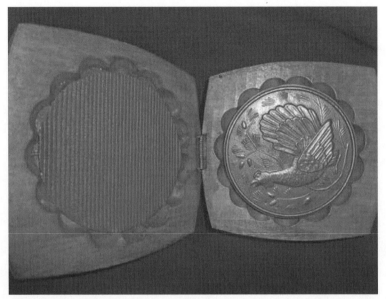

• Close-up of medal in case on right. (Denny Geurink photos)

After a few more toasts, Kiselev came to each of us, shook our hand, and presented us with a beautiful silver medallion with a capercaillie etched on its face and an important-looking inscription etched on the back. Then he handed us a small, red, hard-covered, passport type of document. Inside, next to a picture of Lenin, was a photo of us, and some official-looking documentation written in Russian. Ah, so that's why Dmitri wanted the extra passport-size photos.

"You have been made honorary members of the Communist Party," Dmitri said to us.

"You're kidding, right?," I said.

"Actually, I am kidding," Dmitri chuckled. "He's made all of you honorary members of the region's Society of Hunters. It's a prestigious honor."

We were surprised by what was happening here in the middle of Siberia. This was, indeed, an honor!

On our last day in camp, we decided to give Boris a nice tip for all the hard work and hospitality he had shown us at his hunting lodge. Tipping is an American tradition. That evening we didn't even recognize Boris when he showed up at the dinner table. He had scraped the scruffy whiskers from his face and was wearing a suit and tie. He grinned from ear to ear and smelled of vodka.

"What's up with Boris?," I asked Dmitri. "He seems really pleased. Is he glad we all are finally leaving?"

"No," Dmitri said, with a hint of disgust in his voice. "Do you guys know the tip you gave him today is almost a year's wages? This guy makes about $200 a month and you gave him more than $2,000 in tips. You shouldn't have tipped him so much. Now he's going to expect that much again if we ever come back. Look at him. He's so drunk he can hardly walk."

Boris was a little wobbly, alright, and he was trying to get us wobbly right along with him. He kept proposing all sorts of toasts, each of which was consummated with a shot of vodka.

We learned a lot more about Russian traditions that night. The reason vodka bottles don't come with screw-on caps is because once you take the cap off, you're supposed to keep drinking shots until the bottle is empty. Also, you must keep the shot glass on the table when you fill it; you are not to hold it in your hand. You can't leave an empty vodka bottle on the table; it must be placed on the floor next to the table. The first toast always has to be to your health. You can't sip the vodka shot; that would be bad manners. You are to slam it.

We all slept in late the next morning.

Our hunt in Siberia was over. Next stop ... Crimea.

Heading For A Spring Tonic

• The term "sticking out like a sore thumb" comes immediately to mind when looking at this neat photo. A dark bear on a white background can't get much more visible. It may seem, to us, that it's a bit early to come out of hibernation, but not to the bear. It is headed for low ground and food, such as the scene below. Warmer there, too. (Photos by Bob Lyter)

CHAPTER 2

HANGING OUT
WITH THE KGB

A FTER SURVIVING A LONG evening of vodka toasts and a first-hand introduction to Russian culture, our entourage of intrepid American hunters flew out of Sverdlovsk late in the afternoon October 3. The next morning we landed in the resort city of Simferopol on the southern tip of the Crimean Peninsula. Simferopol is an old Russian navy town on the scenic shoreline of the Black Sea.

What was ironic about landing in Simferopol is that it is near the city of Foros, where Gorbachev had been placed under house arrest during the coup attempt several weeks earlier. Again, we were right in the middle of a time and place of historical significance.

We were met at the airport by Sergey Kolpack, an interpreter hired to accompany us on the next leg of our journey. Kolpack is an English professor at a nearby university. With Dmitri, this would give us two people to translate at the next camp.

I was the first guy through customs, and as soon as I cleared, Kolpack approached. He was a short, slender man in his early 30s. He introduced himself, then looked up at me and asked, "Are all Americans as big as you?"

I'm 6'2" and weigh 210 pounds, so I'm not exactly a small man, but I don't consider myself exceptionally big compared to many other Americans. After Kolpack asked

I noticed that most of the people were rather short. I guess I did look big in this crowd.

"I'm not really that big compared to a lot of other Americans," I told Kolpack. "You should see my cousin."

At that moment, my cousin Terry walked up to us. Terry is 6' 5" and weighs 250.

Sergey's jaw dropped. "You Americans are really big people. I'm glad we didn't fight you," he chuckled, referring to the tensions that existed between Russians and Americans during the Cold War era. We all had a big laugh over that one.

It wouldn't be the last time we would hear this comment relative to physical size.

On the way to our hotel, Kolpack, still obviously intrigued by meeting a group of Americans for the first time, made another astute observation.

"You are the first Americans I have ever seen," he said, looking us up and down. "I'm surprised how much Russians and Americans look alike. I thought you would look different."

"What did you think we would look like? Did you think we had one eye in the middle of our forehead?"

"No, no," he replied quickly. "It's just that in many other countries, the people look a lot different from Russians. For example, Koreans don't look like Russians; neither do the Japanese or Chinese. There isn't much difference between the way Russians and Americans look."

The way we dress was an exception, as I had seen a week earlier on a bus ride through Moscow with Dmitri. After I noticed many people on the bus were staring at me and whispering to each other, I asked him, "How do these people know I'm not just another Russian?" I had heard "American" whispered several times.

"I haven't said a word to this point, but these people know I'm an American and not a Russian. Same thing when we are walking down the street. How can they tell?"

"For one thing, look how you are dressed," Dmitri explained. "You have colorful clothes. You are wearing blue jeans and tennis shoes. Do you see anyone around you dressed like that? They are all wearing drab clothes. No tennis shoes; no blue jeans.

"Plus, Americans are always smiling. Do you see anyone smiling on this bus? Life in Russia is difficult. Russian people are very stoic, very serious. They don't walk down the street or ride the bus with a smile. They are good, kind people but don't show their emotions."

I looked around. Dmitri was right.

Then I noticed two grandmotherly ladies across the aisle from us looking directly at me with their fingers in their ears. That was weird "Why do they have their fingers in their ears?" I asked, a bit perplexed.

"They know you are an American, and they have always been told that all Americans do is swear." Dmitri smiled. "They don't want to hear it."

How could so many misconceptions between Russians and Americans have developed over the years? That bus ride was an eye-opener.

We were the first Americans nearly every place we went. We felt pressure to leave a good impression, not wanting to look or sound like the "ugly Americans" so many cultures picture us as.

We heard the comment "spoiled Americans" a few times, too. Unfortunately, some rude, obnoxious Americans do travel to countries like Russia. We ran into a few of them on the airplane rides over and back.

Meanwhile, back in Simferopol, we had reached the hotel. No one in the hotel spoke English. That's understandable, as we were in a country which had been nearly closed to U.S. citizens for decades.

This city was not a tourist destination for Americans. it was a Soviet Navy town, so there was no need for anyone to speak English. After another lengthy check-in, we stashed our gear in our rooms and ate dinner.

The next morning we were taken to a small helicopter pad and flown to the top of a large, rugged mountain overlooking the resort town of Yalta. This, Dmitri informed us, was where we would stay on this leg of our journey. As we landed on the helicopter pad beside the lodge, we learned our "camp" was on a giant naval base in the southern part of the Crimea.

Things just kept getting more interesting. While unloading our gear and stashing it in the lodge, we noticed a big, black Mercedes pull up out front. Out popped two men dressed in suits and ties, wearing dark glasses and carrying brief cases.

"Who are they?," I asked Dmitri.

"KGB," he replied, with a straight face.

I didn't know whether to believe him, because we were learning he had a dry sense of humor. They looked like they could be KGB, and we were, after all, on a giant Soviet naval base. If they looked KGB, acted KGB, and Dmitri said they are KGB, they must be KGB.

Were we going to hunt with two guys from the KGB?

• *The KGB is watching! The man on left in suit and tie with briefcase is a KGB agent keeping a careful eye on everyone.(Denny Geurink photo)*

We learned from Dmitri that, basically, the only people allowed to own guns and hunt in the Soviet Union are military people and Communist Party officials. That's a big difference from the way we grew up in the U.S., where hunting is a rite of passage for millions of Americans.

When I told him that on opening day of the firearms deer season in Michigan there are around 700,000 hunters in the woods, he was dumbfounded.

"There aren't that many hunters in all of Russia," he said in disbelief, "and Russia covers 11 time zones!"

Our headquarters for this leg of the journey was a comfortable lodge overlooking a steep, wooded valley, home to the Crimean red deer we would be hunting.

The Russians refer to this animal as a stag. There are a number of sub-species of red deer around the world, including this one and the American wapiti, or elk. While our elk and this species of red deer basically look alike, there are subtle differences. These stags are about three-fourths the size of our elk, and the males have antlers that go straight up and crown, rather than antlers that slant back with points coming off the main beams, as on our elk. Red deer cows and calves look like our elk cows and calves but are a bit smaller.

Roe deer, about the size of a large German shepherd, and with small antlers, also live in this area. There also are a few mouflon sheep and wild boar.

Following a quick lunch of soup and sandwiches, we were introduced to our guides, then prepared for the evening hunt. All the guides obviously were military personnel. They wore Soviet military camouflage and carried Russian SKS rifles. My guide's name was Sergey (not the interpreter, another Sergey). Dmitri said he was the head guide in this camp.

That evening as Sergey and I sat beside a well-used game trail on the edge of a small clearing, I was introduced to stag hunting. Since I had never hunted them,

I really didn't know what to expect and had no idea what they sounded like. I thought that because they looked a lot like our elk, they probably sounded a lot like our elk.

Just before dark, a guttural roar echoed through the woods. It sounded like a grizzly bear with a toothache, and it sent a shiver up my spine. I wasn't planning to run into bears in this camp.

"Bear!" I whispered to Sergey. Actually, it was more of a question. "Bear?"

Sergey smiled. "No, stag. Not bear. Stag."

That's what a stag sounds like? I felt stupid. Here I was, supposedly a big-shot writer with the world's largest outdoor magazine and I didn't know that a stag doesn't bugle, that it roars. At that point I knew one thing for sure -- I'd hate to be in the woods alone after dark and hear , for the first time, a stag roar.

"Stag?," I replied, a bit puzzled.

"Da, stag," Sergey replied, and smiled.

• *Our outfitter, Dmitri Sikorski, poses in front of a big stag we found on a later trip. The stag was starving; it was so weak it couldn't stand up when we approached. It was not injured. (Denny Geurink photo)*

The big stag shook the trees again with a loud roar, then grunted like a pig. Another surprise. Then another guttural roar echoed through the woods. The stag was getting closer. The day was getting darker.

Right at dark, the big stag roared near the edge of the woods but refused to step into the clearing. Either it smelled us or just wasn't going to expose itself. It exhibited the same sixth sense our big whitetail bucks have in Michigan. Whatever the reason, we never saw it.

While I was disappointed that I didn't get to see the animal, this was still a great day in the Crimean woods. This was my first stag hunt, and I learned what a big stag in full rut sounds like. Plus, I was hunting in the Soviet Union with a big shot in the Russian Navy. Great experiences all, and more to look forward to tomorrow.

Back at camp, we learned Terry had drilled a good stag just before dark. He smiled a lot while telling the story, describing his hunt and shot in detail.

Everyone had seen or heard a stag on our first night in the woods. Expectations were running high, especially when guides told us there were five red deer per hectare in the habitat surrounding the lodge. Five per hectare! Did they need traffic stop lights to keep from running into each other?

That evening as we gathered around the table for dinner, I noticed the two men with suits and ties were gone. Dmitri said they had driven back to Yalta. So, no more KGB to worry about. I was feeling a bit more at ease about our stay here in Crimea until a short time later. Dmitri leaned close and whispered, "Your guide, Sergey ... KGB."

"Ya, right," I chuckled, figuring he was pulling my leg. He had noted I was relieved the suits and ties were gone and probably wanted to stir the pot.

"I'm not kidding," Dmitri replied seriously. "Big shot KGB. Five years ago you go in woods with Sergey, you don't come back out."

That brought the hairs on the back of my neck to attention. I had just spent the afternoon in the woods with a big shot from the KGB. I was carrying a rifle and he was carrying a rifle, but we weren't pointing them at each other. We were hunting buddies.

So that's why the suits and ties left camp...they had one of their own on the ground and in the field with us. No better way to keep track of us.

Things became more interesting after we had finished eating. Sergey started asking questions through Dmitri. His first question was a good ice breaker.

"Are all your Marines like Rambo?," Sergey asked. We had learned earlier that in this era of Glasnost and Perestroika, Russians were now getting a chance to watch some of our movies and TV shows. Obviously, Sergey had watched *Rambo, First Blood.*

"Yes, of course," I replied, figuring Sergey was joking. He was, fortunately.

"Glad we didn't fight you," Sergey chuckled. We all had a good laugh. This was the second time a man named Sergey said that, and it was just as funny this time.

A bit later, Sergey began to get serious."Tell everyone we never hated Americans," he said. "We didn't want to go to war with America. All we want is have a place to live, enough to eat, a good job, and be able to take care of our families...to live a normal life and be happy."

"So do we," I replied. "We didn't want to fight you either. It's all politics. We are like you; we just want to live a normal life and be happy."

"Let the politicians fight each other," Sergey chuckled.

"Yeah, let them fight."

"Besides, if we had gone to war with America, you would have defeated us in two weeks, " Sergey continued.

"Yeah, right," I said. "Russia has the largest standing army in the world, more tanks than any other country, more missiles, more guns . . . "

"Yes, but no gas for tanks, no bullets for guns and no food for soldiers," Sergey said, laughing. "You defeat us in two weeks. Time to be friends."

I hadn't thought about that. This country was really run-down. No gas for tanks, no bullets for guns and no food for soldiers. Amazing!

"Now you have the Star Wars missile defense system," Sergey added. "You fire missiles at us and blow us all up. We fire missiles at you and you stop them with protective shield. We don't have Star Wars. Time to be friends."

"We don't have a Star Wars protective shield," I said. "It's just a theory, an idea. We are working on it, but it hasn't been perfected. Yes, time to be friends."

"Now if we have a nuclear war, we all die," Sergey said somberly. "We have nuclear weapons, and the U.S. has nuclear weapons. Politicians start pushing buttons, we all die. Time to be friends."

All the Russian guides and all the Americans sitting around the table raised their glasses to this astute observation and toasted "time to be friends."

Later that evening, Dmitri told me more interesting things.

"The waiters in white shirts and bow ties serving your meals are not really waiters," he said. "There has been heavy poaching and organized crime in this area recently. One of our friends from Sevastopol has provided us with armed body guards posing as waiters. They are here to be sure we are safe and no one bothers us."

The seemingly constant revelation of surprising, even shocking, things brought out continual 'wow' and 'holy cow' responses. Silently, for the most part. I didn't want to appear too shocked or dumbfounded in front of our interpreters.

I do know one thing: I'm glad my mother said she was going to have her whole church congregation pray for us while we were gone. I was beginning to wonder whether we might need some divine intervention.

Mom was not pleased I was going to the Soviet Union for two weeks. She kept trying to talk me out of it. She had grown up during the heart of the Cold War and the thought of her, or anyone in her family, going on a road trip to the Evil Empire was something that never crossed her mind.

• *Dmitri hired a body guard and had him dress as a waiter to protect us on the trip, because everything was so unstable after the coup and then the coup failure. (Denny Geurink photo)*

Later that evening, a few of us decided to get a poker game going to pass the time. One of the waiters/bodyguards began watching us with great curiosity. To make our bets, we were using rubles we had exchanged for some of our dollars in Moscow. None of us would have played poker for U.S. dollars; we aren't the betting kind, and the rubles looked more like play money than real money.

We asked the waiter/bodyguard if he wanted to join us. He declined, saying he didn't have enough rubles to spare on a poker game.

"We will supply you," we told him. "Join the game."

The look on his face was priceless as we each pushed a pile of rubles in front of him. We had no idea what they were worth, but it apparently was quite a bit. He looked shocked.

We noticed that he bet sparingly as the game went on. He just couldn't get himself to part with his new found wealth. The clincher came when the pot got rather large at one point. I had a hand full of aces, so I pushed my entire pile of rubles into the center of the table and quipped "I'm all in. Heck, it's only rubles."

Mr. Waiter/Bodyguard gasped and stammered, "Only rubles! Only rubles? That's two months' wages!"

We had done it again! First with our guide Boris in Sverdlovsk, and now with this man. We kept forgetting how little money these men made in comparison to what we were paid in America.

The game ended when I won the pot. The waiter/ bodyguard tried to give back the rubles we had laid on him, but we told him to keep them as a tip.

Big mistake! Out came the vodka and toasting began!

The following morning, Ed and Bob each dropped a huge stag. Bob's was exceptionally large, one of the largest stags ever taken in this area according to the guides. My turn came that evening when I downed a nice stag just before dark.

The guides were almost as excited as we were, telling us we had all taken gold medal and silver medal stags. (Europeans have a scoring program that ranks animals as gold, silver or bronze medal.)

During the next few days, we tagged two roe deer and a number of small quail, called steppen quail by the guides. They are a bit smaller than our bobwhite quail. While they don't look like our bobwhites, they taste good ... just like our bobwhite quail.

We also tried for wild boar but discovered they had left the area already ... another timing casualty of the coup. We jumped several mouflon sheep but were asked not to shoot them because they had just been introduced into the area.

At the end of the hunt, we were paid another visit by someone in a black Mercedes, and dressed in a suit and tie. This time it wasn't the KGB. It was Igor Markevich, president of the Soviet Black Sea Navy Hunting and Fishing Society. When Dmitri told me this man was coming, I was again flabbergasted that such a high-ranking government official was coming to greet us.

• *The Tea House Lodge. (Denny Geurink photo)*

"It's tough to believe these dignitaries are coming to our camps to meet us," I said in disbelief. "They act like we are ambassadors or something. We're just a bunch of peons compared to these guys. We are just plain, ordinary Americans."

"No, you guys are ambassadors," Dmitri replied. "You are the first Americans these people have met. You are the first Americans to visit these places. So you are ambassadors of America. They want to make sure you feel welcome."

• *View from the porch of the Tea House Lodge overlooking the scenic Crimean mountain range. (Denny Geurink photo)*

A statement like that will humble you and make you mind your manners. We were feeling very welcome.

Around the evening dinner table, after a round of toasts, Markevich gave each of us a laminated card on a lanyard to hang around our necks. The cards gave us honorary membership in the Crimean Society of Hunters.

When the hunt ended, and before heading back to Russia, we spent a couple of days in Yalta, a resort city on the Black Sea the Soviets like to compare to the French Rivera. This is where the elite come to play and relax in the sun along the sandy beaches of the Black Sea.

While in Yalta we also had a chance to visit the place where the Yalta Conference took place in 1945. This is where President Franklin D. Roosevelt, Prime Minister Winston Churchill, and General Secretary Joseph Stalin met to discuss Europe's reorganization after World War II. It was the second meeting between the

Big Three to discuss the fate of post-war Europe; the first meeting was in Tehran in 1943. Many believe that resolutions that came out of the Yalta Conference led to the start of the Cold War.

From Yalta we flew to St. Petersburg to spend a couple of days touring that city. St. Petersburg is beautiful, steeped in Russian culture and tradition. Here we had a chance to visit the Hermitage, one of the largest and most prestigious museums in the world. You need more than one day to take in everything to see in this museum. It was, quite simply, incredible.

We also visited St. Catherine's summer palace, the lavish summer residence of the tsars. We also visited the Winter Palace, built by Peter the Great in the late 1700s. It served as the official residence of the Russian monarchy until the Bolshevik Revolution in 1917.

We headed home October 11. What started out as a hunting trip had turned into much more. We learned about Russia, its people, its culture, its history, and its wildlife during our two weeks there.

There was much more about this trip than I could hope to write in a few short stories. I shot more than 12 hours of video and put together what is, as far as we know, the first hunting video filmed in Russia. I also took more than 1,000 color transparency photos (slides). These will help preserve the fond memories and exciting moments I experienced in the Land of the Bear.

CHAPTER 3

BEAR NATURAL HISTORY

RUSSIA IS CALLED THE Land of the Bear for a reason. Out of the 200,000 brown bears roaming the northern hemisphere in a dozen or more countries, approximately two-thirds, or 130,000, are in Russia. Compare that to the 32,000 in the United States, of which 95 percent live in Alaska, and the 21,000 in Canada.

This shows why the brown bear is so closely identified with Russian culture. It is one of the most widespread and popular animals in Russia, where it has long been considered the country's national symbol. It appears on coins, flags, street signs, maps, billboards, and even beer bottles. In 1980, the brown bear was chosen as the official mascot of the Moscow Olympics.

On a number of occasions while visiting Moscow and St. Petersburg, we saw people standing on street corners, with trained bears, where tourists could take pictures of them. Most bears were cubs, but once in a while someone had a large bear.

While the bears are muzzled, they still can be dangerous. On one occasion we saw a large bear try to steal an ice cream cone from a passing tourist. The handler had all he could do to keep the bear in check as it slapped the cone from the frightened tourist's hand. Had the bear been agitated or angry, the person easily could have lost her hand and arm.

Brown bears are one of the most majestic and awe-inspiring creatures in the world, and one of the most dangerous. Scientists tell us that the brown bears found in

North America are direct descendants of brown bears from Russia. They both belong to the same species, *Ursus arctos.* At some time long ago they crossed a land bridge over the Bering Sea and made their way into Alaska, then down into Canada and the lower 48 states.

The brown bear we call a grizzly is a sub-species, scientifically known as *Ursus arctos horribilis.* Some scientists believe the grizzly evolved from the larger coastal brown when it moved inland and began feeding on other things besides salmon. Others believe there may have been two brown bear migrations into North America from Russia.

Biologists believe grizzlies stem from the narrow-skulled bears of northern Siberia. These bears, they contend, migrated into central Alaska, the interior of Canada, and the lower 48 states.

Meanwhile, they believe big coastal Alaskan brown bears, or Kodiak bears, are direct descendants of the broader-skulled bears found in Kamchatka. Brown bears were at one time widespread in Canada and the lower 48; fossil remains have been found as far east as Labrador in Canada and Kentucky and Ohio in the U.S.

What a bear eats has a lot to do with its size. Brown bears living along the coast in Russia's Far East, for example, can and do grow very large, living on a steady diet of salmon. Weights up to 3,300 pounds have been recorded. Meanwhile, the interior version of a brown bear, which we call a grizzly, may top out at only 700 pounds in the Yukon. These bears live off pine nuts, berries, and whatever else they can find. Without the protein-rich salmon the coastal bears feed on, a grizzly just can't grow as large. So, despite the common misconception that the grizzly is larger than a brown bear, the fact is that the grizzly is a smaller version of a brown bear.

There are several reasons Russia has so many brown bears. First, the habitat is perfect for them. The country is covered with dense forests and wilderness areas flush with perfect bear foods, from the salmon-rich Kamchatka Peninsula to the pine nut-rich forests of Siberia. Second, the human population in Russia is widespread. Outside the major cities, the population is very rural. Third, after the Bolshevik Revolution in 1917, guns and hunting disappeared from Russia. This allowed bear populations to explode. This was good for the bears; it wasn't so good for the rural Russian population.

According to Dmitri, many rural villagers live in fear of bears. Many people are killed or injured when they go to the woods to forage for mushrooms or to the rivers to catch fish. With no way to defend themselves, they are afraid to roam far from their homes. This fact was driven home on our first grizzly hunt in the early 1990s.

We were staying with an older couple in their home in a small village several hundred miles east of Moscow. One day, as we sat at the dinner table, there was a frantic knock at the door. The entire village knew American hunters were staying in this house. One of the villagers had come to plead with us to go with him to his home to shoot the bear that had killed his milk cow.

The bear was dragging the partially-eaten carcass into the woods when the man and his neighbors ran off the bear with pitchforks and sticks. They had made such a commotion the bear had been scared off. The farmer retrieved what was left of his cow, loaded it onto a wagon and brought it back to his barn, where he planned to butcher it and eat the meat that remained. His family was in dire need of the meat.

Unfortunately, during the night the bear had returned and dragged the cow back into the woods. The farmer was afraid to go after it. He didn't have a rifle, but we did, which is why, of course, he came to us

That evening, just before dark, one of my clients killed the bear. There was joy in the village because many other villagers had had their livestock attacked recently by this bear and were just as defenseless. Loud voices and several people shouting is not a long-term solution.

• *Bear searching for food along Sea of Okhotsk near Magadan.*
(Tom Thompson photo)

On another hunt, one of the villagers told us how his grandmother had been attacked and killed by a bear when she had gone to the barn to milk the family cow. Dmitri told us this happened too often in remote villages.

Bears find the domestic animals on a farm to be easy pickings compared to trying to find adequate wild food. Many oat crops also are destroyed each year by bears preparing for hibernation.

With so many bears in Russia, and so many remote villages in bear habitat, no wonder five times as many people are killed by bears in Russia as in the United States. Studies show there are, on average, two recorded fatal bear attacks a year in the U.S. (by all bear species), but at least 10 fatal attacks a year in Russia. Many more people are attacked but not killed. With a poor salmon run or pine nut crop, Russian numbers can double.

There are documented cases in eastern Siberia where a bear has become a man-eater when natural foods are scarce. At least two bears in this region have been identified as killing and eating 12 people each.

The following chapters contain some of the bear stories we've heard while traversing Russia. Be forewarned; some are more than a little gruesome.

• *Bear emerging from den near Magadan. (Tom Thompson photo)*

Tremendous Trio of Trophies

• *All three bears squared more than 10 feet. To the guides and most hunters, any bear in the nine-foot class is considered a trophy. In some circumstances, that could be lowered to eight-and-a-half feet. Of course, everyone would like a 10-footer, and we took a number of them every year. Most hunters are happy with a nine-footer. A bear that size is, indeed, a real trophy. That's about one foot larger than the average bear taken in Alaska now, according to the Alaska Fish & Game Department. (Denny Geurink photo)*

CHAPTER 4

BEAR ATTACKS

A LOT OF THE BEAR encounters which occur in Russia happen along salmon streams where people and bears both come seeking food. I have heard about a number of these attacks over the years from guides, interpreters and residents of the many small villages which dot the Siberian landscape. Most of the attacks occur in July and August during big salmon runs. People from the villages often camp along the salmon-rich streams for several days while they seek to supplement their winter food supply. The bears are doing the same thing. They congregate in large numbers, seeking to build up their fat reserves for a long winter's nap. It's a recipe for disaster and tragedy.

Over the years, I've had the chance to fish a number of salmon streams in Russia's Far East with great success. On most of these trips, we would see either bears or numerous bear tracks along the streams. We always knew there were plenty of bears in the area but, unlike most of the Russian villagers, who don't have guns, we always carried a high-powered rifle for protection. Fortunately, we have never had to use a gun, and I hope we never have to. That's because, generally speaking, bears will avoid human contact. We certainly try to avoid contact with the bears, but it doesn't always work that way.

One of the most heart-wrenching bear attack stories I have ever heard happened in August, 2011. The story was reported by a number of news agencies, including the *Moscow Times* and the *Daily Mail,* and was featured in a story written by Spencer Hawken in *Newsflavor.*

According to news sources, a 19-year-old girl, Olga Moskalvova, and her stepfather, Igor Tsyganenkov, were camping and fishing beside a river near their home in the village of Termalniy on the southern end of Kamchatka Peninsula.

Olga and her stepfather were trying to retrieve a fishing pole Igor had left in the tall reeds along the river when a large female brown bear burst from the reeds.

Olga watched in horror as the big bear knocked her stepfather to the ground, grabbed him in its powerful jaws, crushed his skull, and broke his neck.

As Olga turned to run, the bear saw her and ran her down, grabbing her by the leg. At first the bear just toyed with her, biting and chewing on her leg.

That's when she managed to get out her cellphone and call her mother, Tatiana Tsyganenkov. "Mom, the bear is eating me," she screamed into the phone. "Mom, it's such agony! Mom, help!"

At first Tatiana though her daughter was just joking because she liked to joke, but she quickly realized this was no joke. She knew her daughter was in trouble as she listened in panic to her daughter's screams.

"I heard the real horror and pain in Olga's voice, and the sounds of a bear growling and chewing," Tatiana said later. "I could have died from shock!"

The phone suddenly went dead. She had lost the call. At this point Tatiana called her husband to ask his help, not knowing he was dead. There was no answer.

Then Olga called back. "Mom, the bears are back," Olga cried. "She came back and brought her three babies. They're eating me!"

When this call was also cut off, a distraught Tatiana phoned the police and relatives in Termalniy, pleading with them to rush to the river and save her daughter.

A bit later the phone rang again, nearly an hour since the first call. Tatiana listened helplessly as Olga spoke to her for the last time. The long ordeal was nearing an end.

After viciously attacking and mauling her for nearly 60 minutes, the bears apparently had walked off.

"Mom, it's not hurting anymore," Olga spoke in a weak voice. "I don't feel the pain. Forgive me for everything. I love you so much."

These were the last words she heard her daughter speak.

A half hour after the last call, Igor's brother Andrei and several policemen arrived at the river. They found the mother bear and cubs feeding on Igor's partially-eaten body. They found Olga's body a short distance away. She had been badly mauled and was dead.

"My daughter was such fun," said a grief-stricken Tatiana. "She was so cheerful, friendly and warm. She had just graduated from music school and had just gotten her driving license."

Local authorities sent six experienced hunters to the scene to track down and kill the mother bear and her three cubs, which they did. The bears could not be allowed to live. Once a bear loses its fear of humans, it is more likely to attack and kill humans again.

BEAR DRAGS OFF SLEEPING BAG WITH MAN INSIDE

Elaina Bulatoba, one of my interpreters, told a similar story a number of years ago. It was a horrible experience her father, Sergey Bulatoba, had late one summer while camping and fishing the Zhuponova River.

When Sergey and his friends arrived at the Zhuponova to do some fishing, they fully expected to see bears along the stream during their visit. They had fished the

river several times previously and had always encountered
bears, but they found that if they left the bears alone, the
bears left them alone. As they were soon to discover,
however, this uneasy truce between man and beast can
quickly turn deadly.

Sergey, a police officer in the small town of
Yelizova, had brought his police-issue revolver to camp.
Not much of a bear gun, to be sure, but better than no
gun. They thought they wouldn't need the pistol, as they
planned to avoid confrontations with the local bear
population. The bears had always given the anglers a
wide berth, so they were not expecting problems on this
outing.

While the anglers were storing their gear in one of
the camp's small wooden fishing shacks, they noticed a
sow and her two cubs scrounging for food nearby.
The mother bear did not act scared of the men, who
were busily preparing to fish, nor did she appear to be
aggressive. The fishermen went about their chores, not
overly concerned with the bear's presence yet keeping
one eye on her to make sure she didn't get too close to
camp.

Bulatoba and his friends planned to stay on the
river for several weeks, hoping to gather a larder of
fish and caviar for the winter months ahead. As
usual, the fishing was good. It wasn't long before
they had dozens of fish drying on big wooden racks in
the hot July sun. Nor was it long before the mother bear
and her two cubs began sneaking in, pilfering fish and
caviar. The bears had a den nearby, and they found the
camp fish to be easy pickings.

The men ran off the bears every time they caught the
animals near camp. After a couple of days of camp raids
the bears finally seemed to move off, and the fishermen
began to forget about them.

One particularly hot summer night, Bulatoba had a hard
time sleeping in the stuffy wooden shack, so he so took his

sleeping bag outside and laid it on the ground next to the shack. He had done this many times in the past, because he enjoyed sleeping under the stars. He always took his pistol and kept it inside his sleeping bag, just in case.

During the middle of the night, Bulatoba was awakened from a deep sleep by a strange sensation of movement. At first he thought he was dreaming but, as he slowly began to wake up, he realized something was dragging him and his sleeping bag across the ground. He still didn't know what was happening until he heard a low growl. Immediately, a cold chill began to spread across his entire body and his pulse raced.

"I became aware of the sound of heavy breathing," Bulatoba recalled, "then the stench of rotten fish filled my nostrils. I was smelling a bear's breath. I was about to be eaten alive!"

Bulatoba's heart hammered against his rib cage as the bear dragged him farther and farther away from camp. He was paralyzed with fear. He couldn't even scream for help. His mind raced as he thought about the horrible death he was about to experience. In the pandemonium he realized the mother bear was dragging him to her den to feed her cubs.

"Then I remembered the pistol in my sleeping bag," Bulatoba continued. "I tried to get my hands on the pistol, but my body was moving in slow motion. I couldn't make my arms and hands work. It was like I was trapped in the middle of a bad dream, but this wasn't a dream. My palms were sweating but the rest of my body was as cold as ice. I was shivering and sweating with fear."

Finally, as he desperately groped for the pistol, he felt his pistol's cold steel against his outstretched fingers. Instincts began to take over. He slowly slid the handle of the pistol into his hand and arched his finger around the trigger. He just as slowly pulled the pistol out of the bag and aimed it at the mother bear's body. He pulled the trigger again and again and again. Confused feelings of fear and pity rushed through his head.

The bear roared in pain and fury. It dropped the sleeping bag and charged into the forest. The mortally-wounded beast sounded like a bulldozer clearing brush as it plowed through the trees.

As the roaring and crashing faded into the distance, Bulatoba pulled his shaken, bruised body from his torn sleeping bag. While his nerves were shattered, his body was intact. No broken bones and no bite marks. He was alive!

Bulatoba slowly groped his way through the inky blackness back to the shack, hoping that his bear encounters were over for the evening. This was, however, the time of night the river bank was crawling with hungry bears looking for something to eat.

At last he was back at the shack, where he found his frightened friends waiting for him. They were worried and extremely happy to see him. When they had heard the shots and the roaring bear, they expected the worst.

After a long, sleepless night, the men cautiously headed out the next morning in search of the bear. They found it dead near the entrance to its den. As they approached the dead sow, they could hear the young cubs whimpering inside. Their overwhelming sense of fear gave way to a feeling of sadness for the orphaned cubs.

Knowing that the young cubs would not survive without their mother, the men caught them and carried them to a nearby Forest Service office. Later, they learned that one of the rangers was able to get an older sow with one cub to adopt the two young bears. Soon, the cubs were back along the river, feeding on fish once again.

"I was happy the cubs were able to survive," Bulatoba said, "and that they had something else to eat instead of me."

KILLER BEARS

Sergey Mashkantsewe told of another attack while we were in a hunting camp near the town of Magadan along the Sea of Okhotsk. Mashkantsewe was the head guide in the camp and, with all the time he spent in the woods hunting and trapping, he had plenty of big bear stories to tell. Again, it was the volatile combination of salmon stream, bears, and fishermen that created the tragic story.

Like most young Russian military inductees, Mashkantsewe grew up lean and tough. You don't have a choice when you are sent to a military outpost in the middle of Siberia to help operate a remote weather station. You either survive or you are sent back to the city in a pine box. That is, if the bears don't find you first.

"My job was to provide food for the outpost," Mashkantsewe, then in his early 40s, told me through an interpreter. "I was a professional hunter. I shot moose, bear, wolves, fox, waterfowl, and anything else I could find, for food and hides. The meat we would eat and the furs we would sell to the natives in the remote villages for a few dollars to buy more supplies. If there were streams around, we caught fish. When the blueberries and red berries were ripe, we picked them. We had to live off the land. We received supplies only once every three or four months from the city."

He told me that even when supplies arrived from the city many hundreds of miles away, they were usually sparse and consisted mostly of bread -- which went stale fast -- sugar, salt, and hard tack. So it was shoot something for the table or starve.

Sergey became very good at what he did best -- hunting moose and bear. There were a lot of bears.

However, even the many close encounters he had with ill-tempered bears did not prepare him for the ghastly scene he came upon one gloomy October afternoon. He still had trouble talking about it as he told me the story.

"We were working our way down a wide, shallow spot on the Renzhina River when we noticed a big bear feeding on something along the bank," Mashkantsewe said in a low, sad voice. "We decided to cut our engine and try to float in close to see what the bear was eating. The bear spotted us and slowly walked off, not really afraid of us. It was more annoyed than afraid. That's the sign of a dangerous bear. That's when we saw the body of a partially-eaten man in the bushes. His face had been eaten."

Mashkantsewe paused for a second and swallowed hard. He was visibly shaken. In a few minutes, he composed himself and continued.

"The scene sent a cold chill down my spine," he said in a barely audible voice. "We knew we were dealing with the worst kind of bear, a man-eater. We knew we had to destroy it or it would kill again."

Mashkantsewe and his two partners quickly formulated a plan. They knew the bear would be back to reclaim its kill, so they set up a blind about 50 yards away. Every nerve in their bodies was on edge as they waited in silence,

All the hunters had for firepower were military issue 7.62 carbines. They were using standard issue, full metal jacket cartridges with minimal powder. This is what they had always used to hunt bear, but those rifles and bullets seemed inadequate now. They thought about how nice one of the carbines of their American hunters would be. A .338 or .375, with a 220-grain bullet, would have made them feel safer.

Just before dark, the hackles on the back of their necks stood up when they heard a twig snap. The bear was coming in behind them. It had caught their scent and was hunting them, intending to make Mashkantsewe and his friends its next meal. They were in a bad situation. The brush was so thick behind them they would not see the bear until it was less than 20 yards away. Their skin began to crawl as the big bear stalked closer. They could hear it sniffing the air for their scent as it worked toward them. Their hearts began to race as they thought about the man whose partially-eaten body lay beside the river in front of them. Would they soon join him on the stream bank?

Then, in the waning daylight, they saw a dark form slipping through the shadows. They didn't wait for the bear to clear the brush. With nerves sparking like electrical shorts, they opened fire. The big bruin roared, sounding like a freight train as it charged through the brush toward the men.

"I don't know how many times we shot," Mashkantsewe said. "Maybe 20 to 30 times. We didn't stop until the bear quit moving right at our feet. It was an old bear with bad teeth and a bad hide. That's why it had become a man-eater. We found the man's arms and hands inside its stomach. It made us sick."

A few weeks later back in town, Mashkantsewe learned the man was one of his friends, with whom he had spent a lot of time fishing.

"I have a hard time talking about this, even today," Mashkantsewe whispered as he walked from the tent.

CHAPTER 5

THE PEOPLE

"WE ARE JUST LIKE Americans," one of my guides, a KGB operative named Sergey, told me back in 1991. "We just want to be happy. We want to have enough food to eat, clothes to wear and a place to live. We never hated the Americans. We never wanted to fight you. Let the politicians fight each other. We want to be friends. We just want to live a normal life."

That statement has stuck with me through my many years in Russia. The Russians are like us; they just grew up under a different system of government. They have the same hopes, dreams, and needs we do. The difference is they were always told what to do and when to do it, who they should love and who they should hate. Big Brother was watching.

"We never hated you either," I told Sergey. "We were told bad stories about you too, but we never hated you or wanted to fight you. You're right. Let the politicians fight."

Over the past two-plus decades, I've made many friends from all walks of life in Russia. One of the most unusual friendships was with a colonel in the Russian army in the late 1990s. Because of the sensitivity of an American businessman hanging around with a Russian colonel at that time, the colonel asked me not to use his surname in any story that mentioned him. While we doubted there would be any repercussions, we did not take a chance.

The friendship began when an interpreter, Vladislav Shurin, told me about a high-ranking military officer he knew in Moscow. "His name is Igor," Vlad told me.

"He's a colonel in the Russian army. I went to school with his wife, Larisa. She was a good friend and we still are friends today. Would you like to meet him and his wife? They would like to meet you and talk to you. Let's go to dinner with them in Moscow."

"That sounds really cool," I told Vlad. "A Russian colonel. That would be great. Let's do it."

That evening Vlad and I took a taxi to a nice restaurant, where we met Igor and Larisa. Igor was a handsome man in his early 50s, dressed in a dark suit. His wife, Larisa, a pretty lady, wore a nice dress and fine jewelry. I felt sorely under-dressed in my jeans and Outdoor Adventures shirt, but they were friendly and spoke a bit of English. Between Vlad's excellent command of the English language, their spotty English and my spotty Russian, we communicated very well.

As an American in Russia, I felt no animosity at all from the colonel and his wife. I felt that if anyone had been subjected to a steady stream of anti-American sentiment throughout his career, it would have been Igor, but it didn't show.

We had an excellent dinner and interesting conversation. Igor and his wife were extremely curious about life in America. What was the food like? Were the restaurants in Moscow as nice as the ones in America? Were Russians as well off as Americans? What sports did I like? Why the incredible passion for football in the U.S.? They were extremely curious about my opinion of Russian life, food, housing, clothes, technology.

It was the dawning of the computer age; they wanted to know if all Americans had a computer. Russians were just getting them, but Igor felt they were inferior to the ones Americans were buying, because Russians couldn't afford to buy the expensive ones Americans could afford. Like so many other Russians I came in contact with, Igor seemed to have the perception that all Americans were millionaires . . . or cowboys . . . or both.

The next night it was just Igor, Vlad and me on a guys' night out. We went bowling and then played pool. There was, of course, some vodka involved, not much but just enough to lead to interesting conversations. At no point did I feel intimidated, as I might have been in the presence of a Russian army colonel. Igor was a warm, human being, unlike the perception I had grown up with of a gruff, terrifying Russian army officer.

Of course, afterward, when I told some of my friends about hanging out with a Russian colonel, they said, "Maybe he's with the KGB, and he's just trying to get information out of you." There was plenty of suspicion on our side of the pond as well.

My friendship with Igor and Larisa lasted several years. On later trips to Moscow, Vlad and I met with the colonel and his wife several times. Once, the colonel took us to the horse races. I couldn't believe they had a horse track in Russia. We sat in a special box reserved for VIPs. My, how quickly capitalism was catching on!

Another time we went to Moscow to attend a tennis match; tennis stars from around the world were competing in an international tournament (the Kremlin Cup) at the old Olympic Stadium. The tourney was established by the first President of Russia, Boris Yeltsin, an avid tennis fan. He is generally credited with the surge in tennis popularity in Russia in the early 2000s. This eventually led to the domination by Russians of the international tennis scene for many years. I was impressed when they announced his name and he stood to receive an ovation from the crowd. "I'm at a tennis match with a Russian army colonel and Boris Yeltsin," I said to myself.

I was privileged to watch some of the best Russian tennis players in the world. Among the women were Elena Dementieva, Nadia Petrovo, Anastasia Myskina, and yes, even Anna Kournikova. Many say she was just a flash-in-the-pan tennis player, who had really never played tennis that well. To set the record straight, she won the Kremlin Cup doubles tournament in 2001 and two Grand Slam doubles titles, one in 1999 and another in 2002.

I was thrilled one year when I learned she was on the plane with us on one of our trips from the U.S. to Moscow. While I wasn't lucky enough to talk to her, I did catch a glimpse of her in first class, as did everyone else on the plane. If I had known she was going to be on our flight, I would have purchased a first class ticket.

One of the most exciting evenings I spent with the colonel was when Vlad and I had dinner in his apartment one evening. He met us in town, dressed in full military colors. I was impressed by his rugged look and air of command. This was the first time I saw him in military uniform.

"Now, when we get to the military base where I live, do not speak English," Igor instructed as we hopped in a taxi and headed for his flat on the base. "Do not speak English until we get to my room."

"No problem," I said. "I'll try to keep my mouth shut. You know that won't be easy."

"They might think you are CIA," Igor chuckled.

Didn't think of that. Not immediately, anyway. Not until we got there. We were dropped off at the entrance of an intimidating military compound and met at the closed gate by two sentries. They briskly saluted Igor, and he saluted back. They opened the gate and gave me and Vlad the evil eye as we walked past. Now I felt intimidated.

A couple more times, as we progressed up the sidewalk, we were met and saluted by Russian soldiers. The same at the door to the building, and even in the elevator. I was definitely getting the once-over. Igor didn't have to worry about me speaking English. I don't think I could have said anything had I wanted to. I was beginning to think we should have found a restaurant in town.

Finally, we arrived at his flat. Larisa greeted us at the door and silently motioned to come into the room.

"OK Denny, you may speak English again," Igor chuckled. "This is my flat. Sorry it doesn't look like much for a Russian colonel, but this is what we have. We don't make nearly as much money as an American colonel does, but it's comfortable."

• *Dale Fulkerson, left, a friend, and I on a visit to the Colonel's apartment. We edited his face out at his request. While I don't expect any repercussions, we didn't want to take any chances.*

It was comfortable. Igor and his wife were gracious hosts.

First we were treated with typical Russian appetizers of meat, cheese, caviar, bread and, of course, vodka. Bottles of cognac and wine were on the table. We had a tasty meal of meat, fish, and potatoes, cooked by Larisa.

It was an excellent night. Before it was over and after I had participated in several vodka toasts, I got up the courage to ask Igor if I could have my picture taken wearing his Russian military officer's jacket and hat.

"No problem," he said, chuckling, "but you can't take the uniform with you. You might look suspicious wearing that when you leave."

• *Me in Igor's uniform cap and topcoat. Do I look like a Colonel in the Russia army? (Denny Geurink photo)*

We met a few more times after that, but, eventually, I lost contact with Igor and Larisa, mainly because my company wasn't working with Vlad's outfitter as much, so I didn't have a chance to see him very much.

One more thing: after one of our dinner meetings, Igor handed me a business card with his name on it. "If you ever have a problem with anybody in Russia, like the police, or some business guy, or whatever," he said, chuckling, "just show them this card. No problem."

A "Get Out of Jail Free" card! Never know when you can use that.

Kirsan Ilyumzhinov, president of the Republic of Kalmykia, was another interesting person I met. Kalmykia is part of the new Russian Federation created after the fall of the Soviet Union, and it is the only Buddhist region in Europe. In addition to being that country's president, Ilyumzhinov was also the president of the International Chess Federation. He is credited with advancing an already big interest in chess in Russia during his ICF presidency.

I had the opportunity to meet Ilyumzhinov while on a trip Dmitri Sikorski had arranged with the head of the

Kalmykian Hunting Department. Dmitri wanted to know if I would be interested in meeting the counry's president, who he said wanted to greet us and welcome us to his country. Of course I was interested, especially since I had just started a TV show in the U.S. and was hoping to film this hunt for an episode on the show.

"You think it would be OK if I took my TV camera along to get some film of the president?," I asked Dmitri. "Can you imagine how impressive that would be? Tell him it will help bring more tourists to Kalmaykia. Give him your best sales pitch."

"I'll see what I can do," Dmitri said. He did well. I was given permission to film our meeting.

I'll never forget walking into the president's office and seeing the colorful country flag, a large collection of

• *Denny and Kirsan Ilyumzhinov, the president of Kalmykia, taken during a meeting in 2002. (Dmitri Sikorski photo)*

Buddhist photos, paintings, statuettes, and an impressive conference table. There, sitting behind a huge desk, was Ilyumzhinov, looking presidential. The setting and scene were a bit intimidating.

After a formal meeting at the conference table with the head of the hunting department and another department head, I mustered up the nerve to ask Ilyumzhinov if he would make a statement I could use as an introduction to my TV show. He agreed.

I guessed Dmitri would have to translate what the president said, and I would need to dub in the translation when I edited the show. To my surprise, Ilyumzhinov followed his Russian greeting with one in excellent English.

"I would like to welcome our friends, especially those from America, to come and visit our beautiful country," he began. He went on to say how beautiful Kalmykia was and how many natural resources from flora to fauna can be found in this region. I was impressed.

The surprises and presidential hospitality were not over yet. Later that evening, much to our delight, Ilyumzhinov had a native dance troupe come to our hotel to perform some of the country's traditional dances in the hotel ballroom. Several of the dances dated as far back as the 16th century when the ancestors of the present day Kalmykians migrated to this part of Russia from China.

I kept the video camera rolling.

The next day we were taken to a Buddhist temple in downtown Elista, Kalmykia's capital, to ask for a blessing for our trip. Before entering the temple, we went through a ceremonial ritual where we had to touch a dozen or so large, colorful photos and paintings lined up about 40 yards from the entrance. Then we were told to walk into the temple, ask for a blessing and walk backward out the door.

Another close encounter with the head of a country came in January, 2000. While I didn't get to meet him, I had the chance to hunt stag on the estate of Leonid Kuchma, president of the Ukraine. Accompanying me on that trip was Jay Link from the Jack Link's Beef Jerky Company in Minong, Wisconsin. He was joined by several of his long-time hunting buddies.

As I mentioned, we didn't meet the president, but we almost had a close encounter.

One day he stopped by the main residence on the estate while we were in the hunting lodge a mile away. A security person came to the lodge and told us to stay inside and keep our hunting rifles locked in a storage room. He would watch them until the president left.

We were fine with that. None of us wanted to be roaming around the woods with a loaded rifle while Kuchma and his entourage of heavily-armed body guards patrolled the area.

Kuchma left the estate several hours later, and we went about our business.

Besides Dmitri, I worked with two other main outfitters in Russia over the years. One of them was Michael Silin, a short, thin man from Moscow, who had organized hunting and fishing trips for the Communist Party elite and the military when the country was still the Soviet Union. Michael had close friends in the hunting department and was able to get us in and out of sensitive areas to hunt moose, sheep, and bears.

I always enjoyed Michael's company because he was an easy-going guy with a good sense of humor, but he sure could get nervous helping us clear customs at the airports. That had a lot to do with us being heavily armed and entering sensitive military areas. As mentioned earlier, about the only people allowed to hunt in the Soviet Union were Communist Party elite and the military, so a convoy of Americans roaming around the countryside with high-powered rifles and several boxes of live ammunition was not something the local police and military personnel were used to seeing.

Fortunately, Michael had good contacts in the government and knew how the system worked. A number of times he asked me for "a little money to grease the wheels". I would hand him $50 or $100 and he would take care of the problem. When we encountered these situations, Michael would look at me and say, "What can I do? It's Russia."

The other outfitter I worked with extensively over the years was Andrey Konvolov. Andrey lived in the small town of Yelizovo, located just outside the city of Petropavlovsk on the Kamchatka Peninsula. I always enjoyed working with Andrey because I knew he was covering all the bases. He was a detail-oriented man who took his job seriously. Andrey also knew how to get things done under the table when needed.

In addition to working with me on bear and moose hunts on the Kamchatka Peninsula, Andrey was one of the top agents in Kamchatka for angling trips. The Kamchatka Peninsula had become the premier destination for fly fishermen. Salmon and rainbow trout fishing here was second to none. These pristine streams produced thousands of fish a year for anglers from all over Europe and the United States.

Andrey arranged many of these fishing trips through an organization called Wild Salmon Rivers (WSR), which worked closely with the Fly Shop. There were years when WSR booked more than 200 anglers to various streams on the Peninsula.

One of the most famous streams is the Zhuponova River, just north of Petropavlovsk. I also took clients there, with Andrey's help. I have caught more trout and salmon on a fly rod in one week on the Zhuponova than anywhere else.

I met one of Kamchatka's most prominent fly-fishing aficionados a number of years ago. Andrey had come up to me with a big grin as we made our way out of the small airport in Petropavlovsk.

"You know who that is?," he asked, pointing to a tall man standing just outside the door.

"It looks like Bobby Knight," I said excitedly. "He used to be the coach at Indiana and is now with Texas Tech. How do you know who Bobby Knight is?"

"That's him," Andrey replied. "That's Bobby Knight. He's been here before. He was at the Cedar Lodge, where you fished with me. I worked as an interpreter then and was at Cedar Lodge when he was there. He likes to fly fish here in Kamchatka. Have you ever met him?"

"No, I haven't," I said, "but I'm going to take care of that right now.

"Hi, my name is Denny Geurink," I said as I walked up to Knight and extended my hand. "I went to school at one of your Big Ten rivals. We played some exciting games against you when you were at Indiana."

"Which school was that?" Knight asked, smiling.

"The University of Michigan," I said. "I took graduate courses there."

"Those were some good games," Knight replied.

The conversation then turned to fishing. After talking a few minutes, we shook hands, wished each other luck and and parted. I never saw him again.

Another famous visitor to the Zhuponova in 2004 was President Jimmy Carter and his wife Rosalynn.

Among some of the nicest people I met in Russia were the various interpreters, guides, and cooks who accompanied me and my clients on our journeys. I got to know many of them well.

One year we were in a spring bear camp during the Russian Victory Day celebration, the equivalent of our Fourth of July. It is celebrated May 9 to commemorate the day the German military surrendered to the Soviet Union in World War II. It honors those who fought and died in the war. The holiday is observed with military parades in Red Square and the

• Among the nicest people I met in Russia were some of our guides. I especially enjoyed swapping stories with our Yakutian guides, shown here in front of our tents with Gerald and John Crever. (Gerald Crever photo)

laying of flowers and wreaths at grave sites. It's a poignant reminder of the carnage and casualties of war.

When May 9 arrived, the guides became very somber at the evening dinner table. They wanted to have a vodka toast to honor those who had fought and died in combat. Some of the guides had fathers, friends, and relatives among the casualties.

After the first toast, one of the guides stood up to toast American soldiers who fought and died, because, as he pointed out, Russians and Americans were allies in World War II. The guides made a big deal out of this alliance. It was the one time in history where Russians and Americans stood side by side to defeat a common enemy.

After that toast, I made a toast to Russian and American friendship. I told the guides my father was a World War II veteran, that he had landed on Omaha Beach in France on what is known in America as D-Day, and survived that day, only to be mowed down later by a German machine gun. He took four bullets. Two of them took out a lung, one went through his hip, and another went through his elbow as he fell to the ground. He lived to tell about it.

The looks on the guides' faces showed I had really struck a nerve. From that day on, every year we were in camp, the guides made sure they made a toast to my father. One year, two of the guides, who were in a camp about 30 miles away with some of my other clients, drove their snowmobiles over a mountain to come to the camp where I was staying, just so they could toast me and my father on Victory Day.

Much has been written over the years about the Russians' love affair with vodka, a very potent alcoholic beverage. I can tell you from personal experience most of it is true. It is an integral part of their society. They celebrate with it, mourn with it, party with it, and toast everything you can imagine with it. It's on the table for every occasion, and, of course, it's always in camp. The guides are always toasting something.

Those first few years, the guides would haul out the vodka bottle and shot glasses and say "Denny, wadka."

I didn't want to offend them by not joining in a toast, so I would say, "OK, but choot choot." This means 'just a little bit' in Russian.

The guides would look at me, chuckle at my attempt at speaking Russian, and then pour a full glass.

Undeterred, I kept asking for a "choot choot" shot every time they brought out the bottle, because I had such a hard time getting the nasty stuff past my lips. It burned all the way to the pit of my stomach. Some of the really cheap vodka the guides brought to camp would bring tears to a glass eye.

After a few years of asking the guides for a "choot choot" shot every time they hauled out the "helicopter fuel," as Dmitri called it, the guides began smiling at me and, instead of saying, "Denny, wadka!," they began saying, "Denny, choot choot! Denny, choot choot!"

The nickname soon stuck, and that's how Russian vodka became known as "choot choot" in our camps.

One of the first things we usually did after arriving at camp was meet with the guides and sight in our rifles. We wanted to make sure everything was working properly after our arduous trip from the States to the Middle of Nowhere, Siberia. The guides were just as interested as we were in making sure our rifles shot accurately. A bad shot could spell all sorts of trouble for guide and hunter.

•*Our Russian guides were as tough as nails. Notice this one even is missing the tip of his left index finger, not an unusual occurrence. Many were missing body parts. (Merle Barnaby photo)*

Those first few years the guides were especially interested in seeing what our rifles could do. They were used to old SKS military issue rifles. None of the rifles had scopes, and some were so battered they were held together with duct tape and baling wire. The guides were fascinated by the size and shininess of our rifles. They especially marveled at the scopes and the sizes of our cartridges.

"That's not a bullet, it's a bomb," one of the guides gasped in amazement our first year in Russia, as he looked at one of my cousin Terry Geurink's cartridges. "May I shoot your rifle?"

"Sure," Terry said, handing his .300 Magnum to the guide.

The guide pulled up the rifle, aimed at the target, and pulled the trigger ... just as Terry tried to warn him about the recoil. Too late. The guide got whacked on the eyebrow with the scope. He handed the rifle back to Terry, wiped the blood off his brow, and shook his head.

"Russian hunters don't need such big rifles," he said sarcastically. "We can kill bears with a little gun."

To be sure, our Russian guides were some of the toughest, hardest-working, grittiest individuals you'll ever meet. On one occasion, two of my Kamchatka guides traveled from their village over snow-covered mountains and through dense wilderness for two weeks, just so they could get two extra snowmobiles in camp for my hunters. They ate fish they caught in the streams and squirrels and hares they shot (and who knows what else) to survive so they wouldn't have to eat the food designated for camp. At night they slept on the sleds behind their snowmobiles, waking up frequently to chase bears and wolverines from their campsite.

Several times we had guides do the same thing for our sheep hunts in Yakutia, only then they were taking in strings of pack horses instead of snowmobiles. Again, it was a two-week ordeal, basically living off the land.

We have no comprehension of how tough life was -- and still is -- in many remote areas of Siberia. These guys

*• Life is harsh in the remote villages of Siberia. You can especially
see it in the faces of the elderly. (Ken Horm photo)*

do this all the time without giving it a second thought. It's
part of their normal way of life.

We often complain if the TV remote doesn't work!

Besides having a good command of the English
language, making them easy to communicate with, my
interpreters have always had an insatiable appetite
to learn more about America. Combine that with
my insatiable appetite to learn more about Russia,
and you have the basis for a good relationship. I've
learned to speak and understand quite a bit of
the Russian language over the years, thanks to my
interpreters.

One of the most interesting interpreters I had the
pleasure of getting to know is Vladislav Shurin. He lives in
the city of Donetsk in the Ukraine, and is an English
professor at the University of Donetsk. He has
impeccable language skills, but he was taught the
King's English. His quirky British accent made me
smile every time I heard him speak.

• *Our guides would do whatever it took to get the job done, including hooking up a horse to a homemade sled to haul one of my clients who had broken a leg a week before his expedition. (Dmitri Sikorski photo)*

Vlad and I shared many camps and many more laughs. He taught me a lot about the history and culture of Russia and the Ukraine. He also told me that when his country was part of the Soviet Union, things did not go well.

"The Communist Party leaders were always telling us how much better off we were than the Americans," Vlad said disgustedly. "Now we find out we are a Third World country. We are like a poor African country. We have been lied to all our lives. We were part of a great experiment called Communism, which failed. While the rest of the world evolved and moved forward, we stayed the same. Now we are 40 years behind America."

Another one of my favorite interpreters was Andrey Shutov. Andrey is also from the city of Donetsk. You will read more about him in an upcoming chapter.

I discovered that the Russians, despite having lived through tough times during the Soviet Union era, have quite a sense of humor. A street vendor we met on Moscow's famous Arbat Street in the early 1990s proved that.

Arbat Street has existed since the 15th century. Today it is lined with souvenir shops and street vendors; it has become a favorite tourist destination. When we were first there, not many people spoke English in the shops, but whoever was running the shop would always find someone who spoke English to help us out.

•*Taking a tour of a small Siberian village with friend Boris. (Denny Geurink photo)*

I wanted to buy one of the Russian-style fur hats and asked the street vendor if he would take American money. He didn't know what I was talking about but told me to wait a minute. He was soon back with a young man, who approached me with a big grin.

"How can I help you, sir," he asked, smiling. "Did you want to buy this hat from my friend? What were you saying to him?"

• *The daughter of one of our guides models a beautiful Russian fur hat her father made from a red fox he trapped. (Ken Horm photo)*

"I asked him if he would take U.S. dollars for this hat, and if so, what would it cost in American money."

"Let me see your American money," the young man said. I handed him several one-dollar bills. He looked them over carefully and grinned.

"Your American dollar looks just like the Russian buck," he chuckled. "Of course we will take your American dollars."

We all had a big laugh over that one. Because we were walking around without an interpreter at the time, the young man volunteered to stay with us and   help with our souvenir shopping. What a great gesture! Today you don't need an interpreter on Arbat   Street, as   nearly all the shop owners and vendors have   someone who   speaks English.   They   have   picked   up   on   our decadent capitalistic ways quickly.

In fact, everything about Russia has changed tremendously in the past two-plus decades. Moscow has gone from being one of the poorest cities in the world to the most expensive city in the world. According to Dmitri, on any given day there are more than two million foreigners in Moscow, a far cry from the "closed society" days of the Soviet era.

• Galina Unichanko, one of our interpreters, compares her long fingernails to the claw marks of a bear. Not much difference. (Steve Van Poucke photo)

CHAPTER 6

THE FOOD

ONE OF THE FIRST THINGS I noticed when I arrived in Russia was how different their food was from ours; at least in the way they prepared it and what they considered suitable for each of the three square meals per day.

My introduction to Russian cuisine on that inaugural trip to Moscow was startling. We checked into our hotel and decided to go out for dinner, having no idea what a challenge "going out for dinner" would be.

The first challenge was trying to find a restaurant. We drove all over town looking for a place to eat. It was still the Soviet Union, and it soon became apparent that the communist system didn't put much emphasis on eating out, fine dining, or fancy restaurants.

Here we were in a city of more than 10 million people and couldn't find one decent restaurant.

When we finally found a restaurant, after nearly an hour of driving around, I quickly saw why it took us so long. It was in the basement of a drab building, with a very small sign out front. No one ever would have guessed it was a restaurant. It looked more like a small studio apartment a college student would have rented off-campus. No neon sign. No flashing arrows. No "Open" sign. Absolutely nothing that would lead you to believe someone was cooking and serving food there.

We were met at the door by a stoic man who led us to a small table in an isolated corner of the restaurant. Even though the restaurant was almost empty, Dmitri told us this was the area reserved for foreigners. He told us foreigners and locals were usually segregated in restaurants, hotels, and other public places.

Officials wanted to keep foreigners from interacting with local people. We had first noticed this practice at the hotel. We were lodged on separate floors and generally kept apart in many ways. I guess they didn't want us to poison the locals with our evil capitalistic views.

As we later learned, foreigners paid a different rate for their room than did the locals. Dmitri told me he paid less than half of what we paid for our rooms. Several times on subsequent hunts he would tell me not to speak while we registered at a hotel. He would register me as a Russian rather than a foreigner to save money on the rooms. Anyhow, I digress; back to the restaurant.

As we sat at the table talking about how hungry we were and what we wanted to eat, I felt a presence behind me. I looked up and saw a young lady with a pen and pad in hand, staring hollowly straight ahead.

"Hi," I greeted her with a smile.

She nodded and continued to stare blankly into the smoke-filled air. She never said a word. Never cracked a smile. Didn't even look at us. In the U.S., you are greeted with a big smile and a "How are you?" and "What can I get you to drink?" Nobody in the restaurant seemed glad we were patronizing them.

The waitress handed Dmitri a menu. He said something to her and she just shrugged her shoulders. "Sorry guys, no English menus, only Russian menus," he told us. "So tell me what you want to eat and I will order it for you."

"What do they have?," I asked. "I'm kind of hungry. I could eat a horse."

"I'll see if they have that," Dmitri replied.

As it didn't seem he was joking, I quickly added, "That's an expression we use in the U.S. when we are really hungry. I really don't want literally to eat a horse."

"Well, they do eat horses in Russia," Dmitri said. "I just don't know if they serve it in this restaurant."

"I'll pass on the horse," I replied. I learned several years later on a trip to Yakutsk that Dmitri was right about horse meat on Russian menus. In one of the restaurants we visited, there was a selection of horse meat entrees. Among them were Fillet of Colt, Steak of Mare, and Stallion Meatballs. You could also order a glass of warm mare's milk to go with your Colt Fillet. Yum! Again, I digress.

"It seems they have some sort of steak on the menu," Dmitri told us. "I don't think it's beef; we don't have much beef in Russia. It's probably pork steak. They also have chicken and fish. I would not order the fish. We are a long way from the sea. I'm afraid it won't be very fresh. Who knows how long it took to ship the fish here, and I don't know how well it was refrigerated. So, what do you want to order?"

I was beginning to get a good picture of what Dmitri thought of restaurant food. He had warned me before we started to look for a restaurant that one of the reasons Russians don't eat out is that the food in many restaurants is suspect. Whether that was the reason there were few restaurants in Russia, or whether it was for effect, I didn't know. We had insisted on finding a restaurant, while Dmitri had suggested we buy food and cook it ourselves. Obviously, Russians don't know how lazy many Americans are. Many of us would rather go out than cook.

"Tell you what ... I'll try the steak," I said to Dmitri after contemplating the possibilities.

Dmitri passed my order to the waitress in Russian. She shook her head. Dmitri said something else. She again shook her head, but this time accompanied her head shake with an explanation. Aha, she wasn't mute.

"Ah, sorry, Denny they don't have any steak left," Dmitri said. "Is there anything else you would like to try?"

"How about the chicken?"

Again, Dmitri passed my request to the waitress. Again, the waitress shook her head.

Dmitri spoke to her again. She came back with a curt reply and shook her head one more time.

"Sorry, Denny, they don't have any chicken, either. "Anything else you want to try?"

"How about the pork?"

One more time Dmitri relayed my request. One more time she shook her head.

Dmitri spoke to her again, with a definite hint of disgust. Even though he was speaking in Russian, I knew what he was saying.

It also was what I wanted to say at that point. We all were getting fed up about not being able to be fed.

"They don't have any pork either, Denny," Dmitri groused. "Anything else you want to try?"

We were down to the fish. While I wasn't eager to eat the fish after what Dmitri had told us about it earlier. I was hungry and just wanted to move this whole thing along.

"I guess I'll have the fish," I told Dmitri.

Once more Dmitri relayed my food order to the waitress. She shook her head again.

Dmitri was now definitely irritated; I was glad I didn't understand Russian. As he looked at me and began to speak, I said, "Yeah, I know, they don't have fish. What do they have? Do they have any food? This is a restaurant, right?"

Dmitri spoke to the waitress again. The conversation definitely became tense as they talked. Finally, Dmitri said, "they have hot dogs and rice. Do you want to eat hot dogs and rice? I told you we should have bought some food and cooked it ourselves.

"Do you want to leave? Let's leave and get some food and cook it ourselves."

"I'll take the hot dogs and rice," I replied.

If this didn't show Dmitri how much many Americans detest cooking for themselves, nothing would. We would rather go to a restaurant and eat hot dogs and rice than buy food and cook it ourselves. Pitiful, when you think about it.

A contributing factor in my decision was that the waitress was getting upset. She had a tear in the corner of her eye; I felt bad for her. It wasn't her fault the restaurant didn't have anything but hot dogs and rice. We understood it wasn't her fault. I asked Dmitri to apologize to her for our rude behavior. Dmitri agreed and conveyed our apologies.

A bit later the waitress presented us with our plates of hot dogs and rice. The "chef " had tried to spruce it up a little with a sprig of parsley on top of the pile of cold rice. We tried not to laugh out loud. Let's have a little respect here. As hungry as I was, the hot dogs and cold rice actually tasted pretty good.

After the meal, still feeling a bit bad for the waitress, we decided to leave her a nice tip. Russians apparently aren't much for tipping. When she came back with the change from our bill on a small tray, I told her to keep it. She looked at me quizzically and tried to hand the tray back to me. I don't think she was used to getting tips; she definitely was not used to getting that large a tip.

She said something to Dmitri and tried to hand the tray to him. He said something back to her and pushed the tray away. Right then a look of complete surprise overcame her, and she put her hand to her chest. "For me?" she gasped in Russian. "All of this for me?"

"Yes, for you," Dmitri replied.

She said "spaceba" several times as she walked away... actually, it was more like a skip.

"Spaceba", we learned, was Russian for "thank you." That was the first Russian word we learned.

"She will probably go home now and take the rest of the week off," Dmitri scolded. "Russians usually don't leave a tip. When they do, it's not much, maybe five percent or less. You just gave her a month's wages. You tip way too much."

Our main problem was that we didn't realize how little money these people made, nor had we fully grasped what Russian currency was worth. We were told the exchange rate when we traded some of our dollars for rubles, but it didn't really register. We often referred to the rubles as "monopoly money". It took so many rubles to make one dollar that we treated it like monopoly money. Dmitri said our waitress probably made only $10 to $15 a week. Gives you an idea of what life was like under communism in 1991.

This episode was a unique insight into the stark difference between capitalism and communism. This establishment was owned and operated by the government, not by a private individual. There was no incentive to be cordial, no incentive to smile, and, as we learned, no incentive to offer a large menu of tasty entrees.

With private ownership, the owner knows he or she has to do everything s/he can to offer the best product and the best service possible so the customer will want to return. When you own a business, the amount of money you make is based directly upon the amount of product or service you sell, and its quality. Plus cost control, of course.

Not so when an enterprise is government owned and operated. The people working here couldn't care less if we never came back, and probably hoped we wouldn't. It would make their job much easier. They were paid the same, no matter what. There was no way for them to make extra money, other than meager tips.

We discovered another big difference between restaurants in Russia and America the following year when Dmitri visited the U.S., and I took him to one of our restaurants. It was as much a lesson on the difference in the amount and quality of food we have in the U.S. compared to the lack of food in Russia.

First, Dmitri was shocked by the number of people in America who ate out. We were on a 30-minute waiting list at the restaurant. Second, as we sat in the waiting area, he kept watching the number of half-eaten plates of food taken back to the kitchen.

"My god," he gasped, "Americans throw away more food than we have!"

I never had thought about that. As I began watching the trays going from the tables back to the kitchen, where the trays would be dumped, I felt a bit ashamed of our country. We do throw away more food than many countries have. What a waste!

The next day we took Dmitri to a supermarket to buy groceries. Again, he was flabbergasted by the quantity and variety of food available in the U.S.

"There is so much bread in America it's falling off the shelves," Dmitri quipped. "In Russia, people sometimes have to wait in line more than two hours to get a loaf of bread."

If nothing else, my first trip to the Soviet Union showed me how lucky I was to be born in America. We sometimes take this country for granted. We seldom think about how good we have it.

FISH BREAD

One of the strangest culinary items I encountered in Russia was served by a camp cook. We were staying in a small village about 400 miles east of Moscow. Our cook was a kind, grandmotherly lady named Anna.

She told us that during our stay she wanted to introduce us to some of the local foods she grew up on during the old Soviet Union days. She wanted us to try things we may not have had a chance to eat back home.

One day, however, she really pushed the envelope.

Dmitri and I were sitting at the dining room table having a cup of coffee when Anna walked in with a loaf of fresh bread she had just pulled from the oven. The warm loaf looked and smelled inviting, with its golden brown hue and soft texture.

Anna said something to Dmitri as she set the loaf on the table and handed Dmitri a knife. Dmitri got a strange expression and turned to me.

"Anna says this is fish bread, whatever that is." He gave the bread the evil eye.

"I've never heard of fish bread. I don't know what it is. Maybe she ground up some fish and added it to the flour when she cooked it. A loaf of bread that tastes like fish doesn't sound good to me."

"Can't say I want to eat fishy bread, either," I replied, "but we don't want to offend Anna. Let's give it a shot."

Dmitri took the big knife and cut the bread about a third of the way into the loaf. There, smack in the middle of the loaf, surrounded by baked dough, was an entire fish. Head, tail, fins, scales, and *everything!* The head poked out of the piece Dmitri had just cut, and the cooked fish stared up at us with glassy eyes.

Dmitri gagged and pushed the bread away, cursing in Russian. I don't know exactly what he said, but, believe me, he was cursing. I felt sorry for Anna as she scooped the loaf of bread off the table and rushed out of the room. I swear the fish stuck out its tongue at us as Anna darted to the kitchen.

Later that afternoon, she returned with a fresh loaf of cheese bread. That was more like it! A loaf of fresh, warm bread with cheese baked in the middle of it is much more palatable.

THATS NOT PASTA!

One of my most unusual encounters with Russian food occurred in a moose hunting camp.

A client had scored on a big bull moose, and the guides had brought some of the meat back to camp for dinner. I was eagerly looking forward to my first taste of moose meat.

• *Zoya Abdilina, one of our interpreters, helps prepare a meal in our tent camp. (Denny Geurink photo)*

At dinner time Dmitri called us to the cook tent. We sat down around a large wooden table, flanked on each side by 2x8 planks of rough sawn wood that stretched from one stump to another and served as benches.

The cook placed in front of us a bowl of two- to three-inch by half-inch strips of thin, white pasta in a cheese sauce. It looked like fettuccine. I ate the bowl of pasta with gusto and waited eagerly for the moose steaks to follow. As I could see, the cook wasn't quite ready with the steaks. I asked Dmitri if the cook could give me another bowl while we waited.

"That's a tasty pasta dish he whipped up," I said, handing my bowl to the cook. "Tell him he did a great job."

"What pasta?" Dmitri asked.

"The pasta we just ate."

"That's not pasta."

"It's not?" I said incredulously. "Then what is it?"

"It's the sinus cavity from the moose," Dmitri said with a grin. "You want some more?"

"The sinus cavity of a moose? Aaaaaghh! Never mind, I'll pass."

"But you said it was tasty," Dmitri said, still grinning.

"Not any more!"

MOOSE MEAT SURPRISE

A couple of years later, hunting moose near the city of Yakutsk with a group of clients, we were served another 'moose surprise' dish.

The guides in this camp were local native people called Eveny. They are a warm and friendly people, but they definitely had different ideas than we did about the parts of a moose that are good to eat.

As we sat at the dinner table waiting to eat some of the moose one of the guys had shot a few hours earlier, the first thing the cook set in front of us was the same 'pasta' dish we had in the previous camp. When I declined it, the interpreter, Misha, asked what was wrong.

"I know what that stuff is," I told him. "It's the sinus cavity from the moose, right?"

"Yes, it is," Misha replied, "but the guides consider it a delicacy. It's very tasty. You should try some."

"I have tried it before, and while it doesn't taste as bad as its name sounds, I just can't eat it," I said. "I can't get the thought of nibbling on a moose nose out of my mind."

Misha laughed and said, "the cook is putting other moose dishes on the table. Try one of them."

"Well, what exactly are they? I can't really say I see anything that looks like a steak or roast."

"What's this one?" I asked, pointing to one of the plates.

"That's moose tongue," Misha said. "It also is considered a delicacy. Do you want some?"

"No, I think I'll pass on the tongue," I replied. I didn't feel like French kissing a moose either. "What about that one? What's that?"

"That's the heart," Misha said.

"And that one?" I pointed to another plate.

"Those are the kidneys."

"And that?"

"Those are the lungs," Misha said, chuckling.

"Oh, my God!" I gasped. "Where is the meat? Where are the steaks and roasts?"

"These dishes are considered delicacies," Misha said. "The guides don't like steaks and roasts as much. They will go back and get that stuff later and take it to the village for the others to eat. They save the good stuff for themselves. Nothing will go to waste."

"I think I'll stick with bread and cheese tonight," I told Misha.

The next day I followed one of my hunters with my TV camera and captured his hunt on film. After the big bull was down, the first thing the guide did was cut out one of the eyeballs and take a bite. Eyeball fluids squirted everywhere.

The guide looked at us and offered a bite. I declined as diplomatically as I could, trying desperately to suppress my gag reflex. The hunter also declined when he was offered a bite. We looked at each other with small grins of disbelief.

As the guide began field-dressing the moose, I paid attention to what he was doing. Out came the sinus cavity. Then he pulled out the heart, lungs, kidneys, and some other things I don't even want to talk about. He stuffed everything in a plastic bag and got ready to leave.

"Wait a minute," I said to the guide. "I want the tenderloin to take back for the hunters and me. You guys can eat that stuff; we want the meat."

The guide looked at me quizzically and smiled. He had no

idea what I was saying. I went to the moose carcass and pointed at the tenderloin.

"Denny want tenderloin," I said, jabbing at the inside of the rib cage next to the backbone. "Tenderloin. Denny want tenderloin!"

"Ah, fillet," The guide chuckled. "Denny, fillet."

"Yes, fillet," I smiled. "Denny want fillet."

The guide peeled out both fillets and handed them to me.

They were huge! They must have weighed eight to 10 pounds each.

I had brought a plastic bag, as I was determined to bring the tenderloins back and eat them instead of those other things. I carried them back to camp like a bag of gold. I couldn't wait to eat moose tenderloin for dinner.

That evening, I quickly learned why the guides prefer innards to steaks. The cook pan fried the fillets into little piles of charcoal. Naturally, they were tough and tasteless. The guides polished off the juicy innards.

The next day I cut several steaks from the remaining fillets and marinated them in a mixture of CocaCola, catsup, salt, pepper, mustard, and anything else that looked like a spice. The cook looked at me like I was crazy.

I then found some rocks and built a fire pit. The wood in the fire pit burned all day until there was a nice pile of hot coals.

I found a roll of heavy wire the guides had brought in for some project and made a grill top of sorts.

When the guys came back to camp, I placed the homemade grill over the fire pit, put the steaks on the grill, and cooked them until they were medium-well done. I handed them to my hunters, all of whom waited with great anticipation. The steaks were excellent.

As my clients oohed and ahhed, the guides looked on in disbelief. They were busy munching on heart and lungs.

I offered one of the guides a medium-well fillet. He declined and pointed at the pile of lungs on his plate, saying "Delicatessen, delicatessen!"

• *While we had some unusual meals in our remote camps, most were tasty, and the presentation usually was great. (Denny Geurink photos)*

• *A small woodstove is all that's needed to cook some amazingly good meals, made even better by the fact that we were in the middle of nowhere and didn't have an option.*

"Try it, just try it," I insisted, holding the plate with the fillet in front of him. Reluctantly, he grabbed a fillet in his hand and took a small bite.

"Oohh," he exclaimed in utter shock. "Oohh! Delicatessen! Delicatessen!"

"Delicatessen?," the other guides asked.

"Da, delicatessen!," he blurted.

The other guides each took a bite and began oohing and ahhing like my clients. Now they knew how a fillet was supposed to taste.

The guides and my hunters had me grilling steaks the rest of the week. In subsequent years I took a grill top and marinating sauce to every moose camp.

NOTHING GOES TO WASTE

Over the years I have eaten all sorts of what we Americans would consider strange dishes -- bear paw soup, fried moose tongue, tripe from a Maral stag, horse meat, goat meat, blood meal, mare's milk, Rocky Mountain oysters from red deer and mouflon sheep, plus a host of mystery meats that I shudder to think about. Some of it was eaten on a "don't ask, don't tell" basis.

You have to remember that the people we were hunting with were used to living off the land. They are modern day Jeremiah Johnsons living in the remote regions of Siberia. They ate everything. Nothing went to waste.

Actually, they weren't any different from our ancestors. I remember watching my grandpa butcher a hog. When he had finished processing the hog, there was nothing left but a spot of blood on the garage floor. He could see I was surprised. That's when he looked over at me and winked. "We eat everything but the squeal," he said.

The people we met in Siberia remind me so much of my grandfather and his generation. That's why the guides ate everything but the grunt of a moose.

What we didn't eat in camp, they took back to their

villages   after the hunt. Our moose hunts were an efficient way for them to stock up on meat for the winter, while we were looking at the hunts as a way to get a big set of antlers for the wall. This was quite a conflict of interest in the early years.

One of the contributing factors to the big difference in the perception of what a hunt consisted of stemmed from the fact that we were getting moose tags reserved for the locals for subsistence hunting.

When I first began thinking about setting up moose hunts in the Yakutia region of central Siberia, the outfitter told me there were only three or four moose tags set aside in his area for "foreign" or non-native hunters. The native people could get approximately 18 moose tags a year to gather meat for the villages.

I told him I couldn't set up hunts for just three people a year. It would be too costly.

We began brainstorming. When he told me about the 18 tags reserved for the locals for subsistence hunting, I asked him if there was a way to transfer some of the local tags to foreign tags.

I told him we would gladly give all the meat to the locals, except the little meat we ate in camp. My hunters were coming for the trophy, not the meat. We couldn't get that much meat home anyway. Baggage fees would cost too much, and it wouldn't be worth the importation hassle we undoubtedly would have with the U.S. Department of Agriculture.

He worked out an agreement with local authorities for a reassignment of moose tags. He and the guides were pleased with the arrangement. Not only did the natives get the meat they were after, we bought their tags, paid them to guide us, and brought the meat back to the villages after the hunt. It was a "win-win" situation.

However, this arrangement lead to a problem the first few hunts. The guides were used to shooting the first thing they saw -- cow, calf, small bull or big bull. They were not trophy hunting; they were meat hunting. Consequently, they pushed our hunters to shoot whatever they saw first.

My hunters, meanwhile, were here to shoot as big a moose as they could find.

The guides finally realized we each were going to shoot a moose at some point in the hunt, whether it be the first one we saw or the last one we saw. They were going to get their meat, regardless. That's when they got excited about trying to find the biggest bulls possible.

We hired a chopper to fly us out and drop us at camp, then come back after the hunt to pick us up. It now was much easier for the guides to get the meat back to their village. Normally, they would have had to walk or take a horse to camp, meaning many trips to pack out a moose. Now the meat was coming to town at one time, and all the villagers knew it was coming.

When we returned to town those first few years with the helicopters loaded with moose meat, as soon as the villagers heard the chopper they poured out of their homes with buckets, wheel barrows, axes, saws, and plastic bags. It was free moose meat day in the village!

One year the locals waited for us in a large field just outside of town. They had a long table set up with an assortment of snacks and drinks. It was like a hero's welcome. As soon as we climbed out of the helicopter, they escorted us to the table and asked us to sit down. Then they waited on us like we were dignitaries. We were a bit humbled by the experience.

Talk about nothing going to waste! When a bear is harvested, the Russians even scrape the fat off the bear's chest. They take this fat back to camp and boil it down to a thick, clear liquid, then store it in a jar. They use it for medicinal purposes. Some Russians eat a tablespoon of fat every day for preventive maintenance, much the same way my mother used to make me take a tablespoon of cod liver oil when I was a youngster.

One year when I was sick in camp with a cold, the cook tried to get me to take a tablespoon of the boiled fat. I wanted to but just couldn't get it past my nose. He then told me to rub it on my chest like Vick's. I did. I smelled like a dead fish for several days but it cleared my head cold. Many old home remedies have been handed down for generations, because they work!

After several years of eating strange foods on these trips, I planned a standardized menu for the camps. While we thoroughly enjoyed much of the Russian cuisine -- borscht soup, fried cheese bread, flat chicken, and other local delicacies -- I wanted to phase out a few things. Bear paw soup, for one. I created a full menu for the entire hunt and had the outfitter give it to all our cooks before we arrived at the camps. It included many good Russian dishes, plus a few American favorites. Ham and eggs and bacon for breakfast, anyone?

Author's Note: As mentioned earlier in this chapter, we found it almost impossible to find a place to eat on that first trip because restaurants and eating out were not a cultural part of the Soviet Union. This changed quickly when the communist government fell. Once capitalism moved in, restaurants began popping up like morel mushrooms after a warm spring rain. Just one year later, in 1992, we had a wide selection of great eating places to choose from. Today you can find everything from McDonalds to TGI Fridays to Pizza Huts and Subway shops. God bless capitalism!

The word in neon lights is MOSCOW, in the Cyrillic alphabet of the Russian language

Just wanted to show what is available in Moscow now compared to 25 years ago when we couldn't even find a restaurant. There are many top-end restaurants in Moscow today.

Sometimes you pay more for the presentation than the meal.This small plate, lower left, was at a restaurant that served fancy food rather than large portions. The gargantuan meal of king crab legs was toward the other end of the volume scale ... and delicious.

Photos by Denny
Geurink

CHAPTER 7

THE CULTURE

BEING A HISTORY BUFF, I was especially fascinated by the cultural and social differences between the United States and Russia on those first few trips back in the early '90s. I was intrigued by how differently our countries had evolved over the years under two drastically different forms of government. The contrast between communism and capitalism was dramatic. You could see it in many facets of the everyday lives of the Russian people; it was evident in the clothes they wore, the cars they drove, the food they ate, the places they lived.

It was especially evident in their homes. There were very few "houses" in the cities. Everyone lived in a government-owned apartment complex. These apartment buildings were large, ugly, and run-down. Even recently-built complexes looked at least 50 years old. There was absolutely no emphasis on design or beauty. Buildings and communities were basic and functional, giving the impression of a cold existence.

As we drove through St. Petersburg one day, I commented to Dmitri about how dull and drab the apartment buildings' exteriors were. They all could have used a coat of paint. The yards were messy and uninviting, and there was very little grass or shrubbery to make them look "homey." The hallways and stairways were dark and dingy, almost creepy. Yet, when I had a chance to visit a guide's and a cook's apartments, they were bright and cheerful.

"That's because all these buildings are government-owned," Dmitri explained. "The people who live there aren't going to spend their money fixing up the outside of the building they don't own. They spend money on the inside, because that's where they live. It's not like in the U.S. You usually own your home, so you want it to look good inside and outside. You don't mind spending money on something that belongs to you, but you're not going to spend money on something that isn't yours."

This -- the ownership of private property -- was an eye opening, first hand look at one of the major differences between capitalism and communism.

I also learned from Dmitri that all Soviet citizens were required to have passports and personal documentation with them whenever they moved about in their own country, as foreigners do when they come to visit. If they stayed more than three days in Moscow, they had to register with local authorities. If a Russian wanted to move from one city to another, he had to get permission. The Soviet Union was paranoid about keeping track of its citizens. Big Brother was always watching.

The transportation system was another thing that really intrigued me those first few years. In the States, just about everyone owns a car or pickup truck. In Russia at that time few people owned a private vehicle. They walked from one place to another or used public transportation. That's why Moscow's underground metro system is one of the largest and busiest in the world. That's also why, above ground, streets today are choked with streetcars and buses. No country in the world has more public transportation than Russia. It was one of the core principals of communism.

Most of the cars we saw on the roads were small, plain, boxy cubicles called Ladas. The Lada is a Soviet-engineered car that was first built in the 1970s. It's a dull, drab, and purely functional vehicle designed to get people from Point A to Point B. No frills, no sport, no speed. In the early '90s, I didn't see convertibles, pickup trucks or brightly-colored vehicles in Russia.

By comparison, in the U.S. at that time we were in love with our cars and trucks. (Still are!) Many people saw their vehicle as an extension of their personality. Our cars and trucks were big, beefed-up road hogs with bucket seats, chrome wheels, and leather interiors. There was nothing even close to that in the Soviet Union in the early '90s.

Today, just 20-some years later, the streets of Moscow are jammed with cars. In fact, traffic has become a major problem in Moscow because the road system wasn't designed to hold the level of traffic that now exists.

As in any other major city around the world, you will now find every make, model, and size of car for sale in Russia. We drove past a huge Ford dealership every time we went from the airport to our hotel.

• *Red Square: Once off limits to foreigners but is now one of the most popular tourist destinations in the world. (Denny Geurink photo)*

Toilet paper can be used as another tool to compare capitalism and communism. Toilet paper? A tool? I know what you're thinking: this guy's missing a card. Please indulge me. I was introduced to what I call the "Toilet Paper Effect" on my first trip to the Soviet Union. It began one day when I got into an interesting discussion with one of my interpreters about, of all things, toilet paper. I asked him why Russian toilet paper was so coarse and rough.

• *Red Square. Notice the heavy police presence. This was right after the coup. (Denny Geurink photo)*

"Toilet paper in the U.S. is much thicker, softer, and smoother than the brown paper bag material you use," I said, chuckling. "We use that kind of paper in a butcher shop to wrap meat. Our toilet paper even looks and smells good."

"That's easy to explain," my interpreter replied. "In the U.S. all toilet paper companies are privately-owned. Each company tries to make its brand of toilet paper better than the other companies' toilet paper, so they can sell more product and make more money. Your toilet paper is always improving, getting softer and smoother. Here, the government owns and operates the only toilet paper manufacturing company. There is no competition. They don't have to bother making it any better, because you can't go anywhere else to buy better toilet paper. If you want toilet paper, here it is. You use the government's toilet paper or you do without.

• *Changing of the guard in front of Lenin's tomb on Red Square. (Denny Geurink photo)*

"In some of the villages, people use old newspapers or magazines instead of toilet paper," my interpreter chuckled, "because it's softer."

The toilets you threw the paper into were worse, than the paper. This was especially true of the toilets found in public "restrooms". I use the term 'toilet' and 'restroom' here very loosely. Again, there was no emphasis on comfort or convenience in the Soviet Union. Most of the toilets found in public places were nothing more than a hole in the floor. There were no 'toilets' per se. No porcelain throne to sit on. There was nothing to sit on. You need to take a number two, you squat over an open pit, praying you don't lose your balance. I have no idea how 70-year-old ladies managed it. My wife has a fit when I leave the seat up!

When we had to make a pit stop while traveling down the road, we would pull into a 'rest area' --again, I use the term loosely -- and try to hold our breath the whole time we were in the pit area. You would know the definition of gag reflex when you entered one of these facilities.

We finally started doing the same thing most of the local Russians did; that is, we would take care of business behind the building, where you could at least breathe while you relieved yourself. You could see the locals were avoiding going into the building by the toilet paper and 'droppings' scattered around.

I discovered another big difference between capitalism and communism on that first trip when Dmitri and I got on the subject of productivity. Dmitri told me the Soviet Union was talking about increasing the work day from eight to 10 hours in its factories to boost productivity. Workers just weren't getting enough done in eight hours.

"People in the factories seem to be working slower and getting less done," Dmitri explained. "That's one of the problems with communism. There's no incentive to work harder and get more done so you can make more money. Everyone gets paid the same, no matter how hard they work. Why should Boris work hard when he gets paid the same as Anatoly who sits around all day and does nothing? The slower Anatoly goes, the slower Boris goes. Instead of getting more done, they get less done. This system doesn't work."

"Communism breeds lazy people," another interpreter chimed in. "It just doesn't work. The problem is that it's taken 75 years to prove that it doesn't work. So now we are 75 years behind the rest of the world."

This negative attitude toward communism was especially prevalent with the younger generation in Russia. One time we were in the town of Shushenskoye after an ibex hunt and went to visit the home where Lenin had been placed under house arrest from 1897 to 1900. He had been exiled there by the Czar for advocating the overthrow of the monarchy. His brother, Alexander "Sacha" Ulyanov, had been arrested on May 8, 1887, for trying to assassinate the Czar. The Lenin family was bent on revolution.

During our sightseeing visit, the tour guide, a young man in his late twenties, put everything in perspective.

"This is where Lenin worked out his Marxist ideas that led to the Bolshevik Revolution in 1917," our tour guide stated. "This is where all the bulls**t started that led this country into chaos, isolation, and poverty. If only the Czar had executed Lenin instead of putting him under house arrest, this country would have been much better off."

Wasn't expecting that one!

As Dmitri and other interpreters had so colorfully pointed out, their life under the communist brand of socialism was harsh. Because there was no way to earn extra money by working harder or producing more, many people at that time resorted to more 'creative' ways of supplementing their income. This became especially prevalent during the transitional period between the break-up of the Soviet Union and the establishment of Russia's own brand of democracy. At that time, Russia was much like the old American Wild West. It was a freewheeling time of discovery, graft, and corruption. There was a strong "anything goes" attitude in the country until they found their way into the 21st century.

During those early years, we regularly had to grease wheels to make the system work efficiently. All my outfitters were good at greasing wheels; Dmitri was particularly good at it.

For the first few years we were in business, Dmitri had me bring gifts to give to local officials to help speed up the customs process. The presents ranged from hard-sided gun cases, Swiss Army knives, and Gerber tools to cartons of Marlboro cigarettes. One year I brought a fancy display of the different kinds of rifle cartridges made in the United States. It had been specifically requested by one of the customs agents.

Even with grease, it sometimes took a while to get anything done. People didn't seem to know how to do anything quickly, to say nothing about caring to do so.

• *St. Basils Cathedral is one of the most iconic sights on Red Square. It was built in 1555 by Czar Ivan the Terrible. (Denny Geurink photo)*

I think it was a holdover from the communist days when nobody was in a hurry. In the U.S., time is money. In the Soviet Union time was, well . . . just time.

Because my clients were accustomed to the way things are done in the U.S., they had a hard time dealing with how slowly things moved in Russia. To make things easier for them, I always told them before we left home to forget about the Western time clock and be patient, really patient.

We have what I call the McDonald's mentality in the States. You order your food at one window, pay for it at the next window, pick it up at the next one, and are back on the road in five minutes. No such concept in Russia.

"In the U.S. we have Eastern Standard Time, Central Standard Time, Mountain Standard Time and Pacific Standard time," I noted to my clients, to drive home the point.

"In Russia there is one time -- Russian Standard Time -- even though there are 11 time zones. This means things get done when they get done. There is no set time schedule. No one is in a hurry. If someone tells you it will take an hour to do something, it could take 30 minutes, or two hours or two days. There is no concept of time management."

After several years of bringing gifts to Russia and handing them to the customs agents, that changed one year. As I was unwrapping a gift for one of the agents, Dmitri pulled me aside. "Don't give that to him. He can't accept gifts any more. It's against the law. Give it to me; I will give it to him later."

It was now illegal to give a gift to the agent. It still happened, but not in the open.

One of the most interesting episodes of greasing the wheels occurred in downtown Moscow in the mid-'90s. I could have used the colonel's "Get Out of Jail Free" card on this occasion, but, unfortunately, I didn't yet have it.

I had just finished checking into the hotel and was hungry after my long flight, so I decided to catch a cab to a local restaurant. On the way to the restaurant, we were pulled over by a policeman. I suddenly realized I had left my passport at the hotel registration desk. Not good.

(Back then, a hotel would take your passport and keep it several hours, even overnight, to complete the registration process. I usually waited to get my passport back before leaving the hotel.)

After checking the taxi driver's papers, the policeman looked at me in the back seat.

"May I see your passport," he asked in decent English, obviously knowing I wasn't Russian.

"I left it at the hotel so they could register me," I replied nervously. "I can get it and show it to you."

"Big problem," he said with a steely stare. "You need to have passport."

"I do have a passport, but they took it from me at the hotel," I replied. "I can show you if you want to follow me back to the hotel."

"Oh no, can't go to hotel," the policeman said. "Must have passport with you. Big problem. Please come with me to my car. Maybe we need to go to police station."

I did not want to spend the night in a Russian jail! I thought my knees were going to buckle as we walked to his cruiser.   In the cruiser sat two more cops. This was getting worse by the second.

The officer turned and looked at me in the back seat with a bit of a smile. I thought that odd, not realizing it hinted at 'a solution'.

"No passport is a big problem in Russia," he said the third time. "What to do? Maybe we go to police station?"

I cringed, trying to figure out what to do. Then it hit me. He asked me "What to do?". He has that small smile. He is looking for money. The solution is in my wallet.

I pulled a $50 bill from my wallet and showed it to him. "Will this solve the problem?"

"There are three of us," the officer said. "Still big problem."

I pulled out two more fifties. I'd have given him my entire wallet to stay out of a Russian jail cell. "Here are three fifties," I said. "Problem solved?"

"Problem solved," the policeman replied, smiling broadly as he took the cash. "You can go back to taxi now."

Then he added insult to injury. "Have a good day," he chirped.

You will never see anyone hop into the back seat of a taxi faster than I did. Solemn vow and guarantee: From now on, I will have my passport with me whenever I travel in Russia or any other country where I need it.

Many Russians in those early years disliked policemen because of incidents like this. It was a fairly common practice for a policeman to pull over a person, come up with an infraction, then hint at a bribe to solve the problem.

One time Dmitri and I were pulled over when we were with a group of hunters. We had all our gear, including several cases of hunting rifles and ammunition, with us in the van.

Dmitri was not happy. I can't print the words he called the police officer; they were not kind and endearing. Although we had the proper paperwork, Dmitri said we were going to have a problem.

"We have enough firepower in this van to take over a small village," he said. "These guys are going to freak out when they see the rifles and ammunition. They will try to find something wrong. Someone may have forgotten to dot an "i" or cross a "t" on their paperwork. They will find it. They are going to want to get some money from us, but I'm not giving these *#@**# anything!"

Sure enough, the policemen got excited when they saw the van was full of Americans, lots of luggage, and firearms, to boot. First they went through our passports and paperwork. Then they made us take all the rifles out of their cases and checked serial numbers against the paperwork we had for them. Then they counted the cartridges and said we were off by one or two.

Aha, an opening for them. They were about to have us take out all our luggage and open all the suitcases when Dmitri finally gave in and offered them $200 cash.

They took it, and we were on our way, just that quick.

I could complain about the under-the-table cash transactions we had to make over the years, but I'm not that upset. Some clients got a bit bent out of shape when we slipped cash to an official, but when I pointed out this faster, smoother route to a solution, they usually saw the benefits of the practice.

The beauty of this system was that you could solve a problem on the spot, such as when clients gave me the wrong serial number, or the wrong make and model of their rifle, or the wrong caliber, for the paper work we had to submit for their rifle permits.

All those things happened, and more than once. "Just call it a fine for giving me the wrong information," I told offending clients. They were happy with that.

One guy on a stag hunt in Crimea was extremely happy with the Russian way of doing things. We had just finished eating in a nice restaurant and were walking out the front door and down the steps when this client, who had consumed too much vodka, stopped and began to urinate on the steps in front of the restaurant! You can understand my shock when I saw this moron urinating in public. Before we could get to him and stop him, a policeman grabbed him by the arm and hauled him to his cruiser.

Dmitri quickly followed the policeman and our client to the cruiser and began talking to the officer.

This drunken client was going to spend the night in jail. No ifs, ands, or buts. He was in big trouble.

Not so fast; this is Russia! After a few minutes of dialog, and the transfer of some cash, Dmitri returned with one humble, frightened client.

Dmitri and I gave him a tongue-lashing, put him in our van, took him back to the hotel, and put him in bed.

The next morning I asked him if he knew how close he was to spending the night in a Russian jail cell. He said he certainly did, and just the thought of it had scared him sober. He thanked Dmitri profusely.

The willingness of some Russian airline ticket agents to earn a little extra cash on the side helped me upgrade to first class a number of times. The first time I became aware I could get a first class upgrade simply by slipping the ticket agent a crisp Benjamin Franklin happened on a flight from Moscow to Petropavlovsk. I was at the ticket counter getting processed when the ticket agent pulled my interpreter close and said something to him in the "Pssst, hey buddy, want to buy a watch?" tone a guy on the sidewalk in a big city would use as he rolled up his coat sleeve.

My interpreter then came close to me and said in a low voice, "Denny, do you want to fly in first class?"

"Sounds good, but I checked out first class ticket prices before I left home," I replied. "They are double the cost of a coach class ticket, so I think I'll pass."

"You don't have to pay double for first class," my interpreter said. "Just give the guy a hundred bucks and he will upgrade you. He's trying to make a little extra money. His job doesn't pay much."

"A hundred bucks to upgrade to first class?," I gasped. "I'll pay a hundred dollars for an upgrade to first class!"

I grabbed my wallet, pulled out a hundred dollar bill and was about to hand it to the ticket agent when my interpreter stopped me.

No, no," he whispered. "Don't hand it over the counter in plain sight. Put it in your passport and hand him your passport."

I put the hundred dollar bill in my passport and handed my passport to the ticket agent. He lowered the passport, let the hundred dollar bill fall into his lap, and handed back my passport along with a first class ticket.

I tried this several other times after that. Sometimes it worked; sometimes it didn't.

I also worked it with flight attendants in the early years, but I wouldn't try it today. There have been big changes in this type of activity in Russia the past two-plus decades. The last time I tried it, in 2005, I got the evil eye from a flight attendant.

Russia has pretty much made it through its Wild West stage and is no different today from most modern countries. A lot of the things we did in the '90s wouldn't work today. You can even buy Charmin toilet paper in the stores.

Ah, I miss the good old days!

CHAPTER 8

SURROUNDED BY BEARS!

"ARE YOU SURE IT'S safe?" Tom Moore asked anxiously, the worry creeping into his voice. "I don't mind telling you, I'm a little nervous about this hunt. I'm afraid of bears, especially grizzly bears. I think I'd rather go stag hunting. You think we can talk Dave into a stag hunt? I really don't want to hunt bears. And in Russia? That doesn't make me feel any better!"

This was the second telephone conversation I had with Tom, a Traverse City, Michigan, native. He was trying to ease some of the fear that had been preying on his mind as time got closer and closer to an upcoming grizzly bear hunt in Russia. His son, David Moore, from Illinois, had booked the hunt several weeks earlier for himself and his father. From the beginning, when Dave and Tom began debating whether to go on a Russian brown bear hunt or Ukrainian stag hunt, Tom had made it quite clear that he was voting for the stag hunt. Dave wanted to do a grizz hunt and since he was paying for the hunt, by golly, they were going to go grizz hunting.

"Dad, you're going on a grizz hunt," Dave chided his father every time the topic surfaced. "Quit making a big fuss. You'll be fine. Don't worry about it. Denny will take care of everything."

Tom was plenty worried. He had a healthy respect for bears that verged on outright fear.

He continued over the phone. "You said we'll be off the ground in a stand, right? We're not going to be on the ground with these things, are we? How far away are the shots? We won't be too close will we? A hundred yards or so, right? The guide has a big gun for back-up, right? Has anybody ever been attacked by a bear on this hunt? I'm telling you, I'm a little nervous about this whole thing."

I assured Tom everything would be fine, and we would make sure his guide kept him safe. "Besides, you'll have a big gun with you, Tom, so don't worry about it. Just make a good shot," I assured him. In an effort to lighten the mood, I said, "We haven't lost anybody yet."

"I don't want to be the first one," Tom fired back. "That's another thing ... we're going to be out in the woods with a Russian guide? Can't we have an American guide? Can't you guide? I don't mind telling you, that makes me a little nervous, too."

Tom had grown up in the Cold War era when the Soviet Union and U.S. were mortal enemies. The era of Glasnost and Perestroika hadn't caught up with him yet.

"The Evil Empire and all that stuff," Dave chuckled when he told me about his father's fears of going to Russia.

"Throw that in there with a genuine fear of grizzly bears and you can see where my dad is coming from."

After several more telephone conversations on the same subject, it was time for the hunt. Tom and Dave arrived in St. Petersburg in late August with two other hunters from the States. My outfitter, Dmitri Sikorski, and I met them at the airport and escorted them to our camp in a small village about 400 miles east of Moscow. After a good night's sleep and a leisurely day in camp, it was time for the evening hunt. We sighted in the rifles and were ready to hit the bear woods.

Our Russian grizzly bear hunts are conducted much the same way a Canadian black bear hunt is run; they are evening hunts done from a stand overlooking a food source. The big difference? Our food source is a food plot, not a bait pile. The guides plant a number of these food plots throughout their hunting areas. Most of the plots are planted with a high-protein grain like oats. The bears hammer these food plots in the fall in preparation for the long, cold Russian winters.

Once an oat patch is established, the guides construct a small shooting platform 15 to 20 feet off the ground overlooking the plot. The clients are taken to their stands a few hours before dark to wait for bears to come out and feed in the oat patches. The guides sit with the hunter on the stand to be sure the client remains safe.

Finally, it was time to go hunting. Dmitri introduced the hunters to their guides, went over the safety rules, and addressed questions the hunters and guides had for each other. The hunt of a lifetime was about to begin for Dave, Tom, and the rest of the group.

Almost . . .

"I might stay in camp," Tom mumbled as the other hunters began loading gear. "I'm not feeling too good. Maybe I'll skip tonight and go out tomorrow."

"You're going out now," Dave admonished! "Don't give me that 'I'm sick' stuff. There's nothing the matter with you and you know it! You'll be fine."

After some lively discussion, and a bit of prodding, Tom finally agreed to go hunting. He jumped into the four-wheel drive vehicle with his guide and disappeared down the road heading out of town.

Dmitri and I walked back to the apartment house that served as our base camp. This was one of our nicer camps. It was a two-story structure with individual rooms for each hunter, complete with hot running water, showers, and flush toilets. It also had a large dining area where we could enjoy our meals and hang out.

Dmitri and I headed to the dining area for a cup of coffee while we waited for the hunters to return.

The hunters left camp around 6 p.m. It usually gets dark around 10 o'clock. Dmitri and I expected them back between 11 p.m. and midnight. Of course, the time a hunter gets back to camp depends on whether or not he shoots a bear. If a bear is shot, it takes longer to get back to camp because the guides usually let if lay a while before they retrieve it. Finding the bear, loading it into the vehicle, and getting back to camp, might take a couple more hours.

The later a hunter got back to camp, the better we liked it. Dmitri and I were hoping everyone would get back late that night.

You can understand the sick feeling in our stomachs when we heard one of the vehicles returning to camp less than two hours later. It wasn't even dark yet. I looked out the second-story window and saw Tom get out of the jeep. 'Rats,' I thought, Tom chickened out.

Dmitri and I hustled down the steps and out the door to where Tom and his guide stood.

"What happened?," I asked. "Why are you back already? You're supposed to hunt until dark."

"What happened is I shot a bear!," Tom shouted."I shot a bear. Take a look. It's right here in the back of the jeep. I shot a bear!"

"You're kidding me. You got one already? That didn't take long. Congratulations! It wasn't as bad as you thought it would be, was it?"

"Actually, it was," Tom replied. "It was a pretty scary hunt, but I couldn't be happier right now. I actually shot a bear. I really didn't think I would get one."

As we admired Tom's bear, he continued. "I have a bone to pick with you. You told me most of the shots are 80 to 100 yards. You said I would be up in a stand and not on the ground with these things. Well, let me tell you what happened.

"After parking the jeep on an old logging trail, my guide and I walked for a while until we reached the edge of an oat field. As we started sneaking through the oats toward the shooting platform, the guide all of a sudden grabs my arm and whispers, 'Tom, stop! Big bear to right.' He motions for me to get my gun up and swing right.

"I slowly brought up the rifle and eased right. I was looking for a bear 80 to 100 yards away. Then I see this bear just 30 yards away with its head down in the oats. I started shaking like a leaf as I tried to get the scope on it. About the time I'm on it, the guide grabs my arm again and says, 'Tom, stop! Bigger bear to left!'

"Now I'm really getting nervous! I started easing back around toward the left, again looking for a bear 80 to 100 yards out. But what do I see? Another, even bigger, bear just 35 yards away! Oh my! Now I'm starting to shake even harder as I try to bring the rifle around to the left. Just about the time I get the gun around, the guide grabs my arm again and says, 'Tom, stop! Biggest bear in front!'

"I looked back around toward the front and saw this big bear standing on its back legs with its nose high in the air trying to smell us. This bear was 100 yards away but ... I lost it! We were surrounded by bears!

"By now I'm shaking so bad I can't hold my rifle steady. The guide grabs my rifle, takes me by the arm, and we start sneaking toward the stand. We would wait for all three bears to put their head down and start eating, then we would take several steps. We could walk only a few yards at a time. It took us 20 minutes to reach the stand. We climbed into the stand, moving only when we were sure the bears weren't looking in our direction.

"We were finally in the stand! We were finally off the ground! I didn't think we would ever get there. The guide leaned my rifle in the corner of the stand and started patting me on the knee, telling me to take deep breaths. He was trying to calm me down. After about five minutes, I regained my composure. The guide then motioned toward my gun and said, 'Tom OK? Shoot?'

"I slowly picked up my rifle and shot the closest bear to the stand. I didn't care which one was the biggest. I just wanted to shoot one. The bear growled, popped its teeth and dashed into the woods. I breathed a sigh of relief.

"I was feeling pretty good until what happened next. You won't believe it!

"The guide climbs down the stand, pulls out a pistol and runs into the woods after the bear! I'm thinking, 'You got to be kidding me!' I'm out in the middle of nowhere, in Russia, in a field surrounded by bears, and my guide just ran into the woods after a wounded bear. Oh my gosh! If he gets eaten by the bear, I have to walk back to the jeep -- if I can find it -- in the dark, through a woods full of hungry bears! I'm screwed!

"After a few minutes of sheer terror, my guide finally comes out of the woods, puts his thumb in the air and yells, 'Tom, good shot!' What a relief! I was never so glad to see anybody in my life!

"And here we are."

"Now, that's a story," I said. "It would have to happen to you. You were already more than a little anxious before heading out, to put it mildly. That's the first time anyone has had that kind of an experience. I guess the bear gods put this one together for you."

"My guide wants me to have a toast with him," Tom laughed. "I imagine it has something to do with vodka. I don't know how to tell him I don't drink vodka."

"Well, maybe just have one little shot with him and switch to cola or something," I chuckled. "It's a tradition to have a shot with the guides after a successful hunt. He will feel insulted if you don't have just one small shot with him. It's totally up to you. If you really don't want to drink any vodka, just tell him you're allergic to it or something."

"Well, maybe just one shot won't hurt," Tom replied. "I just don't like the taste of it."

So up to the dining room Tom and his guide went. Dmitri and I followed. The toasting began. First we had a shot to toast the successful hunt. Then another shot to toast Russian and American friendship. Then one to good health. Then one for our families. Then one for love ... and so it went. True Russian tradition, faithfully observed!

Soon, Tom was feeling no pain, and as each of the hunters came back to camp, Tom retold the story a little louder, followed by another round of toasts. By the time Dave got back to camp near midnight, I had heard the story enough times to tell it myself.

•*Tom Moore celebrates surviving his grizzly bear experience with a shot of vodka and a cigar. (David Moore photo)*

When Dave rolled into camp, I went out to meet him to ask how his hunt had gone. As he got out of the jeep, the first thing he asked was "Is my dad back yet? He didn't chicken out, did he?"

"Yeah, he came back early," I answered, "BUT he didn't chicken out. He shot a bear. He's up in the dining room telling the story right now."

As we unloaded Dave's gear from the jeep, he paused a second then looked at me with a puzzled expression.

"Is that my dad I hear up there?" Dave grinned. "He sounds kind of loud. He hasn't been drinking, has he?"

The window to the dining room was open and you definitely could hear Tom telling his bear story. I smiled at Dave and replied, "that's your dad, and he's had a couple of shots."

"But my dad doesn't drink hard liquor."

"Well, he started tonight."

Dave and I walked to the dining room and were met by Tom as we walked through the door. "Dave! I got one!," Tom yelled as he wrapped an arm around his son and gave him a big hug. "I shot a bear! Can you believe it! I shot a grizzly bear my first night out!"

Dave looked at me with a big grin and said, "I can't believe this is my dad. I've never seen him like this. He's not a drinker. This is almost unbelievable."

As Tom repeated his story one more time for his son, everyone had yet another toast. Soon Dave had caught up with the rest of the group and everyone was in a festive mood. After the victory party finally wound down in the wee hours of the morning, everyone went to their rooms to catch a little shut eye. A few minutes later, Dave walked back into the dining area and approached me.

"I just want to tell you how happy I am right now!" He smiled, choking back a tear. "I can't believe my dad got a bear already. I don't even care if I get one or not. I'm just glad my dad is happy, and what's really nice is we are really bonding here. My dad and I were never real close when I was growing up. Oh, he was a great father and a great provider for the family, but we were never really close. That's why I wanted to do this hunt so badly with him. I wanted to get to know him better. Now here we are with our arms around each other, hugging each other and telling hunting stories. This is great! This is what I came for. Thank you, Denny! Thank you!"

By the time Dave finished with his story, my eyes were getting moist as well. Too much vodka, I told myself.

As Dave ambled back to his room, I said, "I'm happy to hear that. Glad it worked out for you and your dad. By the way ... don't worry, Dave, you'll get something too."

He did. Before the week was over, Dave bagged a bear and a wild boar. While it was a great hunt, it was an even better personal journey for Tom and Dave. I know I'll never forget that camp. It brought back great memories of my dad and our first Canadian fishing trip together.

• *David Moore, center, celebrates successful hunt with Russian guides. (David Moore Photo)*

Many groups of hunters saw more than 100 bears a week

(Denny Geurink photo)

In Russia, hunts are five or six days, and most hunters fill their tag within two or three days. In Alaska, most hunts are 10 to 12 days, because it may take that long to get a bear.

Everything broke right for this group of hunters. They filled their tags by noon on the first day of the hunt. The bears were just coming out of hibernation in mid-April, and, as usual, we were in a camp that was over-run by bears.

Some of the people in our camps saw more than 100 bears a week. Easy to see why Russia is called The Land Of The Bear.

The largest number of bears ever spotted by a group of hunters in one week was more than 250!

It's just the result of a huge population of bears and no hunting pressure from the Russians, who never were allowed to own guns under the Communist system. As a result, the average Russian doesn't grow up hunting as we do.

All our camps were pretty much perfect for bear hunting.

CHAPTER 9

A LESSON ON FEAR

"I GET THIS STRANGE FEELING right in my chest," sputtered Andrew Shutov, flapping the shirt pocket over his heart for emphasis. "It is how you say, very funny feeling. Kind of tingling feeling."

"The word I believe you are looking for, Andrew, is fear," I offered as we listened to our new Russian friend describe a close encounter with a large grizzly bear. "It's called total, absolute, unbridled fear."

"Yes, fear." He nodded. "Very much fear."

"And how about your shorts, Andrew? Do you need clean shorts?," I chuckled.

"Yes I think clean shorts would be good," Shutov grinned. "I have very funny feeling in shorts, too."

This conversation about fear and soiled shorts took place at a September bear hunting camp south of St. Petersburg. Shutov was filling in as a cameraman for Bob Coker, one of three hunters who had joined me on a bruin hunting expedition to the Land of the Bear. Coker, from Eufaula, Alabama, was filming the hunt for a video he was working on. He wanted to film one of the first – if not the first – Russian bears shot with a bow and arrow. Shutov was supposed to have been along as an interpreter, but he got a little more than he bargained for when Coker's cameraman was unable to make the trip.

Coker had been sitting in a tree stand overlooking a patch of oats when the action began to heat up. Coker had positioned Shutov in a ground blind a fair distance from the tree stand, hoping to capture the action from ground level. The bears were supposed to come out into the field under the tree stand Coker was sitting in, a safe distance from Shutov. But that's not how it worked out.

As Coker watched four bears feeding in front of his stand, a fifth, very large, bear stepped out of the woods. The other bears immediately scrambled for cover. One of them almost ran over Shutov, who was so frightened he forgot to turn on the camera.

Shutov was still recovering from this harrowing experience when a herd of 20 wild boar began moving down a trail behind him. Two large and ugly boars broke from the herd and began feeding toward Shutov. As they fed closer and closer, Shutov decided to stand up and wave his arms to scare them away. Instead of running off, however, the two Russian boars charged.

Fortunately for Shutov, they broke off their charge at the last second and ran into the woods just a few yards shy of ripping him with their huge, razor sharp tusks. That's when the "very strange feeling" in Shutov's chest became even more pronounced. Again, he was too frightened to turn on the camera, missing some great action footage, but who could blame him?

"They were as big as the bears," Shutov said back at camp. "They had very long and very sharp tusks. Tomorrow I sit in a tree, too. No more sitting on the ground."

The next day Shutov was sitting in a tree stand next to Coker when Coker arrowed what may be the first interior brown bear taken in Russia with a bow. The big bear walked right under and out in front of Coker's stand. He drilled it at 35 yards. It was a clean, swift kill and, indeed, a very nice bear.

The guides estimated the bear to be an eight-footer.

Another person who can tell you about the meaning of fear is Tom Thompson from Danvers, Illinois. Thompson had a close encounter with a big bruin near Magadan. He wrote a story about his hunt that offers a unique

insight from a client's perspective about what goes into one of these trips. Here are excerpts from his story.

***

Late April found me and my hunting partner, Keith Jeffries, on a Magadan Airways flight from Anchorage to Magadan, Russia. The purpose of the trip was a long awaited and highly anticipated two week hunt for the Siberian version of *Ursus arctos horribilis*. We had heard stories about these bears being much more plentiful and aggressive than their Alaskan cousins, so we were extremely excited about our adventure.

After a layover of several hours for customs and immigration at the Petropavlovsk airport, during which we learned what Denny meant by 'Russian Standard Time', we were on our way to Magadan. There we met Mikhail, our translator, and were escorted to camp.

The camp was located at the mouth of a small river on the coast of the Sea of Okhotsk. The snow-capped mountains and rugged coastline made for some of the most beautiful scenery in the world. The only problem was that an early spring had melted much of the snow, making the use of camp snowmobiles impossible. Our mode of transportation would be via LPCs, or leather personnel carriers -- our boots. We would be doing a lot of walking. If the sea was calm, a rubber boat would be used, too.

I will say the camp was impressive. The tent frames had been made from driftwood using chainsaws and hand tools. The tents even had hand-sawn plank floors. Wood stoves and cots made them very comfortable. Cooking and dining was in separate tents, and a sauna had been constructed for bathing.

After introductions, we shared a few vodka toasts with our new friends, and the adventure began.

After six days of walking mile upon mile through some of the toughest terrain on earth, and seeing close to a hundred smaller bears, the sea finally calmed. The camp had a 16-foot Zodiac boat equipped with a 30hp outboard. Using it greatly expanded our hunting area. The guides wrapped me in heavy rubber rain gear, life jackets, and hip boots. They put me in the boat, and out to sea we went.

The operator ran the boat parallel to shore, staying out 100 yards or so. We saw plenty of wildlife, including waterfowl, snow sheep, seals, eagles, and, of course, bears. They had just come out of hibernation and were ravenous. They fed on pine seeds, last year's berries uncovered by the recent snow melt, and any dead salmon they could find. Their favorite food, however, was kelp that had washed ashore and left on the beach during high tide. As the tide went out, the bears would head for the beach and gorge on the kelp.

Using a mixture of sign language and some key words from a small Russian-to-English translation sheet, my guide Alexi indicated that we would beach the boat near a tall ridge that protruded into the ocean. We would then leave the boat and, using the ridge as cover, ascend the cliffs, find an elevated observation post and glass for bears feeding on kelp.

We found a crevice in the cliff that was full of loose shale but passable. We used this crevice to access the top of the cliffs. There the landscape opened into miles of dwarf spruce, spruce bushes that had been flattened by the snow and were slowly straightening up after the melt.

The only way through them, or over them, was to step on the branches and ride them down while holding onto other branches, kind of like walking on springs. We had to pay close attention to our footing; one misstep would find us at the bottom of a six- to ten-foot-tall jungle of needles and branches. Near the top of the ridge, the spruces gave way to tundra and a beautiful view of the coastline.

We stepped out into the clearing, thankful to have a few yards of easy walking, and headed to the crest of the ridge to get a view of the beach below. Alexi motioned for me to move ahead to the crest and peek over the edge.

I moved forward, slowly scanning the landscape ahead of me. Just as I cleared the top of the ridge, I spotted a huge bear coming up the trail on the other side. It was a mere 15 yards away, walking straight toward me. At that moment my entire body was gripped in sheer panic. I had nowhere to go. I could hear it breathing. I could see its breath. I could see its beady eyes sizing me up. I was screwed!

Dense spruces lined both sides of the trail in front of me and behind me. I was caught out there in no-man's land. The bear showed no sign of backing off. In fact, it began picking up speed as it closed on me. Was this where my hunting career was going to end, on some remote mountain top in the middle of Siberia? There was no way I could stop this bear from getting to me, even if I shot it right through the heart. It could cover the ten yards left between us in less than a second.

My memories of the next second are a slow motion blur. Somehow my instincts for survival took over. I shouldered my .338 Winchester Magnum, found the base of the bear's neck in my crosshairs and pulled the trigger. That was the only shot that would stop this grizzled blur of tooth and claw at this short distance.

As I was chambering another round, the bear stood on its hind legs and raised its front paw to take a swat at me. I took aim to put a second round in it before it could complete its swipe, but it wasn't necessary. The bear fell with the claws of its front paw inches from my boot.

I had just gone toe to toe with a big Russian brown bear and survived unscathed. It was a miracle. It took a long time for me to stop shaking. I still have a hard time believing I survived such a close encounter with a brown bear and lived to tell about it.

Alexi circled the bear carefully to make sure it was dead. When he was sure it was dead, I pulled the bolt back on my rifle to clear the chamber. At that point I realized

I had already ejected a live round onto the ground. I would never have thought I would have been the type to do that.

After the adrenaline rush was over and Alexi and I shared high-fives, we took some pictures. Then, when I had a chance to sit down, I tried to run through my mind what had just happened. It took me a while to realize how lucky I was to be sitting there enjoying the view.

As it worked out, my buddy Keith also shot a really big bear only a few miles away. He was with another guide hunting a river valley. We picked them up with the boat on our way back to camp. When we learned we had each tagged a bear, we spent the two-hour boat ride back to camp telling and retelling our stories and high-fiving all the way back.

All four hunters in camp tagged nice bears. The hunt was a great adventure. We had not only harvested nice bears, but Keith and I also made two great new friends on that trip. We still get together with them once a year or so. The guides and the camp personnel were all great. We became friends and, were it not for the distance, I am sure we would see them often.

One highlight of the trip was that we had the honor of celebrating Victory Day with the guides while in camp. Victory Day is a Russian holiday to celebrate the end of World War II and to honor the memories of all the people they lost. It is the equivalent of our July 4th. We fired a 21-gun salute and toasted our countries, veterans, and each other. All in all, I can't imagine a better trip, although I am willing to try.

Two Of Many Book Bears

At the moment, we have 30 bears in the top 50 spots in SCI's world record book, more than any other bear hunting company in the world.

• One of several bears taken over the years that squared more than 11 feet. It was taken on a fall hunt in Kamchatka. (Photo by Dmtri Sikorski)

• Chris Fuller from Michigan with a bear just about as big as the cabin wall. It squared more than 10 feet. (Photo by Dmtri Sikorski).

Many of our bear camps today are fairly new cabins built by the guides for fishing and trapping work.The cabins are nice inside, with wood heat, comfortable bedrooms, a full kitchen and a cook to prepare good meals.

CHAPTER 10

AN ENCOUNTER
WITH THE WWF

I KNEW IT WAS JUST a matter of time until she asked me "the question." I was on a flight from Anchorage, Alaska, in April of 2003 heading for the Kamchatka Peninsula for the start of the spring bear hunts. Also on board Magadan Air Flight 802 were a number of people from the World Wildlife Fund. While not as hostile and fanatic as some of the anti-hunting groups, I think it would be fair to say the World Wildlife Fund is not a pro-hunting organization.

I had been engaged in pleasant conversation with several members of the contingent, including Margaret Williams, editor of the organization's *Russian Conservation News*, and Managing Director of the WWF's Arctic Field Program. I knew the group was excited about this field trip and were looking forward to visiting park and wilderness areas in Kamchatka, where they hoped to see some bears coming out of hibernation. Their enthusiasm was evident. They were here to save the bears! Then came the question.

"So, Denny, what is it you are going to do in Kamchatka?" Williams asked.

"Just the opposite of what you are going to do." I replied with a smile, trying to introduce my profession in a neutral way. The smile left her face immediately.

"What do you mean?"

"I organize and lead bear hunting expeditions on the Kamchatka Peninsula," I replied, still trying to keep a smile, and still trying desperately to keep the mood open and friendly. "I've been coming to Russia for 12 years. My company is the number one brown bear outfitting service in the world. We harvest more big brown bears than any other hunting company in the world."

I don't know why I said those last three sentences. They just blurted from my mouth. Part of my sales pitch in more hunter-friendly crowds, I guess, but it was certainly not a good choice of words for the present time and present company. I didn't know what to say. I just wanted to fill in the dead silence that suddenly spread over rows one through six.

"You shoot bears?," she asked, as tears began to well. "How can you do that? There are hardly any bears left in Kamchatka. How can you be part of an activity that is wiping out the bear population in Kamchatka?"

"Well, for one thing, the bears aren't almost gone in Kamchatka," I quickly responded. "There are more bears in Kamchatka now than there were 12 years ago when we first started hunting here. My business is saving the bears."

A look of utter disbelief slowly crept over her face. "How do you figure that?," she asked.

"Well, before we started bringing bear hunters here from the U.S., the Russians were actually carrying on a sort of commercial hunting program," I explained. "The guides were shooting bears to cut up for profit. They were selling hides, gall bladders, claws, meat, and teeth. To make enough money to feed and take care of their families, they had to shoot a lot of bears.

"For example, if a guide needed to make $5,000 a year to support his family, he had to shoot four or five bears. Now I pay him more than $5,000 for just one bear. I also tell him if he shoots any more bears on his own to make extra money, I will not come back to hunt in his camp.

"I have made bears in Kamchatka much more valuable to keep alive for my clients than to be shot on sight. Bears used to be shot indiscriminately. It didn't matter if they were boars, sows, or cubs. They were mowed down for their body parts. The first few years we hunted in Russia, the guides kept shooting bears on sight to make extra cash, even while we were hunting with them. If my clients passed on a bear because it was too small, the guides shot it. I was in one camp where the guides had nearly 40 bear hides stashed in an old building. I was very upset.

"After I dropped several camps because of this practice, the rest really started cleaning up their act. I bring in hundreds of thousands of dollars to these people every year. I told them if they shoot the bears, there won't be any left in a few years for my clients. My business will die. They won't make any more money from me. On the other hand, if we shoot only surplus, we can keep hunting bears forever. It's taken them a few years to accept this concept, but I have won over most of them. We have instilled a desire to manage the resource, not waste it."

I could see this was making sense to some in the group. You could have heard a pin drop as I continued.

"It's the same thing that happened in Africa with the elephants some years back," I explained. "When several countries there passed laws to shut down elephant hunting, the elephant population nosedived. That's because the elephant now was worth much less as a resource than it had been. Because no money was coming in from hunters, poachers took over.

"They began slaughtering elephants for their ivory, feet and tails. The rest was left to rot in the sun. Many of the very same people who used to guide hunters and protect the elephants became poachers and killed elephants indiscriminately. Without a way to support their families on the income they made from hunting, they turned to poaching. Because the individual elephant now was worth a lot less, they needed to kill more of them.

"Fortunately, government leaders in those countries realized their mistake and reinstated hunting on a limited basis. There was again money for elephant protection, and guides could make enough money to feed their families again.

"They went back to protecting the elephant. The elephant population came back.

"I know this may be hard for you to accept, but animals are a renewable resource, just like trees, corn, and wheat. If managed properly, they will never become extinct.

"You also must understand there are no social safety net programs in Africa or Russia like in the United States. There is no welfare, food stamps, aid to dependent children, or unemployment benefits. If I don't pay them to guide and feed my clients, and buy bear tags, they will shoot bears anyway just to survive."

Williams looked at me in a little different way and said, "That's a very interesting concept. I edit a magazine for the WWF here in Russia. Would you mind if I interview you for a story when we get to the hotel in Petropavlovsk?"

"No problem," I replied.

The next day we sat down in the hotel café and I explained it to her again. After she left the table, a gentleman approached me and introduced himself.

"Hi, my name is Andrew Meier, and I'm the editor of *Outside Magazine*," he said. "I overheard you talking to the lady from the World Wildlife Fund. We publish a magazine about things outdoors, like hiking, camping, climbing, and so forth. While we are not pro-hunting per se, I would say we aren't as anti-hunting as the WWF might be. We do some nature-related stories. I would like to interview you about the brown bear here in Kamchatka. Would that be all right?"

"Have a seat," I said and told my story one more time.

I don't know whether Williams published a story on our interview. I asked her for a copy if she did but never received one.

I asked Meier the same thing with no response. I did find out later that he mentioned a little bit from our interview in a story published in the December 2004 issue of Outside Magazine titled "A Message In Blood," which certainly was not a pro-hunting story.

Over the years I encountered other organizations that frown on hunting in general and bear hunting in particular. However, after presenting my point of view, most at least came away with a different perspective. While I'm sure I didn't convert any of them to my side of the aisle, at least they realized I had good points.

It's a proven fact that sportsmen contribute much more money and time to conservation efforts than any other group of people. Hunting sportsmen are responsible for the comeback of many wildlife species in the U.S., such as the wild turkey and pronghorn antelope. Hunters and fishermen have contributed billions of dollars to wildlife conservation programs through license fees and excise taxes on sporting goods. Without their license dollars and contributions, most of the states would not have a conservation department.

The monies raised by organizations such as Ducks Unlimited have bought millions of acres of wildlife habitat that supports millions of animals, from ducks, geese, swans, and songbirds to whitetail deer, elk, moose, wild turkeys, and, yes, even bears!

• *Birch trees near pond in Siberia in late summer.*
(Denny Geurink photo)

• *Mountains in late summer. (Michael Shutt photos)*

• *Horses and hunters taking a break high in mountains in Siberia in late summer. (Michael Shutt photo)*

• *Guide glassing mountains in Siberia in late summer (Michael Shutt photo)*

*• A waterfall found in a mountain range in Siberia.
(Denny Geurink photo)"*

*• Snow-covered mountain on the Kamchatka Peninsula with
a dormant volcano in background. (Mike Muster photo)*

CHAPTER 11

AMERICAN HUNTER TAKEN TO POLICE STATION

"PLEASE TAKE CARE OF Ray and make sure he comes back OK," Norma Brenner pleaded with me as we were about to board the plane in Grand Rapids, Michigan, for a fall stag hunt in Russia. Norma's husband, Ray Brenner, from Shelbyville, was pumped for the hunt and eager to get started. Dick Davis from Otsego; Don and Tom Mabie from Cedar Springs; and Wesley Wiggers from Hudsonville, all in Michigan, were also excited and ready to hunt.

Norma, not so much. Worry was written all over her face. She pulled me aside to express her concerns.

"Don't let them take Ray and put him in jail," Norma continued. "I really don't like him going over there. Are you sure it's safe?"

Ray and Norma Brenner were in their early 70s and had grown up in rural Michigan during the heart of the Cold War. They had heard all the Cold War rhetoric. Some of it definitely had made an impression, especially the stuff about people the Soviet government didn't care for, getting arrested and thrown in a gulag. Norma was worried Ray would wind up getting arrested and thrown in jail. Ray also was a little nervous. Norma's open fear and pleading with me wasn't helping his confidence.

I joked with Norma, trying to lighten the mood.

"What   does Ray plan to do that will get him arrested? Don't worry, he'll be fine. I'll make sure he stays out of trouble and gets back safely," I assured her. "We have done this many times."

It's rather amusing how many people in the early years of my tourism business were afraid to take a trip to Russia. Their fears ranged from being afraid the guides would purposely leave them out in the woods, to traveling on broken-down airplanes and helicopters, eating unsafe food, having their guns taken away, to the fear Ray Brenner had of being arrested and thrown in jail because he was an American.

Once we arrived in St. Petersburg, we were met at the airport by my outfitter, Dmitri Sikorski. After we cleared customs, Dmitri took us to a nice restaurant. We then loaded our gear into a waiting van and headed for the stag hunting area.

The camp itself was on the edge of a small Russian village. It was a motel set-up, with separate rooms for the hunters, a kitchen where meals would be served   by professional cooks, and a nice lounge where we could kick back after a day in the woods. So far, so good. Ray was losing his fear of being in Russia.

The next morning we sat down to a breakfast of eggs, fried kielbasa, cheese, bread, and hot coffee.

After breakfast, Dmitri took us to meet the guides. Each hunter would have his own guide and hunt in his own area. After introductions, the hunters began loading their gear into waiting jeeps, getting ready to go. Dmitri and I headed back to the kitchen for a second cup of coffee.

What Dmitri and I didn't know was that Ray had forgotten something in his room. He tried to explain this to his guide, telling him to wait, that he would be right back.

When he came back to his jeep, the rest of the group had left. One jeep was left, with the driver standing next to it smoking a cigarette. Ray approached and told the driver he was ready to go. The driver   seemed a bit perplexed at first, but when Ray jumped in the jeep and gestured he wanted to go, the driver jumped behind the wheel and sped away.

In about 20 minutes, the jeep rolled into a small town. Ray had been chattering away the entire time about how excited he was to be in Russia hunting stag, that it was his first time to Russia. The driver nodded and smiled respectfully. The two seemed to be getting on splendidly, but now Ray was a bit puzzled. He thought he was heading for the forest and was a bit surprised to be pulling into a small town. Maybe the guide, like Ray, had forgotten something, and they were going to make a quick pit stop.

Ray's feelings and thoughts changed dramatically when the jeep stopped in front of the police station. After turning off the engine and stepping outside, the driver motioned for Ray to get out and began talking in Russian. Ray was reluctant to get out, telling the driver he would rather stay in the jeep. The driver opened the door and insisted Ray get out.

That's when Ray realized the driver apparently didn't speak or understand a word of English. Second, that badge on the driver's shirt didn't look the same as the badges on the other guides' shirts. This was a policeman's badge.

Ray's bewilderment was quickly turning to panic. The driver, uh, police officer, led Ray into the station and motioned for Ray to take a seat. Ray's worst fears were coming to life. He had been arrested and taken to a Russian police station. He was going to be locked up in a Russian prison. Norma was right! He would never see his wife again!

It was about then that Ray got a worse feeling. Not only was he sitting in a Russian police station dressed in full hunting camo, he still was carrying his rifle. What was going on? Was there going to be a shootout? Ray was sweating profusely.

The longer he sat there the more confused he got. The policeman was chatting with another officer and seemed in no hurry to put Ray behind bars. In fact, he was smiling and pointing around the room and didn't seem a bit concerned that Ray was sitting there holding a powerful hunting rifle.

Ray kept saying to him, "What am I doing here? I want to go back to camp. Does anyone here speak English?"

After nearly 30 minutes of total panic and confusion, a young woman walked into the police station and overheard Ray speaking English. "What is the problem?" she asked in perfect English. "May I help interpret?"

Ray was visibly excited finally to find someone who spoke English. "Please tell them I want to go back to my camp," he pleaded. "I don't know why they brought me here. I just want to get out of here and get back to camp."

The lady spoke to the police officer. They both looked at Ray, pointing and chattering, and then they started laughing. The officer pointed at Ray and motioned for him to follow him outside and back to the jeep. Ray quickly jumped in the jeep and prayed the guy was going to take him back to camp and not off to a gulag.

In 20 minutes, the jeep pulled into camp. Ray scrambled out and nearly jogged to the kitchen where Dmitri and I were just finishing a third cup of coffee. We were surprised to see him, of course.

"What are you doing back?" I asked. "You couldn't have shot a stag already. Did you forget something?"

"They arrested me and took me to jail," Ray blurted. He was as pale as someone who had just seen a ghost. "I've been sitting in the police station for the last hour or so. I was scared to death. I'm just glad to be back"

"What?," Dmitri gasped. "What are you talking about?"

"My driver took me to jail," Ray replied. "I don't know what's going on."

"What do you mean he took you to jail? Where is your driver now?" Dmitri asked.

• *Ray Brenner poses with stag, a much happier moment than his trip to a Russian police station. (Denny Geurink photo)*

"He's outside in the parking lot," Ray answered, still visibly shaken.

Dmitri quickly got up from the table and hustled out the door. While Ray and I waited for Dmitri to come back, Ray told me the story of how he had forgotten something, went to his room to get it, and when he got back to the loading area, everyone else was gone. That's when I started to think there was some sort of mix-up.

"Where were Dick and his guide when you went back out to the parking lot?," I asked. "You were supposed to ride to the hunting spot with Dick and his guide. They were going to drop you at your spot with your guide. Didn't you go with the guide Dmitri introduced you to?"

"I thought he was my guide," Ray replied. "He had the same kind of green camo shirt as the other guides, and he had a badge like the other guides. I didn't notice until later that it was a policeman's badge."

A few minutes later, Dmitri arrived back in the dining area with the police officer. Both were smiling ear to ear.

"There's been a very funny mistake," Dmitri said with a laugh. "Did you know this guy is a police officer and not a guide? Didn't you notice this wasn't your guide?"

"I didn't know it until we got to the police station," Ray replied. "He is wearing the same kind of shirt and has a badge just like the other guides. I thought he was my guide."

"When you came up to him and started motioning that you wanted to go for a ride and jumped into his jeep, he thought you wanted him to take you for a ride to town," Dmitri continued. "He didn't know you wanted him to take you hunting. He doesn't speak English and he's not a guide. He figured you knew that, since he was wearing a police badge. Also, by the way, didn't you see the police insignia on the side of the jeep?"

"I didn't see it until we got back," Ray said sheepishly. "It looked like the insignia on some of the other jeeps."

"The badges some of the other guides were wearing were game warden badges," Dmitri explained, "and the insignia on some of the other jeeps were game warden insignias. Your guides are local conservation officers. A lot of times the guides we hire in Russia to take you hunting are local game wardens. They are in the woods all the time and know where all the game is. They make perfect guides. Here in Russia they can be hired as guides. Probably something you aren't used to in America."

"When you jumped in this man's jeep, he thought you wanted to go to town," Dmitri went on. "Since he is a police officer, he wanted to show you where he works. He was proud to show an American the place he works. When you were jabbering at the police station, he could see you were getting nervous, but he didn't understand a word you were saying. Thankfully the lady who spoke English came in and explained. Then he understood you wanted to go back to camp, so he brought you back to camp. That's it. That's what happened. You weren't arrested. You just went for a tour of the local police station."

Ray looked at the police officer. Then he looked at me and Dmitri. A big grin swept over his face and he burst out laughing. We all started laughing hysterically.

"You got to be kidding," Ray said with a big grin. "I don't mind telling you I was scared. I thought sure my wife was right. I thought I would be thrown in jail and never see her again. I can't wait to tell her what happened."

The following morning Ray stuck tight to the other hunters. He took all his gear with him to breakfast. After breakfast, he was the first one to jump into the vehicle with his guide. He was never late for another thing on the hunt.

But Ray's adventures, or misadventures, weren't over yet. On the way back to St. Petersburg, Ray sat in the front seat of the jeep with our driver, enjoying the ride, when he noticed the cool fur hat the driver was wearing. He began pointing at the hat and jabbering to the driver, telling him how much he liked his hat.

"Denny, when we get back to town, is there a shop or something around where we can buy fur hats like the driver has?" Ray asked, pointing at the hat. "I'd love to take one of these Russian fur hats home as a souvenir."

"No problem," I replied. "There are a lot of places that sell fur hats in St. Petersburg. I'll take you shopping when we get there."

All this talking and pointing didn't go unnoticed by the driver. He could see Ray was interested in his hat. The driver then began eyeing Ray's hat. It was one of my logo Outdoor Adventures hats I give to my clients before each trip. It was a nice green, brushed cotton hat with my logo of a fly fisherman, pine trees and an eagle. Pretty sharp hat, if I do say so myself. The driver began pointing at Ray's hat, nodding, smiling and giving the thumbs-up sign. In other words, he liked Ray's hat.

Ray pointed at the driver's hat and gave it the thumbs-up sign. As they both sat there admiring each other's hats, the driver motioned to Ray that they should switch hats. Ray looked at me and said, "Denny, I think this guy wants to trade hats with me. If I trade with him, will you give me another one of your hats when we get home? I'd like to have one of your hats, too."

"No problem," I responded. "I think you're right. He wants to do a hat swap with you."

Ray then motioned to the driver that he would like to swap hats. The driver grinned from ear to ear and handed Ray his fur hat. Ray took his hat off and they made the deal. I don't know who was prouder at that moment. The driver had an American outfitter's hat and Ray had a Russian fur hat. How cool was that!

After a few minutes admiring his new fur hat, Ray asked me if I knew what kind of fur it was. "It looks like fox fur," Ray said. "The fur is kind of reddish and long like a fox. Can you ask him if this is a fox hat?"

I told Ray I wasn't very fluent in Russian but I knew a few words and fox was one of them. "Lisa? Lisa?" I asked the driver as I pointed at the hat on Ray's head. "Lisa?"

Lisa is the Russian word for fox.

"Nyet," the driver answered. "Ne Lisa. Sabaca! Sabaca!"

"Sabaca?" I replied in disbelief. "Sabaca?"

"Da, sabaca," the driver emphasized.

Sabaca is another Russian word I knew. It meant dog. Ray had the skin of a dog mounted proudly on his head.

The driver then explained to me that his dog had died and it had such nice fur he decided to make a hat from it, something I later found out wasn't all that unusual in many of the remote villages in Siberia. If the villagers had a dog or cat with luxurious fur pass away, they would make a fur hat from their expired pet. "Nothing goes to waste in Siberia," they would tell me. "Fur is fur, right?"

"Well, is it a fox hat?" Ray asked after the driver finished explaining the hat's origin.

I didn't have the heart to tell Ray he had a dead dog curled up atop his head. He was sitting there proudly, like a king with a shiny new crown. His chest was puffed out like a tom turkey in full strut. Ray had just made the deal of the century, trading a ball cap for an authentic Russian fur hat. I figured he had been through enough already, with the ride to the police station and all, and I wanted to spare him further embarrassment.

"Yeah, it's a fox hat," I told Ray. "It sure is a sharp hat, isn't it?"

I don't think Ray took that hat off the rest of the trip. He wore it everywhere we went, even on the airplane ride back to the States. I never saw a guy so proud of a hat. He received frequent compliments on that hat, too. Unfortunately, I made the mistake of telling one of the other hunters later that the hat was made from the guide's dog and not a fox. He had kept asking me about the hat and said he knew it wasn't fox fur. I told him not to say anything to Ray. He promised he wouldn't.

Well, he didn't say anything to Ray about what the hat was made of, but every once in a while he would rub and pat the hat while saying, "Nice hat. Good hat. Good boy. That's a gooood hat."

This perplexed Ray no end. I don't think Ray ever did find out his hat was made from a dog hide. Up until now, that is.

When we got back to Grand Rapids, Norma was there to greet us. She came up to me and gave me a big hug for bringing Ray back safely.

"Oh, Ray, I'm so glad to see you," Norma gushed. "I was so worried about you. I thought I would never see you again. I'm so happy you made it home all right!"

"Well, let me tell you what happened," Ray said with a wry grin as he and Norma walked toward the exit doors of the terminal. "The police took me to jail the first day I was there . . . "

"Oh My God," Norma gasped. "I told you so! I told you that would happen, didn't I."

Ray looked back over his shoulder and gave me a wink from under his handsome new fur hat. I have no idea what he told Norma, but I know he made it exciting.

More than just bears and moose...

Snow Sheep / Bighorn Sheep

• *Robbie Russell from Tennessee and his Kamchatka bighorn ram taken in August 2016. Age was estimated at more than 10 years; normal life span is 10-12 years. Robbie Russell photo.*

The snow sheep and Siberian bighorn sheep are pretty much one and the same. They live in the mountainous areas of northeastern Siberia. The snow sheep is most closely related to the North American bighorn sheep and Dall's sheep. There are seven sub-species of snow sheep.

We specifically hunt sheep. I've taken a number of sheep hunters into the mountains.

Spectacular hunting; spectacular game; spectacular scenery.

CHAPTER 12

THE GOOD, THE BAD, AND THE UGLY

YOU ALWAYS HEAR STORIES about bad outfitters when people start talking about booking trips with guide services and lodges. It seems like everybody knows someone who has a cousin who had a friend whose brother's best buddy had a bad experience. Someone who got screwed by an outfitter who didn't know what he was doing. Or worse, the outfitter misled them. To be sure, there are unscrupulous outfitters who do mess up hunts by being inept or untruthful.

Fortunately, there aren't as many bad outfitters as there are stories about bad outfitters. That's because in this business, you live and die by your reputation. Bad outfitters come and go like bad reality shows. It's like any other business; if you make a habit of screwing your clients, believe me, you won't last long. I've run into a few of those outfitters myself. They do exist but don't last. You can figure any outfitter who has been in business more than 10 years is running a good operation.

Of course, even a good outfitter can have a bad hunt. Many factors can spoil a hunt, with weather at the top of the list. It's no different from a good carpenter driving a nail in the wrong place once in a while, or a good restaurant messing up a meal time to time. Everyone has a bad day. It's not a perfect world. Anyone who tells you they never had a bad day, or never messed up something, is lying or delusional. In all the years I took people to

Russia on hunts, I had a few bad hunts. When that happens, all you can do is try to make it up to the client by replacing his bad hunt with a good hunt.

One thing I have learned over the years in this business is that many of the bad outfitter stories you hear are actually the result of having a bad hunter in camp. Yes, a bad hunter. It's not always the outfitter's fault. It's often the hunter's fault.

A magazine called *The Hunt Club Digest* published a story by Tracy Breen in 2006 focusing on bad hunters. It was titled "The 10 Worst Hunters To Have In Camp." It was a hard-hitting story that revealed the ugly side of the hunting profession as not shown before. Until then, all the focus had been on bad outfitter stories. Nobody took into consideration the fact that the sources of some of the bad outfitter stories were actually bad hunters.

Ms. Breen starts her story with this paragraph: "We all have met him in camp. The guy who thinks he is the greatest whitetail hunter since Fred Bear." She then lists the 10 worst kinds of hunters:

(1) The Movie Star	(6) The Drunk
(2) The Shooter	(7) The Abuser
(3) The Know-It-All	(8) The Great White Hunter
(4) Mr. Tough Cookie	(9) The Rhinestone Cowboy
(5) The Wanna-Be Hunter	(10) The Whiner

If you are a hunter, you can pretty much figure out what each of these individuals is like. You probably have encountered one or more of these types in a camp.

At the time this article was published, I was in a transition period from being mostly a hunter who booked hunts with outfitters for myself, to an agent who booked hunts with outfitters for my clients. I was now seeing both sides of the story clearly for the first time. I realized that not all the bad outfitter stories you hear were the fault of the outfitter, and many were the result of a bad hunter.

During the nearly quarter of a century working on the outfitting side, booking more than 1,000 hunters into dozens of camps, many of whom I've spent weeks with in the bush,

I have encountered all 10 hunter types outlined in the magazine article. Some over and over! Here are the stories of a few of them.

THE KNOW-IT-ALL

It was a spring bear hunt in the early 1990s when I traveled to one of our camps on the Kamchatka Peninsula with four guys from Michigan. We were hunting in the Milkovo region in early May, about halfway up the peninsula. We arrived at camp to find there was still almost 10 feet of snow on the ground. It was up to the roofs of the cabins. The guides had to dig steps down through the snow to get in the cabin door.

Our hunts were designed to coincide with the time the bears start coming out of hibernation. This occurs when spring weather arrives and the warm sun begins to melt the snow away from their den sites.

During a normal year, the spring melt begins in mid- to late April on the southern end of the peninsula so, naturally, we held our first hunts there in late April. We conducted a second hunt in early May a little farther north on the peninsula where spring arrives later, and the bears wake up later. We ran a third hunt even farther north where the bears come out in mid-May.

This schedule works fine and dandy during the course of a normal spring. Unfortunately, not all springs ... or summers ... or falls ... or winters ... are normal. Sometimes spring comes early so the snow begins to melt several weeks ahead of schedule, causing the bears to wake up early. Sometimes spring comes late so the snow melts several weeks later than usual, causing the bears to wake up later. The arrival of spring not only has a big effect on bear hibernation, it also affects the number of bears a hunter will see. Can't see them if they're not out.

Trying to predict when spring will be late, when spring will be early and when spring will be normal is a fool's game. All you can do is schedule the hunts based upon the average spring break-up over the past century. Early and late springs are aberrations you cannot predict. Most hunters are aware of this, but not all.

When we got to camp early that spring and saw there was 10 feet of snow on the ground, and the guides told us bears were still sleeping, the hunters were a little uptight. They also told us the rapidly warming weather should wake the bears any day soon; we shouldn't get discouraged. I figured the clients understood this.

The first day the hunters didn't see a thing, not even a track. They were understandably disappointed but not ready to quit the hunt.

That didn't happen until the third day. After the morning hunt on the third day, all four clients refused to go out after lunch. Even though none of them had hunted brown bears in their lives, they all had suddenly become experts on brown bear behavior. If they weren't seeing any tracks, that could only mean there were no bears in this area.

"There aren't any bears around here," they complained. "We just keep going around in circles in the same area day after day. The guides are stupid and lazy and don't know what they are doing. They are lost. You took us on a wild goose chase. You will be talking to our lawyers when we get home."

Ah, the gang-up-on-the-outfitter strategy. It's always a pain when one guy becomes irate on a hunt, but when he talks a few others into the "let's get together and gang up on the outfitter," things go south in a hurry.

I explained to them that this was a good camp and that there were a lot of bears around. I had been here before and knew this to be a fact. The reason they weren't seeing any bears yet was because the snow was too deep for the bears to dig out of their dens. I assured them the bears would be coming out any time now. Because the weather had been very warm the past few days, the bears would be waking up soon.

I also explained the reason the guides kept going back to the same areas was because this was where the bears were hibernating. It only made sense to go to where the den sites were located and check for awakening bears. If you were deer hunting, wouldn't you keep going back to the same area you had been seeing that big buck all summer? It's just common sense.

Ah, but not common sense to a guy who is bound and determined he's getting screwed by the outfitter and the Russians.

"By the way," I continued, "another reason the guides keep snowmobiling in the same area over and over is because the noise from the snowmobiles will actually help wake up the bears. You're on a seven-day hunt. Don't give up after only three days.

"I can remember a number of hunts in the States when I didn't get anything until the last day, or even the last hour. You can't throw in the towel yet. You still have four days to hunt."

However, they knew it all. I was full of it. Even though I had been doing this for many years, they knew more about spring brown bear hunting than I did.

Thankfully, one of the hunters decided to give it another try. He agreed the group shouldn't give up after only three days.

"I know things don't look good up to this point," he said, "but I paid $10,000 to go bear hunting and, by golly, I'm going bear hunting. I think Denny is right. The bears will be coming out of hibernation any time now."

The other three men were not convinced. They went back to the cabin, laid on their beds and sulked. All they could do was moan and threaten me with a lawsuit.

By now the guides were also getting upset. They were upset because the hunters refused to hunt.

•Snow covers one of our camps on a 2010 trip. In the background only the peaks of cabin roofs stick above the deep snow. (Denny Geurink photo)

• This shows you just how much snow many areas of Siberia receive each winter. The snow on the roof of the house is taller than the house itself. (Seafriends.org photo)

Things were getting ugly fast, but redemption was close.

Two hours later that fourth morning, the client who went hunting rode back into camp, screaming at the top of his lungs. We could hear him hollering a hundred yards out.

"I shot the God Bear!," he yelled. "I shot the God Bear!" He was referring to a local legend about a species of super-sized brown bears living in this part of Russia as recently as a couple of decades ago. Based upon skeletal remains, scientists say these bears grew 12 to 16 feet tall. Some say they still exist in the most remote areas of Russia. Locals call them God Bears. My hunter apparently had read about the legend, and, apparently, had shot a very big bear.

"You should see all the tracks out there now," he stammered with unbridled enthusiasm. "You know where this trail leads to camp," he said, pointing to the snowmobile trail he had just ridden in on. "There are tracks from at least six bears crossing the trail not 200 yards out. On the lower elevations, where we have been circling, you can see where at least two bears dug out of their dens right through the snowmobile trail.

"Denny was right!"

• *Guides sometimes need to dig steps down into deep snow to reach the doors of our cabins. (Mike Muster photo)*

The "I told you so" look was plastered all over my face.

Naturally, the other three guys were now chomping at the bit to go hunting, but now we had another problem.

Their guides were so upset that the "spoiled American hunters" had refused to go out and hunt with them, calling them stupid and lazy and saying they were lost, they were now refusing to hunt. It took all my diplomatic efforts to get the guides to agree to take the other three guys out the next morning.

The next day all three were back in camp by noon with bears. Moral of the story: never give up.

THE LAWYER

I really don't know where a lawyer belongs on the 10 worst hunters list. Maybe they are a compilation of all of them, or maybe this should be a chapter about "The 11 Worst Hunters To Have In Camp" and lawyers should be listed as No. 11 "The Lawyer".

I'm being a little facetious here. Of course, not all lawyers are bad; many are good people and good hunters. I've had a few in camp who were amazing people and great hunters. However, some of them, unfortunately, contributed to the negative perception many people have of lawyers. One of the worst experiences I ever had in a hunting camp was with a lawyer whose real name I will, of course, not mention. Let's call him Jack.

I was on a moose hunt with four guys in September in the late '90s. We were going to a remote camp in Siberia near the Arctic Circle. It always took at least two days to get to this camp, but the moose hunting was fabulous.

One of the hunters on this trip was a lawyer who apparently had a hard time leaving office and courtroom behind. We weren't long into the trip when I noticed he was writing everything in a little notebook he had brought along. He noted every word I said and every observation he made. He asked all sorts of leading questions, then jotted the context of the replies in his little book. This soon became obvious to the other hunters in the group.

"Did you notice Jack is writing down every word you say on this trip," one of the hunters asked me on the second day of the expedition. "If you say someone burped but he actually belched, he is writing it down. If you say we are going to turn left and we actually veer left, he's writing it down. **#@8^* lawyer!"

"Yeah, I noticed," I said, with an undisguised hint of disgust. "That's why I am saying 'I think' and 'almost' and 'usually' when I answer him. This guy is beginning to be a pain in the butt."

We soon learned his ulterior motive. After we boarded the helicopter that would take us to camp, Jack asked me how long the helicopter flight would be.

"About an hour," I replied.

I hate having to watch every word I say because some guy is going to twist them around to screw me later. After about an hour, I spotted the camp site from the air. This was where we would land to set up the tents and do our hunting. I had been there many times before.

"There's camp," I announced as the helicopter pilot began to take us down. "Everyone ready to hunt?"

Everyone, except Jack, responded with a loud "yes."

"You said it was an hour to camp," our lawyer friend litigiously announced. "We have been in the air only 50 minutes. I figure this helicopter can fly 125 miles an hour. So, if we have been in the air only 50 minutes, we could be 20 to 30 miles from the real camp. I think we are in the wrong spot. This helicopter pilot is lost and took us to the wrong spot. I just want to tell you that if I don't get a moose here, I will see you in court."

My jaw dropped to my chest! So did the collective jaws of the rest of the group.

You're kidding me, right?," I asked, gritting my teeth. "I said ABOUT an hour. Isn't 50 minutes about an hour?"

• *The only way to access most of our camps in Siberia was with a helicopter. Where there was deep snow they often sank to their belly when we landed. (Denny Geurink photo)*

"No, I'm serious," Jack replied. "I think we are in the wrong spot."

This was not a good way to begin a hunt. The rest of the guys in camp didn't have much good to say about lawyers that week. Lots of lawyer jokes were told when Jack was out of camp. Some e v e n were told while he sat at the dinner table with us. The other hunters were nearly as unhappy with Jack as I was.

Nor is that the whole story!

Our interpreter had heard and understood everything said since we left Moscow. The Russians don't have much use for our legal system or lawyers anyway, so this incident did not sit well with him. He could see the handwriting on the wall. If Jack has a bad hunt, he sues Denny, and Boris (not his real name) gets dragged into court with Denny. This could cost Boris a lot of money just to get to the U.S. to defend himself. That's how the U.S. legal system works. Even if you're innocent, you spend a ton of money to prove it.   Boris was getting upset and told the guides and cook what was going on.

Besides writing   down   everything that happened in   camp, including whether the soup was hot or cold, Jack asked the guides questions through the interpreter.

He   also   tried   to   question   them   on   his   own. Things like: "Is this the camp we are supposed to be in?" "Are   you   sure?" "Where   are   we   going?" "How   far do we   have   to walk   today?" "What   is the   terrain like?" "Have   you ever   seen   any moose here?" "Is this area over-hunted?" "Have   you   really been   here before?" "Why this camp?" and on and on.

Some of those are legitimate questions when asked by a hunter without an ulterior motive, but in Jack's case he was trying to trip up the guides. They soon figured him out. When he asked how far they would walk today, and the guides said five miles but they walked six, it meant   the   guides   didn't   know   where   they   were going   and   were   lost.   Even   more   amazing,   Jack thought he   could understand Russian after just a couple days in camp and was telling me what the guides were telling him. It was different, of course, from what I had told him.

Jack had no clue what they were saying, of course. When Jack yammered at the guides, they just yammered back. There   was   no   real   communication,   but   that didn't stop Jack from interrogating the guides, the cook, and the interpreter, every chance he got, then writing everything in his notebook.

After about the third day, it hit the fan. One of the guides and the interpreter took   me aside. "These guides,   the cook,   and I don't like this lawyer   you brought to camp," Boris whispered in a low voice. "He is nothing but trouble. He's a first class jerk. It could cost both of us a lot of money if he takes us to court.

he guide proposes that he take Jack very far away from
ip and leave him in the forest. What do you think?"

Just like Jack was serious about taking me to court if he
didn't shoot a moose, this guy was serious about leaving
Jack in the forest. We were in BFE Russia. This was
Siberia, not a woodlot in Michigan. Lots of people had
disappeared here during the czar and communist periods of
this country. I was hunting with indigenous people who live
by the seat of their pants and live by their own set of
rules. They don't much care for anyone, American or
otherwise, who disrespects them every chance he gets. When
you see the phrase "Ugly American" in the dictionary, you
will see Jack's photo next to it.

All I had to do was give the word. As tempting as it was
(not really!), I told the guide: 1) we couldn't do that, 2) take
good care of Jack because I need to get him home safely or
I will have more problems than him not shooting a moose.

I was shaking like a leaf. I kept thinking of what
Dorothy said in the *Wizard of Oz*, "Toto, I have a
feeling we're not in Kansas anymore."

Fortunately, the lawyer shot a big moose. I never heard
from him again, which was just fine. As we boarded the
plane back to the U.S., one of the other hunters quipped,
"I hope you learned a lesson from this."

"What's that?"

"Never take a lawyer hunting."

THE WHINER

This is probably one of the most common 'bad' types
you encounter in a hunting camp. You know, the guy
who complains about everything. This guy can ruin a
camp in a big hurry with his whining and negativity, and he
usually turns the mood of the entire camp sour. Negativity
spreads like a disease. It's the 'one bad apple spoils the
barrel' syndrome. Soon enough -- too soon, actually --
everyone is whining and complaining.

Fortunately, sometimes when you get a whiner in camp, the other hunters see him for what he is and help you try to get him under control. This happened in a moose camp a few years ago.

The expedition started in Chicago, where we met at the airport and boarded a plane for Moscow. One of the hunters -- call him Bill -- began complaining as soon as he boarded the plane: The seats were uncomfortable; the food was cold; the service was bad; the ride was rough; the plane was old, and on and on and on.

In Moscow, the taxi ride to the hotel was too long; the people at the hotel desk were too slow; the room was too small; the bed was too hard; the shower was too small, blah, blah, blah.

Bill's glass was always half empty, never half full. No matter what you do to make a person like this happy, he is determined to be unhappy.

It didn't stop once we got to camp: the soup was cold; the bed was uncomfortable; the food was awful; the guides were stupid; he had to walk too far, yada, yada, yada.

On the second day of the hunt, one of the other guys -- call him Jim -- asked if it would be all right if he had a word with "The Complainer," as the other hunters had by now nicknamed Bill.

"This guy is ruining my hunt," Jim said in disgust. "I paid a lot of money to come on this hunt and want to have some fun, but his continuous complaining and whining is driving me and the other guys crazy. I know you have been talking to him and trying to get him to stop complaining, but it isn't working. Maybe if I had a talk with him it might help."

"Have at it," I told him. "Maybe if it comes from one of his fellow hunters instead of me it might help. He's driving me nuts too!"

I had no idea what Jim was going to say. He had been rather quiet and shy, so I was wondering just how he was going to talk with Bill, who was loud and verbose.

I just hoped it would help. By the way, Jim was about six feet five inches tall and weighed about 250. Bill was about five feet nine and weighed around 175 pounds.

When Bill walked into the cook tent that evening, Jim asked him if he would step outside the tent for a minute so he could talk to him. The rest of us craned our necks, trying to peer out the tent door to see what Jim would say.

Our jaws dropped when Jim took the index finger of his club of a hand and thrust it into Bill's chest, knocking him backward.

"Listen, you whiny, complaining little son of a bitch," Jim growled, "I paid a lot of money to come on this hunt. I came here to have a good time, but you are ruining my trip with all your griping. I'm sick of it and so is everyone else. You complain one more time and you will be breathing out the back of your head because that's where your nose will be. Got it?"

"G-g-g-got it," Bill stammered, taken aback to the point of being terrified. He had no doubt Jim would make good on his promise. Jim was one tough, bronc-bustin' son-of-a-gun from Nebraska. One crashing blow from his big right hand would send Bill to the Promised Land, to paraphrase Jimmy Dean's "Big John" song. That song immediately came to mind.

There was no more complaining or whining in that camp, particularly not from Bill.

MR. TOUGH COOKIE

Once in a while you will get a guy on a hunt who thinks he can bully and boss his way through the trip because he has a lot of money. This guy is accustomed to getting his way and doesn't mind bulldozing everyone to get what he wants. He is going to tell you what to do because he paid good money for this hunt. Because he gave you money, he owns you, and you will do what he says. He will order you around like one of his hired hands. I call it the "Daddy Warbucks" syndrome.

When I am on a trip, I try to make sure everyone has a good time. I try to keep the Tough Cookies happy, as long as they don't get too obnoxious.

On a bear hunt a few years ago, I had one; call him Frank. One day as I was coming into the bunk house, Frank yelled, "Denny, bring me a Coke."

The soft drinks were often stored in a snow bank just outside the bunk house to keep them cold. It was no problem to step out and grab a Coke for Frank.

"You mean, 'Denny, please get me a Coke'," I said, chuckling, as I handed the bottle to Frank. I was hoping he would get the hint, but he didn't.

This happened a few more times over the next several days. I was beginning to get a little irritated, but I bit my tongue and remained civil. It wasn't long before Frank began ordering around a few of the other guys as well. "Hey, Steve, bring me a Coke!" "Hey, Bill, bring me a Coke!"

'I can't wait until he tells Nick to bring him a Coke,' I thought. 'Then we are going to see some fireworks, because you don't order Nick around.'

Nick had hunted with me several times. He is a really nice guy and would give you the shirt off his back if you asked him nicely, but you don't tell Nick what to do. Maybe with a 'please' he would do it, but not on a direct order. I found myself hoping Frank would soon bark an order at Nick. Then it happened.

"Hey, Nick, get me a Coke," Frank barked one evening.'YES,' I whispered to myself. Here it comes.

"Get your own @#%#@ing Coke," Nick shot back. "You got a @#**@ broken leg? You bring me a Coke you (bleeping) lazy SOB! I've got more money than you do. Get me a (bleeping) Coke @**%@*!"

You could have cut the blue air in the cabin with a knife. Frank was dumbfounded. His face turned bright pink as he stared at Nick.

He wasn't going to mess with Nick. Nick was a construction worker with sledgehammer fists.

Frank just stared for a second and then began sputtering. "Hey, Nick, I apologize for my behavior," he began. "I apologize to all you guys. I know I'm in a camp with my peers. It's just that I'm so used to barking orders at work I sometimes forget where I am. I'm really sorry I've been acting like a butthole. Sorry guys."

You have to give Frank his due. He learned a lesson, and he apologized. That's more than some guys do. Frank was a great guy the rest of the trip and on several trips after that. He never ordered anyone around after that, at least, not in camp.

THE GOOD!

I guess I mixed the order of "the Good, the Bad and the Ugly" theme of this chapter. I started with the Bad and the Ugly. I don't want this chapter to sound like most of my clients have been jerks, as that couldn't be further from the truth. In reality, most of them have been great people and fun to be around. More than 95 percent of my clients have been wonderful people. Only about five percent fall into "The 10 Worst Hunters" category. (They do, though, make interesting story material.)

The good guys create interesting memories. Quite a few of the people I took to Russia as clients came back home as friends. You've read about a few of them in previous chapters and will read about others in subsequent chapters, such as Nick Jorae, Jim McDivitt and Earl O'Loughlin, all of whom went on more than one hunt with me. Jorae has been on seven or eight hunts. There have been many others who started out as clients and became friends.

Another client who became a good friend is Chris Fuller from Jackson, Michigan. He went on six or seven hunts with me, so we got to know each other well. Fuller is an upbeat guy whose favorite saying is "Life is too short to spend it worrying and complaining". Ain't it the truth! A chapter titled "The Good, The Bad, And The Ugly" wouldn't exist if everyone subscribed to Fuller's philosophy.

Dale   Fulkerson   from   Livonia,   Michigan,   is another former client who became a lifelong friend. Dale bought into my business in the late '90s and helped me take clients to Russia for several years until he contracted Lyme disease.

He   had   survived   wild   and   woolly   experiences in Siberia,   only   to   contract   this   debilitating disease while mowing grass in his back yard. He is one of the most upbeat, fun-loving guys you will ever meet. My clients and   I   really   missed   having   him   along   on our later expeditions.

A couple of real characters I met along the way were Fred Lemmon from Georgia and Ken Horm from Ohio. Both   became   good   friends   with   whom   I   have spent time   back   home.   Like   Fulkerson,   Don   Nixon from Luther, Michigan, is   a   former   client   who   later bought into   my   business   and   helped   escort   trips   for many years. He remains a good friend, and we still see each other on a regular basis.

Michael Elmore, who for a time, owned and operated Outdoor Adventures, also was a former client who became a good friend. He had gone on a number of trips with me and fell in love with Russia just as I had. He enjoyed going there so much he bought my business in 2011, giving me a chance to retire and write this book.

Another   client   who   became   a   close   friend   was Lynn Hunt from Edmore, Michigan. He and his wife Mary Jo have   been   to   the Ukraine and Africa with me several times. Shortly after their first expedition in 2004, Lynn invited   me   to   hunt   turkeys   with   him   on his Michigan farm. We had been talking about turkey and deer hunting in camp, and he knew I was an avid gobbler chaser.

Lynn filmed me for an episode on my TV show. He later invited me on a deer hunt, and so began a long and wonderful friendship.

We became such good friends over the years that I bought a house and 40 acres across the road from him. My family spent ten great years hunting, fishing, and hanging out with Lynn and Mary Jo. They were the best neighbors a family could have. Sadly, Lynn passed away in February, 2013. This has left a big hole in my life. I really miss him. He was one of the kindest, gentlest people I ever met.

One of the most emotional trips I ever set up for a client began with a call from Robert (Bob) Killion, from Monrovia, Maryland. Killion called one evening in January or February, just before our spring bear hunts, to ask about our Russian adventures.

"Hey, Denny I saw your ad on TV about bear hunting in Russia," Bob said excitedly. "I've wanted to go on a big brown bear hunt all my life but kept putting it off for one reason or another. It's been a dream of mine for a long time, but I can't put if off any longer. I have terminal cancer. My doctor says I have only six months to two years to live."

"Oh, man, I'm sorry to hear that," I said, startled by Bob's sad revelation. "I'd like to help you make that dream come true."

"I probably shouldn't be doing this because of the shape I'm in, but my wife says I need to fulfill this dream. I really want to go on this hunt."

"What kind of physical shape are you in?" I asked. "Can you ride on a snowmobile? Could you make a short stalk if the guides got you close to a bear?"

"I think I could do that all right," Bob said. "I've been through some intensive chemo and lost a lot of weight and all of my hair, and I'm pretty weak and have a hard time keeping food down, but I'm determined to do this. Will you take me? I heard that all your hunters always get a bear. I really want to get a bear. You think you could get a bear for a person in my condition?"

"I'll try my best," I replied. "I'll talk to the outfitter and the guides and tell them to get you as close as they can to a bear so you won't have to walk far. When I tell them your story, they will do everything in their power to make your dream come true. They are good people."

"OK, sign me up," Bob enthused. "I'm really looking forward to this. Just one more thing: if I don't make it long enough to go on the hunt, what happens to my money?"

"I'll tell the outfitter not to pay any of the food, lodging, or guide fees up front," I replied, "but I do need to get you a license, rifle permit and CITES permit. You would be out just the deposit."

"OK," Bob said. "I'll see you in a couple of months."

That shook me. I had never had a guy tell me he might not live long enough to go on a hunt with me.

Bob made it to Kamchatka in the spring. He was thin and weak but determined to make his dream come true.

I was proud of the other hunters, who went out of their way to help Bob however they could, especially Denis McClure, who shared a camp with Bob.

I was proud of the guides, who bent over backward to get him into the field.

I was proud of the cook, who tried to prepare meals he could keep down.

I was especially proud of Bob, who, despite being in obvious pain and distress, lived his dream.

Bob had a great hunt. He took a big brown in the nine-foot class. You never saw a guy so happy. He had tears in his eyes when he told me the story. When he was finished, I had a tear in my eye.

Less than two years later, Bob's wife called one afternoon to tell me Bob had passed away. She wanted to

⹀⹀⹀⹀ me for helping him make his final wish come true.

"He talked about that trip just about every day for the rest of his life," she said, her voice cracking. "He was so happy that he could do this before he died."

So was I.

I've told Bob's story quite a few times. And I always finish the story with the lesson Bob taught me. "Tell people not to keep putting off things they really want to do," Bob explained to me one day. "You tell them to follow their dreams while they can because you never know when your time is up. Your whole world can turn upside down in an instant. Don't keep saying you're going to do something next year, because next year may never come. Do it now!"

Something to remember!

Jeff Gorski was one of my favorite hunters. Jeff lived in Texas and had a heart as big as Pecos County. He has been on a number of hunts with me. He's a down- to-earth guy who loves to hunt and have a good time. Jeff calls himself "a redneck with money". One of his favorite expressions is "Go Big or Go Home." Jeff loved to go big.

Returning from one hunt we flew back to Moscow to spend the night before returning to the States. As we left the airport in a van to go to our hotel, Jeff asked me if we were staying in the same hotel we had stayed in before the hunt. I told him we were.

"That hotel wasn't bad, but I prefer to stay in something a little nicer," Jeff said. "Do they have any nicer hotels here in Moscow?"

"Yes, they do have some nice ones -- the Sheraton, the Hilton and the Marriott are three, but they're expensive. We stay at the Izmailovo. It's only around $150 a night."

"Do they have a Ritz Carlton in Moscow?," Jeff asked. "I always like to stay at the Ritz when I travel."

"They just built a new Ritz Carlton near Red Square, but I hear it's expensive. If you want to stay there, go ahead. We can meet you in the morning. I can't afford to stay there."

"Don't worry about it, I'm buying."

"There are five of us," I said, with a bit of hesitation. "That's going to cost too much. We'll just go to the Izmailovo and meet you in the morning."

"No," Jeff said. "I insist. It's on me."

Jeff called his American Express hotline number.

He has access to a 24-hour concierge. He told the lady to book five rooms at the Ritz and cancel the five rooms at the Izmailovo. We were all a bit shocked. I had never been to a Ritz Carlton but knew its reputation.

We had just spent a week in the bush hunting moose and sheep. We were dirty, sweaty, grubby, and dressed in camo head to toe. Throw in a week's worth of stubby whiskers and muddy hunting boots, and you can imagine the look on the receptionist's face when we walked through the front door and up to the counter at the Ritz. We were toting aluminum gun cases and moose antlers, too. Our group, gear and trophies nearly filled the registration area.

"Can I help you?," the registration desk attendant asked in shock, backing away from the desk. We must have looked like a commando unit fresh off a Special Forces operation.

"Yes, you can," Jeff said as he walked up to the desk and plopped down his American Express card. "My name is Jeff Gorski. My concierge recently called and made reservations for us."

"Oh, Mr. Gorski," the receptionist exclaimed as she quickly stepped back to the counter, color returning to her face. "Yes, we have your reservations right here."

The American Express platinum membership card made quite an impression. After completing our registration paperwork, the lady looked up and asked, "How will all of you be paying for this? With credit card or cash?

"I'm paying for all the rooms," Jeff said.

"All of them?," she gasped. The rooms cost $956 each.

"Yes, all of them."

"All of them?" the receptionist asked again. "Are you sure, Mr. Gorski? All of them?"

"Yes, all of them," Jeff said again, with a chuckle.

When I got to my room, I could see why the room cost $965 a night. There must have been 10 pillows on my bed. Chocolates were everywhere in the room. The shower and tub had more lotions and soaps than a pharmacy aisle. Robes and slippers were everywhere.

After showering, I went to the lobby. I was the first one down, so I found a comfortable couch and waited for the other guys to show up. As I sat there listening to a man in a tux playing a grand piano, a young lady dressed in evening wear approached and asked if I cared for a cup of tea. I told her that sounded good. When each room is $956, I guessed a cup of tea would be included.

She returned a few minutes later with a silver teapot on a silver tray, and a porcelain tea cup and some crumpets. Pretty fancy, I thought, as she set it on a mahogany table in front of me. I thanked her.

She smiled, dropped a piece of paper on the tray and walked away. I picked up the piece of paper. Yikes! The cup of tea cost $28. I've stayed in a Motel 6 in the U.S. for what one cup of tea cost at that Ritz.

I drank the tea and went back to my room to get more money. It looked like I would need it. In the few minutes I had been gone, a housekeeper had remade the bed, resupplied the chocolates, cleaned out the shower and replaced the wet towels with dry ones. This place was off the charts! I could rhapsodize about the meal we had later, and the wine we drank, but you get the picture.

That's a Jeff Gorski story. In some of the subsequent chapters, you will read about other clients I have had the pleasure of meeting.

CHAPTER 13

TALES FROM GRIZZLY CAMP

SOME OF THE MOST exciting and enjoyable camps the last two-plus decades were our Siberian grizzly camps. They were espcially memorable in the early years when I took people to Russia who had grown up during the Cold War. My clients didn't know what to expect when they got to Russia. They had misconceptions on how they would be treated, what the camps would be like, and, of course, wondered if they would even get back home. Remember, this was the "Evil Empire". There were plenty of horror stories going around; few were true.

Many of my clients would go to Russia only if I went with them. So I began personally escorting the trips. More than 90 percent of my clients would not have gone without me.

These hunts were considerably different from any hunt they had done before. It wasn't like going to Colorado or Wyoming, where you can hop in your pickup truck and take off. Now you were traveling to a strange new world full of boogeymen and mystery. The hunters who went those first few years were brave souls who conquered their fears for the sake of knowledge and adventure. They were thrill seekers with open minds who were eager to see a land shrouded in mystery, a country that had been cut off from the rest of the world for more than half a century. It's fairly easy to go to Russia now, but it wasn't then. Here's a look at some of my clients' thoughts and impressions of their adventures to "The Final Frontier."

The accounts are excerpts from my newspaper columns, all of which were written and published shortly after the trips.

BIG BEAR, BEAUTIFUL BIRDIES IMPRESS GROUP ON TRIP TO RUSSIA

"I'd like to propose a toast," Mike Morey Sr. said, as he stood at the table surrounded by his son and hunting buddies in September,1997. "I would like to toast the many good people I've met on this trip. I've been fortunate to hunt all over the world. I've been to Africa, I've been to Alaska and Canada, and I've hunted out west in the United States. I honestly say I've never been treated so well, never hunted with better guides, never saw more game and never had a better time than this week. I thank everybody for making this a trip of a lifetime."

"Here, here," the others chimed in as they rose to their feet and clicked their champagne glasses together. "I'll toast to that."

We were in Vologda, a fair-sized city about 400 miles east of Moscow. We had just finished another successful week of bear hunting and had stopped at the house of one of our guides for dinner before heading back to Moscow to do some touring.

Mike Morey, of Mt. Pleasant, Michigan, had brought his son, Mike Jr., to pursue grizzlies. They were joined by Michigan-based friends Steve Lambert and John Seibt from Clare; Bill Gehoski, from Remus, and Charlie Momber, from Grand Rapids.

The action started slow the first night, with several sightings and a couple of misses. It was raining fairly hard and threatened to continue to rain all week. Fortunately, the wet weather didn't spoil the bears' appetites, as they continued to come into the oat patches in front of the hunters' blinds each evening. Mike Jr. and Seibt were the first to score. Seibt's bruin was huge.

"I had been seeing bears every night," Seibt said, "but this was by far the biggest one of the bunch."

His bear was a dandy, estimated to be more than 16 years old by the guides, who scored it as a Gold Medal animal. Seibt later had it scored by Safari Club International (SCI). It placed high in the record book.

Mike Jr's bear was an average size, so a few nights later he went out and tagged a bigger one, this one estimated to be nine years old. He also shot a big wild boar.

It's remarkable how some guys seem to have all the luck. It's like ice fishing, where you can fish one hole, using the same bait, the same teardrop, and at the same depth, and not catch anything, while your buddy not three feet away catches his limit.

The same sort of thing happened on this trip. It seemed that every time Seibt and Mike Jr. went out, they were covered up by bears and boars. Seibt even took his video camera one day and just filmed bears. Both he and Mike Jr. had a few opportunities to shoot a bear, while Lambert and Momber had only one shot each, which they unfortunately missed.

"I had my chance," Lambert said. "That's all I can ask."

Gehoski and Mike Sr. fortunately got a second chance. They each downed a bear after missing their first opportunities. They didn't see as many as Seibt and Junior, but the bruins they shot were nice.

One highlight of this trip was playing a round of golf at the posh Moscow Country Club after the hunt. It was the only golf course in Russia at the time. Mike Morey Sr. had done some research on Russia before his hunt and learned that Moscow had just constructed this new golf course. Being an avid golfer who has traveled to a number of countries just to golf, he was especially eager to get a chance to golf while in Moscow.

"Is there any chance we could play a round of golf at the Moscow Country Club?," Morey asked one evening via a late night telephone call. "That would really put the icing on the cake on this trip for me and my friends ."

"I didn't know they had a golf course in Moscow," I replied, a bit surprised by his request. "Let me talk to Dmitri and see what he can find out about the course. It does sound like fun. I wouldn't mind trying it myself."

Dmitri told me Morey was correct; there was a new golf course in Moscow. Construction began in 1988 and was completed in 1994. Problem was, according to Dmitri, the Moscow Country Club was an exclusive course for members only. The membership fee was $100,000. That's steep for somebody who wants to play a round of golf on vacation.

"When I told them there were some Americans who wanted to play a round of golf while they were traveling through Moscow, they said they would waive the membership fee and let you play one round for $125 each," Dmitri said. "You will be some of the first Americans to golf at that country club. What do you think? Is it worth $125?"

Morey was ecstatic when I gave him the news.

"Heck yes, we will pay the $125 greens fees!," he gushed. "I'd have paid a lot more than that."

So we played a round of golf at the Moscow Country Club. It was a blast! We probably spent more in the club house buying logo T-shirts, golf balls, tees, and other trinkets and souvenirs than on greens fees.

Bears and birdies in the same week ... not a bad trip. By the way, anyone can play a round of golf at the Moscow Country Club today. In fact, a five-star resort has been built on-site, where you can book a room, then golf to your heart's (or wallet's) content. Several major golfing events, including the Russian Open, are held at the club each year. It is one of the stops on the European PGA tour. A round of golf there today will cost you $250 on weekdays and up to $400 on weekends.

MICHIGAN MAN IS LOCAL HERO IN RUSSIA

When veteran hunting guides in Russia sit around a wilderness campfire at night swapping bear hunting stories, the name of one Michigan man will be spoken during those highly animated conversations. The name of that man is Nicholas "Five Bears" Jorae. That's the name local guides in that part of Siberia gave Jorae at the campfire one starlit evening. The ceremony was accompanied, of course, by shots of vodka.

Jorae had been inducted into the local Bear Hunters Hall of Fame. The 53-year-old contractor from Laingsburg, Michigan, was on his fifth trip to Russia. Three of the trips were in quest of giant brown bears. As Jorae has learned in recent years, they don't call Russia the "Land of the Bear" for nothing.

"I just love to hunt bears," Jorae said, "and if you want to hunt big bears, this is the best place in the world to do it. Some people like to hunt African game; some like to hunt deer and elk; some like small game. Me, I like the big bears. That's why I keep coming back."

On each of his two previous bear hunting trips to Russia, Jorae had tagged two brown bears. On this most recent trip, he shot number five, thus earning the colorful nickname of "Five Bears." (His nickname was later changed to "Six Bears" after he returned from a successful giant moose/brown bear combo hunt that fall on the Kamchatka Peninsula.)

"This might be my last bear hunt for a while," Jorae said. "I want to keep coming back to Russia to hunt. I wouldn't mind going on an interior grizzly hunt again. I really enjoyed that hunt. It was one of my favorites."

"You will be back to hunt bears," the guides chuckled as they lifted their glasses to toast his deeds. "You're a bear hunter, and you can't get the bear out of your soul. You and the bear are one."

Jorae loves hunting in Russia, not only because of the abundance of big brown bears, but also because he enjoys the land, the people, and the culture.

• *Nick "Six Bears" Jorae shows off some of the hides from wolves the guides trapped in the area where he harvested one of his bears. (Denny Geurink photo)*

"Over the years I've met a lot of good people here," Jorae said, as we swapped stories with the guides. "The guides are among the best in the world. I've made a lot of friends here and like coming back to see them."

The friendship Jorae has cultivated with the guides over the years was highlighted on one trip when his guide, Victor, invited Jorae to his son's wedding. Victor's son was getting married in the middle of one of our trips, so he took the night off from guiding Jorae, and they went to Victor's son's wedding. It was quite a thrill for Jorae.

"I was treated like royalty," he said. "Victor took me around and introduced me to all his friends and then toasted me at the reception. I can tell you one thing; these people really know how to celebrate a wedding. They were dancing and drinking vodka toasts all night long. All the old ladies kept trying to get me out on the dance floor. I told them I didn't know how to dance, but that made no difference. They treated me like a long lost friend. These Russian villagers are really kind people; some of the nicest people I've ever met."

GRIZZLY BEAR HUNT GETS HEART POUNDING

"I doubt my heart has ever beat harder," John Fiddelke said as he relived his bear-hunting adventure back in camp. "It felt like I had two hearts in my chest. I didn't know I could get that excited." His September bear hunt was going great.

You couldn't blame Fiddelke for getting geeked; this was his first bear hunt. He, Gary Athey, and Dan Martin had joined me on this grizzly bear-hunting expedition a few weeks earlier. The three were accompanied by their wives, who came along to tour St. Petersburg while their husbands chased big bruins.

It all happened fast for Fiddelke.

"I really don't know what to compare it to," he said. "My guide had pointed at his watch and indicated that the bears would start coming out at eight o'clock. He then pointed to the different directions they might come from. Sure enough, at three minutes to eight, we heard a bear coming out of the woods and into the apple orchard.

"First I heard a twig snapping, then another twig snap. I caught movement in the grass. Then I could make out the form of a bear as it approached one of the apple trees. That's when my heart really started to pound. I had only a small opening to shoot through, so I waited for the bear to step into it. It began picking up apples and eating them as it walked. When it stepped into the opening, I squeezed the trigger. It ran 30 yards and dropped. My hands are still shaking.

"I've hunted bears now only an hour and a half in my entire life. it's been an exciting hour and a half."

Fiddelke's trophy measured seven feet and sported a thick, dark fur. It was a beautiful inland grizzly.

While the men enjoyed their time in the woods (Martin also scored on a nice grizzly), the women enjoyed their personal tour of St. Petersburg. This was the first time any group brought their wives along on a hunting trip. Judging from their reactions, it won't be the last.

"It was first class all the way," Jean Bonnaci said. "The city was beautiful. The people were friendly. The entertainment was wonderful, from museums to ballet to opera. I had been a bit afraid of going to St. Petersburg, but when I got there, the fear went away. The whole experience was heartwarming."

Gina Athey agreed. "I enjoyed it immensely. I learned a lot about the people and their culture. Having a personal tour guide was great. We got to visit places you normally wouldn't see. I got a real feel for the city. I especially enjoyed the entertainment. The visit to your hunting camp was great. It was a wonderful trip."

WHY DO YOU WANT TO GO TO RUSSIA?

"I bet I had at least five guys in the last month ask me 'Why do you want to go to Russia?' like it was an awful place to be," mused Ron Shoemaker from Wayland, Michigan, as we chatted on a September hunt. "I told them I was going because I wanted to shoot a grizzly bear, and this was the place I'd have my best chance. I was right."

Shoemaker was exactly right. There are more brown and grizzly bears in Russia than anywhere else in the world. He had just downed a large grizzly with one shot on his second night out, proving the point. "This is a great place," he continued, as we toasted his good fortune. "The people here are great; they treat you great. The guides are excellent, some of the best I've hunted with. I don't know when I've had a better time."

Like so many hunters from around the country who have gone to Russia to experience first-hand the hunting and hospitality, Shoemaker found the pre-conceived thoughts and emotions many people had about Russia were off base.

Many of the nicest people we met in Russia over the years lived in the remote villages of Siberia. Because there are no motels or lodges in these small villages, our outfitter, Dmitri Sikorski, often arranged for us to stay with someone with a house big enough to accommodate a group of four or five American tourists. These people opened their homes to us and treated us like good friends. They cooked for us, cleaned for us, and even washed our dirty laundry. That's what happened on this trip.

We were staying in the home of Michael and Anna, a couple in their mid-60s. They are one of the sweetest couples I have ever met in Siberia. They were so accommodating they even gave up their bed and slept on the floor so there would be enough places for all the hunters to sleep. When I heard they were going to sleep on the floor, I protested and offered to sleep on the floor myself. So did Dmitri. But Michael and Anna would hear none of it. We were guests in their home, and there was no way a guest was going to sleep on the floor. They slept on the floor for an entire week.

I don't know how they were able to get off the floor in the morning. They weren't sleeping on a big, fluffy bed mattress, not even an air mattress They were on a hard wooden floor with only a thick blanket beneath them. I'm stiff and sore after sleeping on a real mattress all night.

Then Anna cooked breakfast before we went to the field each day. When we returned at lunch time, and again in the evening, she had a hot meal waiting, along with a homemade pie, cake, cookies, or some other treat.

All this she prepared on a wood stove. Michael kept busy all day cutting wood for the stove and the sauna, which was ready for us every night.

"This trip has been a lot more than I expected," said Rick Buist of Palatine, Illinois, as he proposed a toast at the dinner table one evening. Buist was with his father, Don Buist, of Grand Rapids, Michigan.

"You told me it would be a great hunt, but it was much more than that. I can hardly describe what a great time I've had. I saw brown bears everywhere, and wild boar.

"Living with Russian people was a real treat. Anna and Michael opened their home to us. They slept on the floor so we could use their beds. I don't know where else you could find hospitality like that."

Rick Buist tagged two bears and a wild boar. His first bear came the first night, after five minutes on stand.

"I sat with Yuri in the middle of the field and looked at my watch," Buist recounted. "I thought 'This will never work. I'm going to sit here for hours and not see a thing. What am I doing here?'

"Then I looked up and a bear was standing right in front of me. I couldn't believe it. I took a deep breath to calm my nerves and squeezed the trigger. It was over in 10 minutes. It's still tough to believe."

His father also was amazed. It had taken him only 20 minutes on stand his first night to pull the trigger on a grizzly.

"This is incredible," Don said. "Ten years ago I never thought I would be standing in a garage in Russia with my son, watching five Russians skin a bear we had just shot. What an experience!"

One day at lunch time we looked out the window and saw three people walking across a field toward the house. They came to the door and knocked. Michael and Dmitri went to the door. After a short conversation, they ushered the three men into the house. The men took off their hats and stood looking at us with big smiles.

"These guys just walked here from a village a couple of hours away," Dmitri said. "They heard there were going to be some Americans here and wanted to meet you and welcome you to Russia. You are the first Americans to visit this part of Russia, and they wanted to make sure you knew that you are welcome here."

Incredible! They walked two hours to shake our hands and welcome us to Russia.

We shook hands and chatted with them a few minutes. Anna offered f o o d , which they accepted, and they were on their way back across the field.

During the course of the week, we became good friends with Michael and Anna. We ate our meals with them and talked with them (via Dmitri, of course) each evening, telling jokes and talking about our families and our lives. At the end of the week, when it was time to leave, Michael and Anna had tears in their eyes.

"We know we will probably never see you again," Anna said in a soft voice. "We just want you to know how much we enjoyed having you stay with us in our home. You are always welcome here. We do hope you will come back. We think of you as our good friends."

There were a few tears on our side of the fence as well.

Camps Along a Salmon Stream May Be In The Path Of Bear Traffic

• *... in which case, slip meat treats to the dog so it sleeps near your tent, should bears wander into camp at night; and keep frying pans handy for noise-makers to frighten away daytime bruin visitors. (Denny Geurink photo)*

CHAPTER 14

IF IT WERENT FOR BAD LUCK, ID HAVE NO LUCK AT ALL!

I N THE LAST CHAPTER you read about the good time my clients were having on their Russian trips. A lot of the success on those trips was because I personally escorted them to make sure everything went smoothly. There was too much red tape and too many things that could go wrong those early years. You needed someone right there to take care of issues as they cropped up.

Most of the other outfitters who tried to set up hunts in Russia did not escort their hunters. They simply booked the hunts with a Russian guide and sent their clients to Siberia, scared and alone. These outfitters didn't last long.

I've been on a number of flights to Russia where I met hunters who were on their own. They were totally unprepared. They didn't know who they were meeting or where they were going. They didn't know how to fill out the necessary paperwork to get into and out of Russia.

I encountered more than one group arriving in Russia without proper paperwork. As soon as they landed in Russia, their rifles were confiscated, along with the bag they carried their ammunition in. They wound up spending a week in a hotel living out of their backpacks while waiting for the next flight home.

Because of the stories of this nature that I began hearing I placed a warning on our web site, advising people not to arrange trips on their own.

Even when you go with an established outfitter or agent, things may not go totally smoothly. Russia was, and still is to a certain extent, a wild and untamed place. At least, with an established outfitter you have a layer of protection. You will generally enjoy better accommodations, better food, and better service, because the Russians want to keep selling trips to an established outfitter or agent. They won't 'cheap out' on the hunt to increase their profit margin like they might with a person they think they'll never see again.

I say this as a lead in to a story a former client, Bob Coker from Eufaula, Alabama, sent me.

Coker went on a grizzly hunt with me in 1994 (see Chapter 9) which went very well, but two years later he went back on a trip he booked on his own directly with the Russians that didn't go so well. Not all of his problems occurred in Russia, however. He had plenty of them in the U.S. as well. I believe the phrase "If it weren't for bad luck, I'd have no luck at all" was coined shortly after this trip. Here's his story.

***

After many faxes and phone calls to Russia, the plans were made and our invitations were received for a brown bear hunt in Siberia. I had been working on this trip for two years, now all I needed was our visas.

It seemed the government departments in Russia were almost non-existent. The Russian Consulate never answered any of my calls on any of the five numbers I had. I overnighted our forms requesting visas along with a copy of our invitations. I also included a fee and a self-addressed, pre-paid overnight envelope.

I continued to phone the Russian Consulate every day with no luck. I was getting really worried. Things were not looking good. Then our visas arrived, at the last minute.

I began to tune the two bows I planned to take. In the process, I cracked a knuckle to the bone and needed about five stitches. Being stubborn, I cleaned the wound and closed the gash with a tightly-pulled bandage. After a week of my own doctoring, I gave in and went to the doctor.

My hand was swollen to twice its normal size and ached terribly. The doctor said I had cracked the same knuckle I had cracked as a teenager, and it was dangerously infected. After trying to talk me out of going to the remote outback of Russia, he decided to prescribe some potent antibiotics and began to explain how important it was to soak the knuckle in hot salt water three times a day. He succeeded in convincing me how dangerous it was and impressed me with the importance of keeping it cleaned, soaked, and covered with Neosporin.

Unfortunately, my hands were so swollen and sore that I could no longer grip my release and pull back my bow, let alone shoot it accurately. I bought a release and rigged one of my bows in a way that required less of a fist grip than my normal way of shooting. This new way still hurt, but it was tolerable enough to pull back my bow and shoot accurately. After all, if you are going to throw an arrow at a brown bear, it better be accurately thrown.

After tuning two bows, I ran out of time, so I decided to set my pins after I got to Russia. I packed my bags and was off to Atlanta. The Olympics were still in town; it took an hour to get to the terminal after I got to the airport. A police officer directed me to curb-side baggage care.

I noticed in retrospect that a line of five tow trucks were parked to the side parallel to the line of taxis. As I was asked the normal questions -- Did you pack your own bags?, Did anyone ask you to carry their bags for them?, May I see your passport?, etc., my car was being towed with three of my bags still in it, one of which had all my money.

The police told me to go to the airport police office for instructions on getting my vehicle back. There they gave me a copy of instructions to get to the towing company so I could get what I needed out of my car's glove box so I could go back to the airport police station to pay my fine. I took a cab uptown to my car, broke into the car to get my bags, money, and car registrations, then took a cab back to the airport just in time to make my flight. There wasn't time to pay the parking ticket, nor to move the car to a proper parking spot, so I left it.

Back at the airport I went to finish checking in. Buzz Howell, one of my hunting partners, met me at the gate. Noel Feather, the other partner, was meeting us in Anchorage. The flight through Seattle to Anchorage was uneventful, except for a bomb threat at the Seattle airport that threw all flights off schedule about one hour.

We had an overnight layover in Anchorage, so we got about five hours of sleep. I realized I hadn't packed my quiver, so we bought one at Brown Bear Archery on our way to the airport. The quiver mounts on my bows were for a quiver the shop did not have. I bought a PSE quiver, then had to figure out how to mount it on my bow.

The limo driver was nice, but he let us off at the International Terminal in Anchorage since, after all, we were flying to Russia. After he left, and we made several trips from the curb to the terminal with our bags, we found that since we were flying on Alaskan Air, we should have gone to the domestic terminal. Go figure.

We caught another shuttle bus and finally got to the right terminal, to find a long line at Alaskan Air. Buzz talked to all the people ahead of us and got their permission to get ahead of them.

We checked our bags and were charged for excess, then learned that our flight had been delayed at least an hour. Finally, my luck had changed for the better, so I thought. The one-hour delay turned into two and, before we knew it, our connecting flight in Khabarovsk, Russia, to Okhotsk was in jeopardy.

I had decided to wear my yellow pants and green deer shirt. I call it that because it has a deer embroidered over the left pocket. Less than one hour into this eight-hour flight, a man hit my arm while I was drinking a cup of coffee. The coffee spilled all over the left side of my light yellow pants. The stewardess brought club soda and a cloth napkin, and for more than an hour I worked on my pants.

This flight had one stop in Magadan before we reached Khabarovsk. We decided to deplane for this brief layover so Buzz and Noel could get a sneak-peek of what we were in for while we were in Russia. We rode in a cold, noisy truck from the plane to the airport building and back.

The airport was like all other Russian airports I had been to -- old looking buildings and wrecked planes and helicopters everywhere. We were thankful for the Alaskan plane we were traveling on.

One hour after take-off, the stewardess brought more club soda to get the coffee stain off my pants. It became a joke on the plane about everything served to me ending up in my lap. I didn't tell anyone how I had earlier spilled hot salt water on my lap soaking my knuckle.

As predicted, our plane was two and a half hours late landing in Khabarovsk. After the usual hassle through baggage search, we missed the last two planes. We caught the next plane, which left at noon the next day.

We'd made it through Russian baggage security when Buzz realized he had forgotten to get back his passport and visa from the hotel desk when they had taken it to register him. Obviously, he couldn't board the plane without it.

Dmitri, our interpreter, phoned the hotel and, for $20, they sent a man to bring Buzz's documents to him. Because we were so late, we had to load our own baggage on the plane. Finally, we were aboard.

We finally arrived in Okhotsk, but not a moment too soon. After several trips from the plane to the truck with our baggage, we were off to get on a boat that would take us on the next leg of the journey. So far, to get to this spot on a small island in the Middle of Nowhere, Siberia, we had taken a commercial jet and two puddle-jumper planes. Now we were about to board a hovercraft water-taxi. It had hundreds of people aboard. It would take us to an even smaller island where a tug boat with four jet boats roped to it awaited.

It had taken us two and a half days to get to the tug boat. Just to make sure we didn't get stranded, several 55-gallon drums filled with diesel fuel were on board.

At the half way point of this part of our journey, in the middle of the night (3 a.m.) while still on the boat, I learned why the crew took shifts staying awake. Those 55-gallon drums of diesel fuel on board were valuable. In Russia -- or anywhere in the world, but especially in Russia -- that diesel fuel was worth a lot of money.

While we were asleep in the bow of the boat in rope hammocks, in the pitch dark of the night, a gang of Russian pirates tried to board our boat by quietly paddling to it as we were anchored for the night. The night crewman was in the crow's nest, on guard with his AR15. The captain was asleep in his cabin, which also was where the steering wheel was located.

Anyway, the crewman had dozed off and had no clue that pirates had boarded the ship. They went into the captain's cabin, held a gun to his head, and made him walk outside. We were all asleep in the bow of the boat when awakened by the sound of rapid rifle fire.

Dmitri ran up top to see what was going on, telling us to stay where we were. After what seemed like an eternity, he came back down, saying all was safe. When we went topside, there was no sign of the pirates. All that was left was some blood on the deck. The cleanup crew had missed it when washing the deck before we were allowed topside.

It took two days by tug boat and, when the water got too shallow for the tug boat, another half day by jet boats to get to the pristine camp that wasn't set until we got there to set it. The guides did most of the work putting up camp while we put our bows together and fine-tuned our sights.

By the time we had finished with our bows and opened all our bags to organize our gear, the guides had a late lunch prepared for us. It consisted of a soup of boiled fish and whole potatoes. After lunch, we prepared our gear and loaded up for the first hunt.

My guide, Nickoli, and I rode by boat for about 45 minutes to a shallow part of the lake. Nickoli got out of the boat and pulled it, with me in it, for more than 1,000 yards until we came to the mouth of a small stream. It was about six inches deep and full of salmon.

Several sets of moose tracks went to and from the lake and bordering forest, but more impressive than that were the six sets of bear tracks, two which looked to be monsters, probably made by the same bear.

We got set up by 6:00 p.m. We sat on the ground behind some grass, 15 yards from the mouth of the stream.

By 10:00 o'clock it was too dark to see. We had seen the backs of several salmon as they tried to swim farther upstream but no other game. I had gotten some dirt in my right eye at 5:30, and by 10 o'clock I had a tremendous headache. When we got back to camp, I ate supper -- noodles and hash -- and went straight to bed.

My bed consisted of a homemade sleeping bag on top of a bed of crushed rocks. The tent was made from scrap bed spreads. I hoped it wouldn't rain. The mosquitoes in Russia must wear goose-down jumpsuits. The temperature got down close to freezing that night, but they still bombarded the three of us all night.

Next morning we had hash and rice for breakfast. The coffee was good, but I don't like coffee.

On the second evening's hunt, my guide built an elevated

stand about 10 feet off the ground. At 7:15 p.m., my guide decided the stand needed more cover. He got down, sawed some trees and brush and began putting them around me. At 7:30, while he was still working on hiding me, I heard a bear grunting. I looked behind me. A 150-pound cub about 30 yards off was running away. The cub had spotted Nickoli and spooked. We saw nothing else that evening.

Back in camp, Noel had an interesting story. He and his guide had been stalking a bear when a sow and cub came out within 60 yards of them. The sow saw them and stood on its hind legs to get a better look. Noel's guide began shooting his rifle, which just about caused Noel to jump out of his skin. After three or more shots, the sow was dead and Noel was dumbfounded. He told our interpreter, Dmitri, who scolded the guide.

Buzz hadn't seen any bears, but he did see a roe deer.

Several days went by without seeing game.

I think our camp cook was the Russian version of Bubba in the Forest Gump movie, except his thing was fish instead of shrimp. We'd had fish three times a day, every day, in some form or fashion, since we'd been here -- fish and potatoes, fish and rice, or fish and noodles. There was hot tea, coffee or vodka at every meal.

On the sixth day, Buzz killed a goose with his bow, so we had goose soup that night. At least, it was something different.

The next day I accidentally dry-fired my bow, which sent my peep sight into never-never land. I made a replacement peep from the cap of my pen. It looked great but didn't work well. I couldn't get it to stay in the string.

That same day, my guide and I tried hunting a new area. We stalked up a creek most of the day. The creek was 10 yards wide and at times deep enough to be to the tops of our hip waders. The creek meandered in several directions through thick brush. It gave the effect of a topless tunnel. It was eerie, especially when rounding a bend and not knowing what was ahead. Salmon were everywhere.

When it became too dark to see, we decided to head back. While wading back, just as we got to the deepest part of the creek, my guide startled a large salmon. It jumped out of the water and caught me in the crotch, knocking me on my back and into the water. After I pulled myself out of the creek and out of my wet clothes, my pants had an extra pleat, right in the butt area. That felt real good on the walk back to camp! That day, we didn't see any game.

That night we decided to try a morning hunt the next day. We talked about how we could get to where I wanted to hunt before daylight without disturbing the bears.

My guide said he had a plan. He decided we should hike to the location now, spend the night at the stand and be in position at daylight. Sounds good! As fate would have it, it rained most of the night. We didn't see anything during the night or on the morning hunt, so we decided to scout and stalk the rest of the day.

The next day I decided to move my stand about 1,000 yards to a spot I had found while stalking in the creek. It had a better vantage point and trails close by, with half-eaten salmon every 100 yards or so.

On that evening's hunt, I saw a 150-pound cub. According to my range finder, it was 123 yards away and back in the woods. I saw it about 40 minutes before pitch dark. I was hunting this stand alone; my guide was waiting for me back at the boat. I had to wade down the creek two or three miles to get back to the lake where the guide waited. It was an exhilarating feeling, to say the least, wading a thigh-deep creek in the dark, with spawning salmon constantly jumping and swimming into your legs. All the while you know there are bears in the creek, too, looking to eat these salmon.

Maybe "terrifying" better describes the feeling I had as I moved carefully through the dark.

Picture a winding stream with eight-to-10 foot banks, six to 10 feet of grass above the banks, seeing things only by the light of a mini-mag flashlight gripped between your teeth. You're alone in brown bear country. The adrenaline is flowing so heavily through your body you tingle and twitch uncontrollably.

You're aware of every sound, every splash, and every movement. You try to keep your wits and not panic. It definitely seems as though it is taking much longer to wade back than it did to wade in when it was light. In fact, when it seems like you've walked twice as far as you did when you came in, you begin to wonder if you started upstream instead of downstream. If you don't stop and think and check the direction of the water flow, you might turn around and start backtracking.

Panic will try to overwhelm you. Just before it does, you see an opening ahead. You're breathing heavily by now, and you begin wading much faster as hope begins to rise from the pit of your stomach. Another 100 yards and you're into the opening. Then another 1,000 yards along the shore of the lake and you finally reach the boat.

You made it! As you tell the guide about the cub bear you saw, you make sure you don't mention the strange feelings you had while walking back. You don't want to look like a wimp.

Back in camp, spirits were getting low. No one was seeing any game. There was talk of moving camp to another spot about three hours away, or just calling it quits and going home. That night the guides shot a cow moose. No more fish soup, we hoped. Buzz, Noel and I explained how we wanted the next meal to be moose tenderloin, battered and fried. The cook's feelings were hurt, but I will long remember that excellent meal.

By the end of the seventh day, Buzz had seen three roe deer; Noel had seen the sow cub, and I had seen the same cub twice. The guide had killed a cow moose for camp meat. That was the extent of the game seen while on our hunt. We decided to pick up camp and move to another place. It took all day, but we lived through it.

Two hours before dark on the eighth day, the new camp was ready. After another welcome meal of moose meat, we took off for the hunt. I didn't know it was going to be and didn't prepare for an all-nighter, but that's what it became. We got back to camp right at daylight and met Noel and his guide as we arrived. Buzz was already asleep in the tent.

No one had seen anything. We were all frustrated and decided to call it quits. On the ninth day of the hunt, the fourteenth day after we left Alabama, I knew things were looking up. I finally had my first semi-solid stool since arriving in Russia! By 1:00 p.m., after debating with Dmitri, our interpreter, for hours, we finally convinced him we wanted to leave, and to tell the guides we were ready to leave. He had tried to change our minds, but our minds were made up.

We had already packed 99 percent of our gear, so by 1:45 p.m. we were completely packed and ready to go. Two guides stayed behind to finish breaking up camp. We were loaded into three small boats with jet engines. We decided to take these boats to Tearz, the closest village, and then catch a hydro boat to Nickolias.

On the way to Tearz, one of the small boats quit working. After we spent 45 minutes trying to fix it, we loaded all the gear from the broken boat into the remaining two boats and continued to Tearz, leaving a guide with the broken boat. That left two guides Nickoli and Valari, to help load our gear.

We caught the hydroplane to Tearz. While waiting for the boat, we met a group of students who also were waiting for the boat. These students were fascinated to meet Americans and hear us talk on this trip. They crowded around Buzz, Noel, and me more than an hour, listening to us talk and practicing their English.

On our boat, I befriended a 13-year-old boy named Vladimir, and his 13-year-old girlfriend Nina. I taught them to say, "What is your name?" and "What time is it now?" in English. They had a blast; so did I. The two-and-a-half-hour boat ride flew by. In Nickolias, we went to the only hotel in town. It was not fit to sleep in.

We decided, instead, to stay at Valari's apartment. His wife cooked dinner and breakfast for us. Dinner was OK, and breakfast was a bacon omelet with fresh veggies. After eating fish for eight days, both meals were delicious.

Buzz and Noel said that while I was still the fly egg king, now I could add mosquito king to my resume. (Inside joke having to do with flies and mosquitoes landing in my bowl of fish soup every day.)

On Thursday morning, Dmitri, our interpreter, had to go to the airport to arrange our early flight out of Russia. They wouldn't allow us to do this over the phone due to terrorist security. It took Dmitri three hours to arrange everything. Valari's daughter, Lonari, sang and played the piano for us while we waited. She was pretty good. At 3:30 p.m. we caught a flight from Nickolias to Khabarovsk. Once in Khabarovsk, we checked on flights to Anchorage.

We had arrived on Thursday, and we found out that Alaskan Air flew from Khabarovsk to Anchorage only on Wednesday and Friday. We couldn't arrange this flight change at the airport in Khabarovsk, however, because Alaskan Air had employees working only on days they had flights, and then only during the hours of service.

I called my wife, Tami, only to learn it was 2 a.m. in Alabama. Our local time in Khabarovsk was 6 a.m. I asked her to arrange the change of all our tickets and told her I would call back in eight hours. We were lucky to get seats on Friday's flight.

Then began our taxi ordeal. All taxis at the airport were compact cars. The drivers wanted all our bags in one car and all of us in another car to go to the hotel. Arguments began, in Russian of course, between our interpreter and the cab drivers. After a lengthy, heated discussion, Dmitri began to look for an independent driver with a van.

In Russia it is common for individuals to pick up people, just as cab drivers do, and for a normal fee take them wherever they want to go. Dmitri found a person with a large new van who agreed to take us to the hotel. As we were loading our bags into his van, five or six taxi drivers came over and began to yell at the van driver and Dmitri. The van driver quickly unloaded the two bags we had managed to load into the van and drove off.

Dmitri began his discussion again with the cab drivers. After about 45 minutes, it was settled. Three-fourths of our bags and Dmitri would ride in one car, and the rest of our bags, Noel, Buzz , and I would ride in another.

Dmitri later explained how the taxi drivers were trying to scam us, but he wouldn't let them. When they refused to take bags and passengers in both cars, he found the independent driver. He explained how, as we were loading the bags into the van, the taxi drivers began to threaten the van driver and to puncture his tires. That was the reason the van driver unloaded the two bags and fled.

By the time we got checked into the hotel and loaded all our bags into the room, it was 9:15 p.m. We caught a ride by an independent driver for $4 to a restaurant that Dmitri had eaten at before. The meat was good, but the proportions were small. We got back to the hotel at 12:30 a.m.. I called Tami at 2 a.m. our time to get our flight arrangements.

Dmitri and I were sharing a room, and there was no air conditioning. After my telephone conversation with Tami, Dmitri talked to his wife four times, trying to set up business meetings in Moscow. I am not sure of the exact arrangements; they spoke only in Russian.

Finally, Dmitri began to pack and rearrange his bags. I tried to sleep, but the lights and television were on. At 4:15 a.m. Dmitri finally finished.

Too soon, the 7 a.m. alarm rang. I called Buzz and Noel to wake them, then took a shower. It was 10:30 by the time we got all bags loaded and to the airport,

Alaskan Air had no record of the flight changes Tami had made. Fortunately, plenty of seats were available, except for the Seattle-to-Atlanta leg, for which they put us on stand-by. They charged us $125 to change the tickets and $108 for each excess bag.

As we tried to go through customs, we found there was a $30 fee to use the airport bathroom facilities. We waited in line to pay this fee, only to find they wouldn't accept U.S. dollars. We waited in line at the foreign exchange center to get rubles, then back to the airport facilities service fees line, long before the hassle through customs.

Now Buzz and Noel realized why I had insisted on leaving the hotel three and a half hours before departure time, even though the airport was only 10 minutes away.

We made the flight with 10 minutes to spare and had a quick cup of coffee to keep us awake. During the seven-hour flight to Anchorage, which included a short stop, we had a snack and a meal. Both of these meals, even though they were your typical airplane meals, were better than any meal we had had since landing in Khabarovsk two weeks earlier. It felt good to be on our way home.

Customs in Anchorage took longer than usual, which caused us to miss our connection. We were re-routed on stand-by through Seattle, where we got bumped. I was re-routed to Salt Lake, again on stand-by. Buzz was re-routed to Cincinnati. In Salt Lake, I got bumped, put on another stand-by flight and finally confirmed a seat on a much later flight, which I finally caught to Atlanta.

My bags reached Atlanta 24 hours ahead of me. It took more than an hour to locate them.

Now I had to deal with my car issue and the towing. I had called my brother the day we arrived in Russia and asked him to pay my fine and do all the paperwork, and try to get my car out of the impound lot. I told him if he was successful, to park my car in a secret location I directed him to.

He and I had not spoken since the phone call from Russia two weeks earlier, so I wasn't sure the car was going to be there. I hoped my brother had been able to get it from the impound lot.

The car was right where I had asked him to park it. I made the three-hour drive home in the rain without another incident. Boy, was it good to be home! I love America. God Bless America!

More than just bears and moose...

Russian Boar, Largest in the World

• *Chris Fuller from Michigan with big wild boar taken in southern Russia.*

Russia is home to the largest species of wild boar in the world. This one weighed more than 500 pounds. Some Russian boars have weighed more than 800 pounds.

Big boars (and sows) are tough. They grow a thick 'shield' of gristle just under the skin on their shoulders and front ribs.This shield makes them difficult to kill if hit wrong. The best shot angle is quartering away, so the bullet comes in behind the shield to reach vitals.

Females and young travel in groups. Big boars go solitary, just like the American bison. They also can be cranky. We have been charged when we accidentally suprised them; we didn't do it on purpose.

Tusks get big, as you see here. When boars get to be five years old, they usually have impressive tusks.

Boars are found only in certain areas. They especially like to live in forests next to crop fields. They root the ground like all hogs.

Boars generally are hunted in the fall in conjunction with our grizzly bear hunts, because they like the same habitat.

Usually they are a targeted species. Some hunters want to go after boars only, so, naturally, they are taken to the best boar areas.

(Denny Geurink photo)

CHAPTER 15

RUSSIAN BEAR STALKS U.S. ASTRONAUT

THIS TRIP HAD ADVENTURE and suspense written all over it from the get-go. It was destined to be one of the most interesting journeys we would ever take to Russia just because of the participants' stature – Apollo astronaut Jim McDivitt and Earl O'Loughlin, a retired four-star general in the United States Air Force. You can't find two more high-profile military men than these two guys. O'Loughlin would be a particularly interesting person to take to Russia because of the nature of his Air Force work. In fact, when I found out exactly who he was, and what he did, I couldn't believe he even wanted to go to Russia.

It started more than a year earlier when O'Loughlin called me one evening to ask about going to Russia.

"This is Earl O'Loughlin from East Tawas, Michigan. My buddy Jim McDivitt and I are thinking about going to Russia on a brown bear hunt with you next spring," O'Loughlin began, "but before we get too far into this, I need to talk to you about a few things. If we go to Russia, will we ever get back out?"

"Everybody always worries about that," I said, chuckling. "Sure you'll get back out. We haven't lost anybody yet."

"It might be a little different for Jim and me," O'Loughlin replied. "I am a retired four-star Air Force general who worked for SAC (Strategic Air Command). I flew RB-47 spy plane missions over Russia in the '50s. Remember Gary Powers, the guy shot down by the Russians in 1960? That's what I did. He was shot down in a U-2 spy plane. The U-2 replaced the RB-47. They know who I am. I'm in their data base."

"That puts a different twist on things, doesn't it?," I stuttered. "Haven't had this type of security concern on previous trips, but there's a first time for everything."

"That's not all," O'Loughlin continued. "My buddy Jim is an Apollo astronaut who's been to the moon and back. Now he'd like to get to Russia ... and back. I've seen from the air the area where you hunt bears quite a few times. I'd like to see it from the ground. I've always wanted to go over there for a visit."

"Let me make a few calls to some of my contacts over there and see what they say," I responded nervously. "We have taken some high-profile people over there without a problem, but nothing like this. I don't want to be responsible for any problems we might run into. I'll get back to you in a few days." Possible scenarios, none good, ran through my mind.

"OK. I'll wait to hear from you," O'Loughlin replied.

A four-star general! RB-47 pilot! SAC! Spy! How's this ever going to fly! Small pun intended.

I called one of my outfitters, Michael Silin. He had some serious contacts with a number of high government officials. He himself was a big shot in the former Soviet Union and was once prominent in the Communist Party. If anyone could find out if this was going to work, he could. I asked him to check with all his contacts. This was some serious stuff. Each time the answer was the same.

"No problem, Denny," Silin assured me. "That was the Soviet Union. This is Russia. Both guys are welcome to come over. Don't worry about it"

That's like telling a sheep herder not to worry about the mountain lion hanging around his stock pen.

I called O'Loughlin and told him what Silin had told me. "We have the green light."

O'Loughlin and McDivitt sent deposits and we began to plan the hunt. Even though we had approval from the Russian government, I was still a little nervous. I made sure everything on their visa applications was filled out properly, especially for the general-in-the-Air-Force stuff. I didn't want any surprises.

I should have known better.

When we landed in Magadan at 10:30 a.m.. on May 14, 2005, I noticed something different from the other times I had flown there -- two men in suits and ties with brief cases stood near the baggage claim area.

Were they KGB? They certainly were. By now I could spot those guys a mile away.

Sure enough, as soon as we cleared passport control, the two men walked up to us. I began imagining the worst. Had I led O'Loughlin and McDivitt into some sort of trap? I imagined a plot for a future James Bond movie unfolding right before my eyes, and it was a sure bet I wasn't going to be cast in the part of 007.

"Which one of you is the astronaut, McDivitt?," one of the suits asked in an interrogative tone.

"That would be me," McDivitt said coolly. I'm glad he was cool, because I wasn't.

"Which one of you is General O'Loughlin?," the KGB official continued.

Here it comes! I could see the headlines dancing through my head: "Former CIA spy and four-star general arrested in Russia." I was feeling ill.

"That would be me," O'Loughlin answered, also cool as a cucumber.

Then -- complete shock, at least to me -- the two suit-and-tie men stuck out their hands and said, "Welcome to Russia." Not only did they welcome McDivitt and O'Loughlin to Russia, they wanted their pictures taken with them, and they wanted our guys' autographs, too. Great welcome!

Everywhere we went, everyone knew "the General and the Astronaut" were coming, and everyone wanted pictures and autographs.

• *Apollo astronaut, Jim McDivitt (left), and RB-47 spy plane pilot, Earl O'Loughlin (right), pose with photo of fellow Cold War era personality Communist Party Boss Leonid Brezhnev, on a building in Magadan. (Denny Geurink photo)*

• *Apollo astronaut Jim McDivitt takes a rubber raft into the Sea of Okhotsk in search of bears feeding along the shoreline. (Michael Silin photo)*

Once we arrived in camp, things didn't get any duller. My Russian outfitter, Michael Silin, promptly informed me there were so many bears around camp the guides were afraid to go to sleep in their tents at night without rifles at their sides. (Full story in Chapter 16.) Their two male Laikas were kept busy throughout the night barking at bears and chasing them from camp.

As soon as we got off the helicopter that carried us to the camp, I saw why the guides were sleeping with their rifles. The cook tent was erected smack in the middle of a well-used bear trail. That trail led off a small rise right to the door of the tent. "Why," I wondered half-aloud," did the guides set the cook tent in such a precarious spot?"

After a quick look around the camp, the answer was obvious. It would have been impossible to set up camp without a bear trail leading into one tent or another. The entire area was covered with bear trails. It was better to have one of the trails leading into the cook tent than leading to the door of my sleeping quarters. Still, it didn't make me feel much better.

The reason the camp site was covered with bear trails was because it was set up near the mouth of a cold, clear mountain stream where it spilled into the Sea of Okhotsk. The stream hosted heavy salmon runs from mid-summer through early fall, attracting bears from miles around. Not a very good place to pitch a tent, but the perfect spot for a bear camp.

Also with us on this hunt were Anthony Nakroshis from Homer Glen, Illinois, and Richard Frye from Middleville, Michigan.

Then 75 years old and certainly not as spry as he was during his Apollo days, McDivitt still got around well and still loved the thrill of high adventure. Since he was retired from astronaut duties, he got his thrills now with both feet on the ground, from wilderness hunting and fishing adventures.

O'Loughlin, 74, was cut from the same piece of leather.

"I wanted to see this place from the ground someday," O'Loughlin said, chuckling, as we stored our gear in the tents. "It's a thrill just to be here. I can't believe I'm really here. Some of these guys probably chased me around in MiGs in the 1950s." Those words were unknowingly prophetic.

I had hunted with four clients in a nearby area for two weeks before McDivitt and O'Loughlin arrived. Four other hunters had been in the camp McDivitt and O'Loughlin were in now.

Those hunters related some exciting tales. Besides having bears in camp nearly every night, they had watched a huge, white-winged sea eagle pick up one of the camp dogs and fly off with it. (Full story in Chapter 16.) The guides told us these gigantic eagles regularly preyed on young snow sheep, plucking them off cliffs near the camp. We were, indeed, in a wild, rugged area.

The four hunters in camp prior to McDivitt and O'Loughlin's arrival were in good shape; they covered a lot of ground during their stay. They also had hit the spring migration of bears to the sea right on the nose. The four of them counted 270 bears during their two-week stay. That's more bears than we had ever seen on one of our spring hunts in the years we had been coming to Russia. We surely weren't putting a dent in the bear population there.

While we normally used snowmobiles to help us get around in the spring, there wasn't any snow this year. This was the first time in our years of hunting in Russia we didn't have enough snow to use snowmobiles. Winter had arrived extremely early the previous fall; now it had left extremely early this spring.

I knew we would be in trouble when I arrived in Anchorage, April 27. It was 70 degrees, and there wasn't a flake of snow on the ground. This left McDivitt and his hunting buddy, O'Loughlin, on foot much of the time. They also spent some time in a small rubber raft they nicknamed the zodiac.

One evening just before dark, the camp radio crackled to life. McDivitt's guide, Alexiy Skorobrekha, was on the other end. He said he and McDivitt were sitting along a well-used bear trail near the coast about a half-mile from camp.

"We have a bear stalking us," Skorobrekha whispered. "It's circling through the bush, trying to get behind us. I don't know how big it is, but it's getting closer. Wait! Wait! It's here! It's right behind us!"

The camp radio suddenly fell silent. We waited, expecting to hear shots from the hillside, but all was quiet. Then the radio crackled back to life.

"We chased the bear away," Skorobrekha chuckled. "We threw rocks at it. It was too small to shoot. Maybe only a seven-to-eight-footer. Wait! It's coming back!"

Again, the radio fell silent. Back in camp we were thinking 'only a seven-to-eight-footer? That's a pretty big bear to have sneaking up on you.'

Again, we waited. Nothing. Several minutes later the camp radio buzzed."It's gone," the guide whispered.

That was the last we heard about the bear stalk until McDivitt got back to camp several hours later.

"The bear got pretty close to us the first time before Alexiy got up and threw rocks at it," McDivitt explained. "I was waiting for him to tell me to shoot. I thought it was a good bear but Alexiy said 'Small bear. Small bear,' so I didn't shoot.

"Then, when it came back the second time, he pointed at the camera I had around my neck, gesturing for me to take pictures of the bear. In the excitement, I had forgotten about the camera.

"It was starting to get dark, so my flash was going off every time I took a picture. That didn't seem to faze the bear. It just kept coming closer and closer. Got pretty exciting there for a minute. I guess I must have looked like a good meal to it.

"It came really close before Alexiy stood up again and started throwing rocks. I had my rifle ready to shoot if the rocks didn't work. I was sure we were going to have to shoot it. The bear finally ran off for good, but I kept looking over my shoulder the rest of the night."

McDivitt wasn't the only hunter who had a bear after him. Two bruins stalked Tony Nakroshis while he and his guide were skinning another bear. Nakroshis watched the guide's back, rifle ready, as the bruins jockeyed for position. Brown bears are cannibalistic and will kill and eat young bear cubs, or devour a bear carcass.

• *Apollo Astronaut Jim McDivitt snapped this photo of a bear that stalked him along the Sea of Okhotsk. (Jim McDivitt photo)*

O'Loughlin learned this first-hand when a trio of bears ate the bear he shot before he could recover it.

The next day we watched a bear bed down in bushes on a mountainside just above camp. Richard Frye's guide motioned for Frye to grab his rifle and follow him. We watched from camp as Frye and his guide sneaked up the mountain, inching closer and closer to where the bear was sleeping. Suddenly the bear stood up and sniffed the air, then looked directly at Frye.

All of us in camp felt the hair on the backs of our necks stand erect as Frye raised his rifle. This was the moment a bear hunter lives for! Frye made a good shot and put the bear down. He had now fulfilled a lifelong dream, taking a magnificent brown bear with long, thick hair.

That evening the excitement in camp became even more lively when O'Loughlin began telling "war stories". We had finished having dinner with the guides, including the mandatory vodka toasts. O'Loughlin started talking about his RB-47 spy plane days. Our interpreter, Silin, translated to the guides everything O'Loughlin said.

"I flew over this area in my RB-47 a number of times in the '50s," O'Loughlin began. "We got chased by MiGs a few times. One of the RB-47s was shot down not too far from here in 1960, but the MiGs were heavier and slower than our planes. We usually could outmaneuver them."

I remember thinking: "Interesting stuff, Earl, but I don't know if I would be telling these guys such stories. All of them are former military ... and proud of it."

O'Loughlin continued and Silin kept interpreting. "We flew quite a few missions over North Korea and China, too," O'Loughlin recalled. "The Russians were sensitive about all this and shot down a South Korean passenger plane in 1983, thinking it was a spy plane."

One of the guides began saying something in Russian. Silin listened intently. "Really!," he exclaimed.

The guide continued. "Really!," Silin exclaimed again.

"What's he saying?," O'Loughlin asked.

"This guy says he was a MiG fighter pilot and chased you a few times when you flew over here."

I don't know whether or not the guy chased O'Loughlin, but he was a MiG pilot. It created one of the most interesting moments I had in a Russian hunting camp.

Everyone started laughing, including the MiG pilot.

"Tell him to come over here," O'Loughlin said to Silin, chuckling. The guide rose from his seat, walked over and stood next to O'Loughlin. They raised their shot glasses and toasted each other. Several more toasts to Russian and American military men ensued.

Then came a moment that will forever be etched in my mind! As O'Loughlin raised his glass with his arm still around the MiG pilot, he looked at me and winked. "Denny, the Cold War is over!"

How historic is that!

CHAPTER 16

EXCITEMENT IN CAMP

SIBERIA IS A WILD and wooly place. Besides being primitive and remote, it's one of the most geologically-active places in the world. The Kamchatka Peninsula, for example, is covered with volcanoes, geysers, and hot springs. There are 160 volcanoes on the peninsula, 29 of which are active. One of the actives is visible from the hotel we stayed in when in Petropavlovsk. You could see smoke wisping daily.

Of course, where you have active volcanoes and geysers, you have earthquakes. On more than one occasion while staying at the Hotel Petropavlovsk after a trip, an earthquake rattled pictures on the wall and shook the glass in windows. Another time, a volcano had erupted near one of our camps and covered it with ash, just two weeks before we were scheduled to arrive.

Over the past decades, a number of years I spent a month in the spring and two or three months in the fall near the Arctic Circle under the stars, in a tent or trapper's cabin. When you spend that much time in the Siberian wilderness, in addition to the geological phenomena, you are bound to experience many exciting, or hair-raising, moments. From almost being struck by lightning while riding a Mongolian pony through the mountains of Tyva, to chasing a bear out of camp with a frying pan, I've seen or been part of many exciting events.

These remote wilderness camps have been visited by bears, wolves, wolverines, and an assortment of other creatures. I could write a book on just these wild encounters, but for now here's a look at some of the most memorable ones.

BEAR IN THE CREEK

When you hunt, fish and camp in bear country, you will have a close encounter with a bear at some point. It's only a matter of time. I don't mind a close encounter when I have a rifle in my hand; it's the close encounters when I am unarmed that scare me.

Early in my expeditions to Russia, I carried a high-powered rifle because I also was hunting. After a few years, I had harvested nearly all the game animals I wanted to pursue so I left my rifle home. It was considerably easier to travel that way.

There were a number of times, however, when I wish I had taken my rifle. The time, for instance, our cook came running back to the cabin frantically screaming "Bear! Bear!" with a big bruin running after her.

We were on a spring brown bear hunt in Kamchatka in early May near Petropavlovsk. We had just finished lunch, and I had gone back to my cabin to read. Natasha had gone to a small creek about 75 yards from the cabin to wash the dishes, as she usually did at this time of day. The hunters were still out in the woods with their guides, so it was just me, Natasha, and our interpreter in camp. Our interpreter had gone back to his cabin to take a nap.

As Natasha ran up the hill toward the cook shack, I stepped outside my cabin to see what the commotion was all about. Terror was spread all over her face. A terrifyingly large brown bear, in the 10-foot class, was hot on her heels. While it's unusual to have bears come into camp during the middle of the day, it occasionally happens, especially in the spring right after they come out of hibernation. At this time of year some bears are driven more by hunger than by fear of man.

I had played out this scenario in my mind many times. It always made me a bit jittery to be in a camp radiating all sorts of food odors, from fried bacon to smoked fish, surrounded by starving bruins and without a rifle. So I hatched a plan to deal with just such a situation, should it ever arise.

Somewhere way back when, I had read that the best way to scare a bear away from camp was to make noise, a lot of noise. The story suggested clanging frying pans together. I always told myself that's exactly what I would do if ever I was without a rifle and confronted by a bear. Naturally, I hoped I would never have to find out whether or not this worked. Well, now it was show time.

I ran into the cook shack right behind Natasha, hoping I could quickly lay my hands on a couple of frying pans.

Bingo ... two big cast iron pans hung on nails near the wood stove. I snatched them up and began banging them together as loud as I could. I walked toward the door, hammering the pans to make sure the bear could hear the noise. To my amazement and relief, the big brown stopped halfway up the hill, whirled, and galloped back into the woods. It worked! By gadfry, it worked!

After making sure Natasha was all right, I went back to my cabin and changed my shorts.

That evening, when we told the other hunters and the guides about the bear-and-frying pan incident, the head guide handed me a shotgun he had brought to camp to shoot grouse and hares for camp meat. "Next time you shoot bear instead of hitting it with frying pan," he laughed.

BEAR IN CAMP

Unlike the camp in the story above, a lot of the bear camps we've stayed in over the years were guarded by dogs. The guides brought along the dogs, usually a breed known as a Laika, for companionship and protection. Laikas are medium-sized dogs that look much like a husky, with tails that curl over their backs. They are a fearless breed, originating from aboriginal dogs found in Siberia many centuries ago. The guides often use them to hunt and track wounded bears. When confronted by a bear they don't back down. I always tried to befriend the camp dog.

Since most of the time I didn't have a hunting rifle in camp, my modus operandi would be to squirrel away a few scraps of meat from the dinner table, much to the consternation of the cook, then use the scraps as treats for the camp dog, hoping to keep it near my tent at night when dangerous animals prowled.

Every time I woke up during the night, I tossed a scrap piece of meat outside the tent door. It didn't take the dogs long to figure out the routine. They usually were sleeping right next to the tent by the second day in camp. That was perfect timing one spring in Magadan.

We were bivouacked in a tent camp in early May along the Sea of Okhotsk. Along with me on this trip were Apollo 9 astronaut Jim McDivitt and Earl O'Loughlin, a retired four-star Air Force general. (You read their story in Chapter 14.)

I knew I had to work the dog -- actually, there were two dogs in this camp -- into my corner as quickly as possible, because I noticed when we arrived at camp our tents were pitched along a salmon stream crisscrossed with bear trails. I also noticed that the guides were sleeping with loaded rifles next to them. Our outfitter/interpreter, Michael Silin, and I bunked with them in one large tent. Our clients were in a separate tent. We told them to sleep with their rifles ready.

The guides were amused by the dogs following me around camp, sniffing at my coat pocket, where I hid the meat scraps. Those dogs had great noses. They always knew when there was a treat in my pocket, and I made sure there was a treat for them in the tent when we hit the sack every night.

One night as we lay sound asleep, I was awakened around 3 a.m. by a guttural growl just outside the tent door. At first I thought it was a bear, and my heart stopped beating for a second. Then I realized it was one of the dogs. The growling became deeper and louder by the second. Then the other dog chimed in. Soon, everyone in the tent was wide awake and sitting straight up in bed. The guides began whispering among themselves, and then one blurted, "Bear!"

"Denny, there's a bear in camp," Silin whispered. "The dogs are growling at a bear."

Flashlights suddenly began blinking on throughout the tent, accompanied by the distinct sound of rifle bolts slamming cartridges home.

The dogs dashed toward the cook tent, barking and growling. At the same moment, the head guide whipped open the tent door and pointed a powerful flashlight beam toward the cook tent. There stood a huge brown bear, sniffing at our food supply. It didn't get to sniff longer; the dogs were on it almost instantly.

The big brown whirled and ran out of camp as fast as it could, with the dogs right on its tail. We sat there and listened to the barking and growling for several minutes until it faded off into the inky darkness. Then everything went silent. The dogs were out of hearing range, a long way from camp.

"The guides said the dogs may chase the bear all night," Silin whispered. "We might as well go back to sleep."

I tried to get back to sleep, but there wasn't any sleep left in me. I was too pumped full of adrenaline. I heard the dogs wander back into camp about three hours later, huffing and panting.

They eagerly gobbled up the little treats waiting for them outside the tent door.

BABY SNATCHERS

One year on a spring hunt in Kamchatka, the head guide took a mother Laika and several of her five-week-old puppies to camp with him. The puppies were a hit with the hunters. As with all puppies, these were playful and mischievous, providing great entertainment when we weren't in the field.

One day, while the hunters were out chasing bears, a red fox came into camp. That, in itself, was not unusual because foxes had checked out our camps many times. Usually they were just curious to see what was going on in their back yard. They were also intrigued by the scent of camp food. A visiting fox generally came in, did a quick inspection, and left.

This one, however, was different. It was bolder than most and didn't seem afraid of us, 'us' being the interpreter, camp cook, and me. We watched it meander in and out of the woods several times before walking off. After it disappeared, we went back to the tent to drink coffee and chat, forgetting about the fox.

An hour later, we heard one of the puppies making a fuss. We looked out of the cook tent and saw the fox trotting into the woods with a puppy in its mouth. She apparently intended to adopt the puppy; she carried it in her mouth the same way a dog or cat carries its young from one hiding spot to another.

We quickly left the tent and followed the fox into the woods; her actions had aroused our curiosity. She gently dropped the squirming puppy near a pile of brush ... right next to one of the other puppies. She already had carried off that puppy without us even knowing it. We quickly ran off the fox and retrieved the two bewildered puppies.

We assumed this was an adoption procedure by the fox, not an attempt to kill and eat them, because she had not harmed them. She easily could have killed them, especially the first one, which we hadn't seen her steal, but the fox had carefully picked up the puppies by the scruff of the neck and carted them off into the woods.

Of course, this would not have happened had the mother dog been in camp, but she had followed her master into the woods that day, leaving us in charge of her puppies. We nearly blew our babysitting assignment.

* * * *

A few years later, another incident with puppies in camp didn't go as well.

We were hunting bears along the Sea of Okhotsk. One of the guides had a trapper's cabin on a big hill overlooking the sea. Like the other guide, he brought a couple of small puppies to the cabin with him. Two of my clients stayed in this cabin for several days with the guide and a cook. We used the cabin as a spike camp. I was in the main camp, another small cabin a few miles away, with the interpreter and a cook.

The area we were hunting along the Sea of Okhotsk is home to a large species of eagle the locals call a sea eagle. It's scientifically known as the Steller's Sea Eagle. This predatory bird is considerably larger than the North American bald eagle. It is the heaviest eagle in the world, weighing 15 to 20 pounds, with a wing span of around eight feet. By comparison, the average weight of a bald eagle is a bit over 10 pounds.

We watched several eagles patrolling the coastline, amazed by their size and agility.

One day, while guides and hunters were chasing bears, the puppies strayed too far from the cabin. The cook, aroused by the squealing of one of the young dogs, ran outside just in time to see a giant sea eagle swoop down, snatch one of the puppies and fly off with it in its talons. Unlike the fox, this was not an adoption procedure.

The cook could only curse as the eagle winged toward the mountains. It was a sad evening in camp.

• *This is a typical Siberian hunting camp. (Denny Geurink photo)*

• *The guides often would bring a dog to ward off bears prowling around camp at night. The dogs are a fearless Russian breed known as Laikas.(Ken Horm photo)*

FIRE IN MY TENT

As mentioned earlier, I have spent a lot of time in wilderness tent camps the past two-plus decades. Most tents were heated with wood stoves of various sizes and metal thickness. Many were made by the guides using scrap metal and a welding torch to fashion these primitive heat sources. There also were commercially-made stoves for tents and cabins. While these stoves were warm and efficient, they would probably not be OSHA-approved. I've seen stoves made of such thin metal they eventually burned through the sides and had to be discarded after just a few years. They are not like the heavy, thick cast iron wood stoves used in the States.

These primitive stoves have caused many a tent and cabin fire in the Russian wilderness, some of them in our camps. Thankfully, the tents we lost burned down while the hunters were in the woods, not at night with hunters inside. We did, however, almost have one burn down with someone inside ... me.

We were hunting the Milkovo region in north-central Kamchatka. I was in a tent with one other hunter. Just before we went to sleep, I filled the stove with wood and 'put the can on the door'. The wood stoves have a soup can-sized hole cut in the door, which is framed with a circular piece of metal that sticks out the front about six inches. This circular frame has holes cut in it. A soup can fits perfectly over the extension and is used to restrict air flow once the fire is going. We always tell guys in camp to make sure they 'put the can on' at night before they go to sleep so the fire won't burn too hot.

These fires can burn too hot because the wood we use in our camps is birch, the only wood available this far north. Birch burns hot and fast. You need to restrict the air flow to the fire carefully once it gets going. I've seen stove pipes get so hot they turned cherry red. Not a good thing ... especially in a tent.

Because the wood is often wet with snow or rain, we generally bring some inside and set it near the stove to dry off. When we need to put more wood on the fire, we have dry stuff available. We had done that this particular night.

Sometime in the middle of the night, one of these pieces of wood rolled off the pile and landed against the stove. I don't know how long the piece of birch lay against the hot stove, but it's a good thing my cot was near the stove. The smell of smoke awakened me. I quickly sat up to see what was happening. Just as I sat up, the log burst into flames. My cot and the tent would catch on fire in a matter of seconds.

I usually have a bottle of water near my bed so if I wake up thirsty during the night, it's easy to get a drink. On this particular night, I had filled an empty two-liter bottle with water pumped through my water filter from a nearby creek. I quickly grabbed the bottle and poured the contents over the burning log. Thank goodness I had it. It was just enough to put out the blazing log.

All the commotion woke the other hunter. "What's going on?," he gasped, choking on the smoky air.

"I just saved your life and mine," I gasped. That episode shook me. I guarantee you one thing -- I always make sure now there are no pieces of wood close to a stove before I go to sleep.

THE RUSSIAN WAY OF DEALING WITH POACHERS

Many times the guides who take our clients into the field are local game wardens in charge of looking after the animals in their region. They conduct population surveys, monitor the health and welfare of animals under their charge and keep an eye out for poachers. Because they also are working as local guides, who depend upon high game populations to attract hunters to their area, they take poaching seriously. Very seriously!

Here in the U.S., when someone gets caught poaching, he pays a fine and loses his hunting privileges for a couple of

years. In certain areas of Siberia that are a long way
from cities and courtrooms where fines can be paid,
poachers can lose more than hunting privileges.

I was out one evening with one of the guides,
checking his food plots out in the middle of nowhere,
when we heard a shot in the forest. I thought maybe
someone other than our crew was in the woods hunting.

You should have seen the look on my guide's face
when he heard the shot. He was hot! This was his
territory. No one else belonged here.

He instantly motioned for me to get back in the jeep.
As soon as my butt hit the seat, we tore down a
muddy trail toward the sound of the shot. I had a
white-knuckle grip on the dashboard as we careened
through the forest. I was afraid we were going to get
stuck in a mud hole or crash into a tree.

Suddenly, there on the trail in front of us,
was another jeep. About the time we came flying up
to the vehicle, we saw a guy coming out of the woods
toward us with a rifle in his hands. I was a bit on
edge right then, imagining all the bad ways this could
end. Were we about to go toe to toe with a guy with a
loaded gun? I was ready to bail out and run for cover.

Motioning for me to stay in the jeep, my guide
jumped out, grabbed his rifle, and pulled out his game
warden badge, practically all in one motion.

He walked up to the man, yelling at him as he
walked. The man, much to my relief, silently handed
his rifle to the guide. After more of the guide's yelling
and gesturing, the guy pulled his keys from a pocket and
handed them to the guide.

He then began walking down the muddy logging
trail into the darkness, while my guide continued to yell at
him. I couldn't understand what he was saying, but I
got the drift. I actually felt a bit sorry for the man at that
point. We were a long way from the village, it was

getting dark, and there were a lot of bears in the woods. Back at camp, I asked my interpreter to talk to my guide and find out exactly what had just happened. I was still a bit rattled.

He told me the guy we had confronted in the forest wasn't just another hunter, he was a poacher. He was not licensed to be hunting and didn't have permission to hunt this area; it was leased to the guide.

"Your guide told the poacher he was confiscating his rifle and his jeep and would give them back to him when he got back to town," my interpreter said. "He should make it back here in a day or two."

"He also told the poacher that if he ever catches him in the woods again, his family will never see him again."

"Are you serious?," I stammered.

"Yes, that's how it works out here," my interpreter replied. "Most poachers around here reform quickly or they disappear. It's just the way it is. This is Russia."

Checking Out Our Camp

• *Bears often checked out our camps, or came directly into them, particularly in the spring. They had just come out of hibernation, were hungry, and looked for food everywhere. Cook tents emitted attractive aromas. One bear came into camp, walked directly to the dog food dish about 10 yards from the cabin door, and gobbled everything in the bowl. It ignored the dog, which was dancing in half-circles behind the bear, barking furiously. Done eating, the bear walked out of camp. (Denny Geurink photo)*

CHAPTER 17

BIG STAGS ON THE BLACK SEA

ONE OF THE THINGS I was always proud of during my outfitting days in Russia was that I made my trips available to women as well as men. This was no small accomplishment in a country that for a long time regarded women as second-class citizens. Some of the guides on those early expeditions were surprised I was taking women on a hunting trip. Others were more than surprised; they were annoyed and upset that I had taken ladies into their male-dominated world.

My wife, Connie, ran into her share of resentment on those early trips and, later on, when I had her escort a few trips for me, the resentment ratcheted up a few notches. Some of the guides didn't want to have a woman telling them what to do in camp. They tried ignoring her, but she wouldn't be ignored. Besides hunting and escorting trips to Russia, Connie had written a few stories about her journeys for my weekly newspaper columns. Here's one she wrote shortly after returning from her first trip to Crimea to hunt red stags.

***

"Oh, my gosh! That thing is huge. It looks like a tree," exclaimed the Continental airline representative behind the service counter, referring to the set of antlers perched atop our luggage cart.

"Where did you get that monster," she continued, directing the question to my husband Denny.

"In Crimea," Denny replied, and proudly pointed to me. "It's my wife's, not mine."

She stared at me open-mouthed for a few seconds then exclaimed, "Way to go! I'm proud of you!"

I'd heard comments like that before. A lot of people still find it hard to believe some women like to hunt, and a lot of people don't think I look 'tough' enough to be a hunter. The reality is that you don't have to look tough, and you don't have to be a man to love hunting.

Denny and I were on our way back to Allendale, Michigan, after a successful red stag hunt on the coast of the Black Sea in the Ukraine. This trip was, to date, the highlight of my hunting career.

We had left Allendale ten days earlier, flown to Kiev, Ukraine, boarded an overnight train and traveled to Crimea. After a two-hour van ride, we arrived at the hunting camp. We were escorted to a comfortable cottage surrounded by olive trees and enclosed within a weathered picket fence. The sound of the Black Sea 500 yards away, and the roar of rutting stags, invaded the otherwise quiet atmosphere. The sun was shining, the air crisp. We were filled with excitement and anticipation.

This was Denny's ninth trip to the camp; it was my first. With us on this trip were Sarah and Terry Snowday from Traverse City, Michigan; Gary "Hoss" Bentley from Stockbridge, Michigan; Stuart Williams from Seattle, Washington, and Dmitri and Irena Sikorski, our Russian outfitters.

This trip was unique in that we had Sarah Fisher Snowday, the granddaughter of the Fisher Body family who started General Motors (GM), and Gary Bently, a high-low driver at GM, in the same camp. Talk about opposite ends of the economic spectrum, but the big gap in socioeconomic status didn't keep Sarah and Gary from becoming good friends on this trip.

Making the trip even more interesting was the fact we had Stuart Williams along. Stuart is a staff writer for the *Hunting Report*, a popular magazine in the States. He wanted to do a story on our stag hunts.

Denny intended to film the women hunting for his *"Outdoor Adventures"* TV show. I wanted to take a big stag to impress the Russian guides, who are not used to seeing women hunt.

The first afternoon we piled into the back of a big four-wheel-drive truck and were driven into the bush. The terrain resembles the African veldt, with small scrubby trees and bushes and large grassy areas. We could hear roaring stags all around.

Unlike the high-pitched bugle of an American elk, the European elk, or stag, sounds more like it is complaining of a bellyache. The roar begins with a long, loud um-um-umph, immediately followed by several short umph, umph, umph bellows. It makes the hair stand up on the back of your neck.

Stags roared all around us. Using our field glasses we spotted a number of stags with harems at different locations in the distance. We also saw fallow deer, mouflon sheep, quail, ringneck pheasants, ducks, red fox, and many species of hawks and other birds. On one occasion, we watched an albino fallow deer buck and doe until they walked out of sight.

That first afternoon "Hoss" shot a very nice stag after a short stalk in tall grass.

The second morning, Terry Snowday shot a nice stag and, later in the afternoon, Stuart Williams filled his tag. We celebrated with stag tenderloin for dinner, along with a bottle of excellent Ukrainian red wine.

The guides skin and butcher the animals, clean the antlers for transport, and distribute meat to their townspeople; they need it far more than we do. We made sure, though, to eat our share during our stay in camp.

The next morning was Sarah's hunt, her first hunt ever. She had not even hunted rabbits. She had a new rifle, a custom hunting knife, and was to be filmed for a TV show. Sarah was under considerable self-imposed pressure; she said she 'had a monkey on her back'.

Dmitri was Sarah's guide; Denny followed with the camera. They spotted a stag in the distance and walked, then crawled, through tall grass to within 45 yards.

Sarah set up her shooting stick and rifle, then waited for the stag to move into position for a   shot. More than anything, she did not want to wound the animal. She waited ... and waited. The stag chased first one cow, then another, performing the age-old mating rites, roaring loudly with triumph, then continuing the performance, but not offering a shot.

Finally, the pressure was too much. Sarah took a quick shot but missed. The startled animals bounded away.

The scene was repeated two more times. Husband Terry tagged along on one stalk. Later, Sarah asked Irena and me to go along for moral support. The men didn't quite understand how she felt, and what inexperience can do to your self-confidence. We were happy to oblige. I couldn't wait to see one of these magnificent animals up close. (I was the outfitter's wife, so I had to wait until all our clients had filled their tags before I was allowed to hunt.) Irena wasn't going to hunt on this trip, just tag along to see what the excitement was about.

Denny and Dmitri were horrified. They looked at each other as if to say, 'This will never work, no way can we get close enough for a shot with a train of five people and a TV camera.' I must confess I too had my doubts, but I was not going to stay behind.

Off we went with Dmitri in the lead, then Sarah, me, Irena, and Denny with the camera bringing up the rear. Dmitri soon spotted the huge rack of a stag above the tall grass in the distance. We headed in that direction.

We walked for what seemed hours, crossing a large open area dotted with small bushes, crawling quickly, one at a time, from bush to bush.

In mid-sneak, two cows started across the opening from the opposite direction, spotted us, and stopped to stare.

We were strung out across the clearing, three or four feet apart in varying degrees of a crawl, frozen in place. My right leg began to tingle, frozen in a half crouch.

If the cows spooked, they would alert any other animals in the area. They walked closer, stopped, and stared. They walked still closer and stared.

The lead cow sniffed the air, but we were downwind. She moved off slowly, looking back every other step. The smaller cow followed. Finally, the cows walked into a grassy swale out of sight. That was interesting. We began to move again.

We belly-crawled to the top of a small, sandy rise on the other side of the clearing. When the big stag lowered its head to graze, we quickly scooted over the top and down the other side. Dmitri and Sarah scooted into position behind a small tree surrounded by scrub brush. I followed.

Sarah set up her shooting stick, slid the gun into position, and sat there on one knee, panting, trying to calm her pounding heart and slow her breathing.

"OK, Sarah, remember to concentrate on your rifle position. Hold the stock tight against your shoulder. Pick your target, aim, then think about how you're holding the rifle, and concentrate hard on that," I said.

She did just that. With a 'whack' the shot caught the stag right behind the shoulder; it jumped, ran about 40 yards and dropped.

Sarah leapt to her feet. She had done it! The biggest stag taken during the week! It sported a mammoth 8x9 rack. The 'monkey' was off her back.

Back at camp, after a delicious dinner of freshly-caught fish, recounts of the day's hunts and much camaraderie and laughter, some of us went for a short walk on the beach and collected shells. Not for long, though; it had been an exhausting day.

On the final day in camp, I got my chance to hunt. The day dawned thick with fog. My heart sank.

I had come a long way and waited patiently for all our clients to fill their tags. This was my only chance at one of those huge bulls, but they had to be visible.

We had a leisurely breakfast and waited for the fog to lift. Finally, around 11 a.m., we climbed aboard the truck and headed out in search of my trophy. It had to be a big one because we needed a good representative of the stags to present at seminars and sports shows in the U.S. In addition, I was being filmed for television. Oh, boy! Sarah had passed the 'monkey' to my back!

We arrived at an area where the guides had spotted good stags the day before. Today, Dmitri was taking Stuart, who had decided to tag a second animal, out for his hunt. My guide was a pleasant gentleman named Vitali. He had a warm smile that revealed several gold-capped teeth. I asked Sarah if she would like to come along. She seemed to attract the biggest animals wherever she went, and I wanted every advantage.

Off we went through the thinning fog. I was not very optimistic but Vitali seemed confident. We hadn't gone far when he spotted a nice set of antlers turning in the tall reeds. We hunched over and crept closer. It became obvious the stag was bedded down. Slowly we inched closer until we were almost 15 yards from the animal. Vitali signaled I should get ready to shoot.

Suddenly, the stag turned its head, caught our scent, jumped to its feet, and ran straight away from us. By the time I got it in my sights and fired, it had disappeared into the tall reeds. Oh, well, I didn't really want to shoot it in the rear anyway.

We regrouped and continued on, with the fog lifting more and more. Vitali suddenly stopped, brought up his binoculars, and scanned the horizon. Then he handed them to me and pointed. I scanned in the direction he pointed. On the horizon, about a mile away, was the 'Hartford' stag, with a TREE on its head. My pulse quickened. This was it, but first we had walking to do.

We headed in the direction of the stag, zigzagging to stay behind various bits of cover to get within range. Vitali crept on hands and knees to the edge of a grassy swale and signaled for me to follow. There was the stag, only 50 yards away, and it had only one cow with it. It was even bigger than I expected.

I got into position and was ready to fire when the stag moved. It had its rear pointing toward me, then slowly began to move farther away into taller grass. No shot.

Vitali signaled Denny and Sarah to stay behind and motioned me to follow. He crawled about 50 yards to the edge of the clearing, then crept along the edge, with me puffing behind. Then we looked out at the massive animal. It was grazing slowly, broadside to us, about 35 yards away. My heart threatened to jump from my chest. I took deep breaths to steady myself.

I set up the shooting stick, slid the rifle into position, and located the target area behind the bull's right shoulder. I drew a breath, held it, and squeezed the trigger. The stag jumped, ran about 30 yards and fell.

Denny let out a yelp and ran whooping from cover, along with Sarah. He had captured everything on film. That's when I began yelling and pumping my fist into the air. Vitali gave me the universal high-five. I had taken the perfect rack, a stag with antlers topped with crowns on both sides, massive and perfectly symmetrical. I couldn't get my hands around the bases.

I'll be back. You men aren't having all the fun!

•*Sarah Fisher Snowday, granddaughter of the founder of GM Fisher Body, poses with stag she took in 1998. (Denny Geurink photo)*

Winter Snows, September Rut Best Times for Big Bull Moose

... see page 248 for September Rut Results

Two bulls were taken in late November; one in early December. Temperatures ranged from 20 above to 20 below zero, usually zero to 10 above. Snow depths vary year to year from six inches to four feet. Shot distances usually are 80 to 120 yards. In winter, guides and hunters use snowmobiles and head to thick cover to find big-antlered bulls like these.

• *Top to bottom: Kody Cesario, Glenn Paula, Matt Stout (Top photo by Greg Cesasrio, center and bottom photos by Matt Stout)*

CHAPTER 18

LADY AND THE BULL

"I GUESS IT JUST WASN'T meant to be," Linda Klass said dejectedly as we sat in the cook tent waiting for the helicopter to pick us up and take us back to town. "I've dreamed about this hunt a long time. I've always wanted to shoot a big moose, but that's hunting. It just wasn't in the cards. I had a great time anyway. It's been a great trip. You don't have to shoot something to have a good time. It's just icing on the cake."

Linda and her husband, Ken Klass, from Ottawa, Ohio, had joined me and four other hunters on our annual fall moose hunt in Russia, just north of the Arctic Circle. All the other hunters had filled their tags by the second or third day, including west Michigan native, Michael Timmerman, from Kalamazoo, who had downed a huge bull destined for the record books. Only Linda still looked for a moose.

Linda and Ken had come on the trip together to share the wilderness experience, but only Linda had planned to hunt. The couple had purchased just one moose tag. Linda was to be the hunter and Ken the observer; just the opposite of what usually happens when a husband and wife go on a hunt together. Unfortunately, the first day out, Linda had twisted her knee and was unable to do much walking after that. Her husband took her rifle and picked up where Linda left off.

In a strange twist, each day while Ken beat the bush, Linda watched moose file through camp. At least one bull walked through the drainage in front of the tents every day. It got to be funny.

Each evening, Ken came back to camp exhausted after a long day of walking through the bush, only to hear Linda talk about the nice bull that ambled through camp that day. If she hadn't videoed the moose, he would have thought she was pulling his leg.

• *One of our clients was renowned wildlife artist Cynthie Fisher, who created an original oil painting of Connie's stag based on photos of her stag and from seeing animals in the setting where the stag was taken.*

"Sure, you saw 10 moose today," Ken blustered the first day after he took up the hunt. "Thanks for trying to make me feel bad. I've been walking my tail off all day and haven't been able to get into rifle range of anything, and you tell me they are walking right through camp."

"I've got proof," Linda chuckled as she pulled out her video camera and showed Ken the film she had taken.

"Take a look at this."

• *Moose camp in Siberia. (Linda Klass photo)*

"What am I doing out there wearing the soles off my boots?," he mumbled in disbelief as he watched video scenes of nice bulls sauntering past the camp.

Each day, when Ken heard about the moose activity in camp and watched the video, he began thinking more and more about staying in camp the following day, rather than heading into the woods again. Each time the guides talked him into going out, telling him the chances of another nice bull walking through camp were slim.

However, the scenario kept repeating itself. Ken hunted hard all day while Linda stayed in camp, drinking tea and videotaping moose.

It was decided, on the last day, that if another bull came through camp, Linda would borrow a rifle from one of the other hunters and shoot it. To keep both Linda and Ken from shooting a moose, Ken and his guide would stay within hearing distance of camp. If they heard Linda shoot, they would not shoot. If Linda heard Ken shoot, she would not shoot. Of course, now that we had a plan and were ready for a nice bull to visit camp, none came.

The helicopter was supposed to land at 2:00 p.m. and take

us back to town. As we watched time tick away, Linda began to feel a bit dejected.

"Wouldn't you know it," she mused. "Now that I am ready to shoot a moose, they don't come into camp. It's like they know what's going on."

Soon it was nine o'clock. Then ten o'clock. Then eleven. Then twelve, two hours from helicopter time. Nothing. Not even a cow.

"Well, it's not over until the fat lady sings," I said, trying to keep her spirits up, "but I do think I hear her clearing her throat."

Just then, one of the other hunters, Rell Spears from Louisville, Kentucky, burst into the cook tent.

"Moose! Moose! A big bull is heading for the camp! Hurry, Linda, you can use my gun."

We all bailed out of the cook tent and scurried to catch a glimpse of the bull.

"Wait a minute," I stammered. "There are two. Look, the second one is coming out of the trees right behind the first one. Both are nice bulls."

The moose were heading into the open drainage in front of the camp. Each sported massive headgear, with wide palms and long points. Linda was so excited and nervous she had a hard time holding the rifle.

"Here," I said, as I grabbed the rifle, "you follow the guide. I will carry the gun. I'll be right behind you."

We crouched as low as we could and scurried single file into the drainage. First Radian, our guide, then Linda, and then me. Radian began to call like a lovesick cow. The two bulls stopped and stared, then began walking slowly on an angle, getting closer to us.

As the bulls closed to within 80 yards, Radian jumped up and jammed a shooting stick into the dirt. I handed Linda the rifle. She nervously placed it on the shooting stick.

"OK, take the safety off and put the crosshairs right behind the shoulder," I whispered, trying to calm her down. I knew I would have to walk her through this, as she was too nervous to think straight. "Put the crosshairs right behind the shoulder, steady the rifle, and then squeeze the trigger."

The big gun roared and the moose staggered. "One more, right behind the shoulders," I barked. The big gun roared again, and the moose fell into the grass less than 150 yards from the cook tent.

Linda threw her hands in the air and screamed in delight. "I did it! I did it! I shot a moose! I can't believe it! I shot a moose!" Tears rolled down her cheeks as we walked over to the giant beast.

"Was there ever a doubt?" I asked as I gave her a big hug. "By the way, is that the fat lady I hear singing?"

• *Linda Klass poses with the big bull she bagged on the last hour of the last day right next to camp. (Linda Klass photo)*

MORE MOOSE TALES FROM SIBERIA

"There must be a log, a dead tree, or something in back of him," I whispered to Maurice "Mo" White, as I glassed the bull moose standing in a small drainage about 400 yards away. "That can't all be antlers. It can't be that big. It is a nice bull, though."

It was September, and I was hunting in Siberia above the Arctic Circle with White, a Traverse City, Michigan, native. We were on our annual fall moose hunt and had just spotted a nice bull in the distance. Problem was, the trees and bushes were still fully leafed. This part of the world hadn't seen a hard frost yet, which was weird because it was well into September. Later I learned it was still very warm in Michigan, too.

White had spotted a cow in the drainage a few minutes earlier. As we watched her munching on grass, a small bull stepped out to feed with her, probably last year's calf. A few minutes later a bigger bull emerged from the brush. This was the bull we now were sizing up, trying to determine whether it was big enough to go after.

It finally stepped into an opening. "That is all antler!," I gasped. "It's a monster! Sixty-plus inches for sure."

"Sixty plus?," Mo stuttered. "You think it'll go 60 or more?"

"For sure. It's an absolute monster."

Our guide, Ferda, also was getting excited.

I pointed to the bull and said, "Let's go." He agreed.

As we made our way down the hillside toward the moose, the cover began to swallow us up, but our experienced guide kept us on course as he led us through the bush.

Twenty minutes later, Ferda slowed to a snail's pace and then stopped. We all froze, staring into the bush ahead of us. There, partially hidden, was the cow, not 30 yards from us. She finally moved off to our left. We sneaked to a small rise in the brush and waited. The wind was perfect, blowing in our faces.

In a few more minutes, the small bull stepped out of the brush. We froze as it stared right at us. Several more minutes passed, then it too moved off to our left. Then we heard the unmistakable grunting of a bull in rut moving in from our right. Suddenly there it was, looking like a bus with a huge white rack, sliding through the brush right at us.

"Oh, my . . .," Mo whispered softly, "look at the size of that rack!"

"Get ready," I whispered back. "Take it right behind the shoulder when it steps out."

It didn't step out. The bull stood there several minutes, then stepped back into the brush and disappeared. Did it spot us? Smell us? Both questions raced through our heads as we stared in disbelief into the bush.

"Now what do we do?," Mo whispered. "Shall we go after it?"

"I think it's still real close," I replied. "I don't think it's going anywhere. The bull isn't going to leave the cow. Keep your eyes peeled. It's going to follow the cow sooner or later. If we go into the brush, we'll spook it."

I sure hoped I knew what I was talking about.

Seconds dragged into minutes. Ferda, who was a good 12 inches or more shorter than us, hadn't even seen the rack. He didn't know the bull was in front of us and was wondering why we didn't move forward. He wanted to keep moving. I kept motioning to him that the bull was right in front of us. He was beginning to think I was crazy.

Then the big bull pushed out of the brush across the drainage. His huge rack twisted and turned as he made his way through the brush and up the other side.

I raised my TV camera and hit the 'on' switch. Mo clicked the safety off again, aimed, and fired. The big bull staggered. Mo fired another round and it fell.

Mo was in a daze. "I can't believe it! It all worked out perfectly," he stammered. "The bull came right in front of us."

"That is one monster bull!," I said in admiration as we walked toward the fallen monarch. "It's bigger than I thought it was. I'm thinking maybe 70 inches. It's the biggest bull moose I've ever seen."

"It's the biggest rack ever taken from this region," our head guide told us. "I have never seen such a moose."

All this excitement got us thinking: How high up in the record book will this trophy go?

"Just got a call from my taxidermist," Mo told me over the phone a few days after we got home. "He scored my rack and said if it's a Yakut moose, it's a new world record. It completely blows away the old world record. It's just over 72 inches wide. The only thing we have to do is find out exactly where our camp was so we can determine which sub-species of moose it is."

There are three main species of moose in Russia: the European moose, the Yakut moose, and the Chukotka moose. The European moose is similar to a Canadian moose. The Yakut moose and the Chukotka moose are similar to the Yukon/Alaska moose, with the Yakut moose being a little smaller.

Mo shot his moose very close to the dividing line between the Yakut and Chukotka moose territories. If his moose was a Yakut moose, it's a new world record. If it was a Chukotka moose, it would be number six in the world for that species.

We shot another 10 moose that fall in the Yakut and Chukotka regions. If Mo's moose becomes the number one Yakut moose, then we also have number 2 and 3 in the world for that subspecies, as two of our hunters took bulls in the 65-inch class in the same area.

The week after Mo shot his moose, we moved farther east and shot six moose in the Chukotka region, one that measured 78 ½ inches in width. That one would be scored; it looked like a possible new world record for the Chukotka species! But that's a whole new story. Bottom line? It looked like we might have harvested the Numbers 1, 2, and 3 world record Yakut moose and the Number 1 Chukotka moose in one month. Not a bad hunt!

Authors Note: We later learned White's moose would be classified as a Chukotka Moose and was listed as Number 7 in the world record books. The 78½-inch moose taken the following week went into the record book as the Number 2 moose in the Chukotka category. It was taken by Wayne Wilde, from Shevlin, Minnesota. The following year we took over the top three spots in the Yakut moose category.

THE COMMANDER

They called the giant moose the Commander, and rightly so. The bull moose did, indeed, command attention, especially from any other bull moose in the area that might have a notion to steal a girlfriend.

While other moose gave the bull a wide berth, my hunters and guides tried to get close. It was October, and we were chasing moose in the Siberian wilderness.

The Commander came from good stock. Its father and grandfather had commanded respect as well. The gene pool for trophy moose in this area was phenomenal. SCI record books showed that several record moose came from this region, including Wayne Wilde's 78-incher and Maurice White's 72-incher.

This bull was hanging out with several cows quite a distance from camp. The hunters had seen its tracks in the snow and knew it was a keeper. Guides and hunters decided to set up a spike camp in the Commander's back yard, rather than walk from camp each day.

It was cold. There was nearly a foot of snow on the ground during this mid-October hunt, unusual for this time of year. Just two years earlier, when White shot his monster bull from the same camp, the temperature had climbed to 70 degrees. This group of hunters, however, was happy to see the snow. It made the animals much more visible and easy to track.

"I had already seen six nice moose up to this point," said Doug Murray, from Silver City, Iowa. "This region has the largest number of moose in the world. They also have unbelievably big moose, the biggest in the world. The hunting here is incredible."

On the fourth day into the hunt, Murray and his guide came across the Commander's tracks again. This time they were still smoking.

"My guide showed me where moose were feeding on the brush," Murray said. "We knew the animals were poking along and probably close by. We saw where the tracks went into the woods, so we made a big circle around the woods to see if they had come out. They hadn't.

"We started making smaller and smaller circles. The guide suddenly spotted a cow feeding and knew the big bull had to be close by. We stood still and watched for about 20 minutes, looking for the bull. Finally we saw its enormous rack sticking out of the brush. It was lying down.

"The bull sensed our presence, stood up and began to trot into the woods. I couldn't believe the size of its rack.

"I tried to get the bull in my scope, but the brush was so thick I couldn't shoot for 20 or 30 seconds," Murray said. "I followed it in my scope through the woods and at about 125 yards, I fired the first shot. I knew I had hit the bull, but it kept going. So I threw more lead.

"After it went down, we walked to it. I couldn't believe how big it was. The bull was enormous. The rack was absolutely phenomenal!"

Later, when a tape measure was put to the rack, everyone involved found out just how phenomenal the bull was. Its rack measured nearly 72 inches across.

CHAPTER 19

THE CAPERCAILLIE TWO-STEP

IT'S 2 a.m., late April, and I'm stretched out on a bench of pine boughs deep in the boreal forest of Mother Russia. Our guide, Alexi Trapezikov, has just made this primitive bed with an ax and pocketful of nails. Next to me is a crackling fire with a boiling pot of tea broadcasting the sweet scent of jasmine and lemon through the inky black night. We are about a quarter of a mile from a capercaillie lek, waiting for daylight.

This had all the trappings of an old-fashioned American snipe hunt. All that was missing was a flashlight and burlap bag, but we were a long way from America. We were in the middle of Russia in search of a bird almost as elusive as a snipe. The Russians call it "glukhar."

This latest Russian adventure had begun with a phone call from fellow writer and friend Tom Huggler. Tom, who lives near Lansing, Michigan, had just finished watching a TV show I had filmed in Russia featuring the holy grail of grouse hunting, the capercaillie. I didn't realize what a prized game bird this large grouse was until I began talking to Tom and other hard-core bird hunters who began calling and writing me after this episode of my television show aired. Ironically, the capercaillie hunt was more of an afterthought than the primary focus of the show.

"Why don't you organize a bird hunt in Russia," Tom suggested. "I'd love to hunt capercaillie and a few of the other species of grouse they have. The European black grouse and the hazel grouse, for instance. The grouse found in Russia are about the only ones I haven't taken. It would help me finish my Grand Slam of grouse."

"Do you think you can get a group of guys together who want to do a hunt like this?," I asked. "I've had several people ask about going over there to hunt the capercaillie, but they haven't been able to find anyone to go with them. The Russians won't open a camp, hire guides, cooks, and interpreters to take one person. We need a group of hunters to make it happen."

"I think I can," Tom said. "I know several guys who might be interested. Let me make a few calls and get back to you."

I knew if anyone could find a group of hunters interested in chasing birds in Russia, Tom could. Besides being on the editorial staff at *Outdoor Life*, Tom was one of the most avid bird hunters in the country. He had written dozens of stories and several books on game bird hunting.

The capercaillie, or "glukhar" as the Russians call it, is the largest species of grouse in the world. It's about the size of a chicken and can weigh more than seven pounds. It also is one of the most difficult game birds to collect because in most countries it has been pushed to the brink of extirpation due to habitat loss.

These birds need huge tracts of mature, diverse conifer forests. Unfortunately, in most European countries these habitats have been cut down and replaced with smaller, single-species plantations. In addition to not providing the right habitat, these smaller, single-species woodlots have become havens for the glukhar's natural enemies -- foxes, hawks, owls, eagles, and a host of other predators.

Only in the remote regions of northern Russia can you still find the extensive taiga forests that have the habitat the Old World game birds need. In countries such as Germany and Scotland, where there once were good capercaillie populations, the birds haven't been legal game for more than 30 years. Programs to bring the birds back have failed from lack of habitat.

I was introduced to the capercaillie in 1991 when we chased them to fill time between our bear and moose hunts. We weren't pursuing them as a game bird but as table fare. We had no idea they were so revered in the bird hunting world.

The European black grouse and the hazel grouse that Tom also wanted to hunt are fairly widespread across Europe, but, again, much more abundant in Russia's dense boreal forests.

The black grouse, or "tetera" as the Russians call it, is a bit larger than our ruffed grouse and can weigh more than three pounds.

The hazel grouse, or "ryabchik" in Russian, is a little larger than our bobwhite quail, and is one of the smallest species of grouse in the world.

While the capercaillie would be our main target, we also wanted to try for these other birds. Our outfitter, Dmitri Sikorski, said he would arrange everything.

Tom soon rounded up a group of guys eager to chase these unique game birds. As soon as I got off the phone with him, I began putting the pieces together. Now, a few months later, here I was on a bed of pine boughs at two o'clock in the morning, trying to get some sleep before our glukhar hunt begins. I was too excited to sleep.

Earlier that day, Tom, Dmitri, and I had driven two hours in Alexi's little Lada from the village of Cmetahno, where we were staying, down a maze of bumpy roads and muddy two-tracks. Several times we had to get out of the sardine can and push it out of a mud hole. Actually, it's amazing what these little cars will go through.

We ended up parking the Lada along the edge of a large farm field that bumped up against a thick, mature forest of tall conifers and hardwoods.

It was early May and there was still a lot of snow on the ground in the heavily shaded forest; in some places snow was waist deep. This made the three-hour hike into the bowels of the forest an adventurous struggle. The forest was thick and heavy and closed around us like dense fog.

We were exhausted when we reached our destination, a small bump on the forest floor a quarter mile from an active glukhar lek.

A lek is a specific area deep within a mature forest where male grouse get together to sing and dance to impress the ladies. The females are attracted to the lek in search of a mate. These age-old mating rituals usually occur in the same spot year after year. Finding an active capercaillie lek is like finding a pot of gold at the end of a rainbow.

After reaching our destination about an hour before dark, Alexi had built benches of pine boughs for Tom and me and told us we should try to get some sleep.

That wasn't going to happen. The crackling campfire bounced eerie shadows off the dense canopy of pine branches enveloping us. The scene reminded me of a Hollywood film set for a werewolf movie. We sipped tea and told hunting stories into the wee hours of the morning.

At 2:30 a.m., Alexi said it was time. We sneaked under cover of darkness to a mating arena of the glukhar and waited for dawn, which comes early in this part of northern Russia close to the Arctic Circle.

Then it happened! We heard the first "click-click-click" call of the male bird tuning up for his signature song.

Here is Tom's report of this first effort:

"At 3 a.m. we began our first single-file stalk on a male that suddenly had opened up in full song. Alexi led, then me, then Denny with his video camera. It was hard going in the snow, trying to step in unison, copying Alexi's start-and-stop tactics. We got to within 50 yards of the bird, which suddenly bolted from its perch and roared over us at 25 yards. It was the size of a gigantic crane I had noticed the day before. I pulled up my 12-gauge, but Alexi brought down the barrel.

"'Nyet!,' he hissed, apparently not wanting me to miss or possibly cripple one of these majestic birds."

After stalking that first bird, Tom and I began whispering and chuckling about how funny the three of us looked sneaking up on the big male perched high atop the conifer trees. Alexi had told us before the stalk began that we must follow exactly in his footsteps and move at exactly the same time he did -- and stop moving when he did, like a game of Simon Says.

This stalking tactic is necessary to get into shotgun range. When you first begin the stalk, you have no idea which tree the bird is sitting in because the forest is so dense. All you can do is hear it call and estimate its location. As you get closer and possibly able to spot the bird, the advantage goes to the bird because of its high lookout point. You must move only when it is at the end of its three-part song.

The song begins with a click-click-click that sounds like someone tapping a pencil on a wooden table. It then moves on to a guttural whooshing sound, followed by a rasping sound that resembles someone raking a metal file over a piece of wood. During this last sequence, the bird stretches its neck straight up and lifts its head high into the air. This final note lasts about two seconds. While it stretches its neck to the sky, a thin translucent membrane covers its eye. This blurs its vision, giving you about two seconds to move in on it. During these two seconds, you can take two giant steps.

With the song over, the male looks around to see if any females heard his beautiful serenade. You can't move at this time because the bird will spot you. You must wait until the bird starts its song again and gets to the last raspy part before you can take two more steps. It almost becomes a game. You have to listen very carefully to the song and move only during the last note. A stalk is both exciting and nerve wracking.

This sequence of take two steps and stop ... take two steps and stop ... take two steps and stop ... was like a simplified version of the Texas Two-Step. That led to Tom and me calling this dance of the glukhar hunter The Capercaillie Two-Step!

More of Tom's stalk notes:

Soon our guide focused on another singing male, perhaps 200 yards away. Progress was good; within five minutes we had halved the distance. There I stood: unbalanced, legs spread, snow above my knees, water seeping into one boot.

The capercaillie stopped singing. We stood unmoving for eight minutes, while my foot went numb with cold. The male began to call again, then it flushed when my trapped boot made a loud sucking sound in the snow.

During a third stalk, we moved to within 50 yards of a huge male back-lighted and highly visible. I wanted to take him and felt I could, having shot wild turkeys at that range. Alexi said no. The bird blew out.

Then, without warning, another male, no doubt a sub-dominant, flew to a branch about 40 yards away.

"Da?," Alexi mouthed. I nodded and began my slow, careful stalk. I shot the bird at 20 yards. It weighed a bit more than seven pounds.

The long, bumpy ride back to the village didn't seem nearly as long as the ride out. At Alexi's house, we met the other members of our group of Russian bird hunters. Tom had brought Joe Zikewich from Lake Orion, Michigan; Jim Gilsdorf from Ann Arbor, Michigan; J.D McDonald from Chicago, Illinois, and Joe Scillierri from Jamesburg, New Jersey. John Baker from Walker, Michigan, also was with us. John worked with me on my TV show as a cameraman/salesman.

McDonald had come to collect a capercaillie for the Chicago Museum of Natural History. Zikewich had come along to collect one for the Drayton Plains Nature Center in Michigan. The rest of us wanted to add one of these rare birds to our own collections.

Of the seven of us, four guys collected a capercaillie the first morning. John, J.D., and Joe Scillierri had scored, in addition to Tom. Not a bad way to start a hunt. The following day, Jim, Joe Zikewich, and I scored. The capercaillie portion of the hunt was over.

It was time to move on to the European black grouse or "tetera". Before we did, however, the guides told us it was time to celebrate the success we had experienced up to this point of the expedition. You know what that means.

• *Dmitri makes tea over an open fire while I sit on a bench our guide built with his hatchet deep in a capercaillie forest. (Tom Huggler photo)*

"I'm not used to drinking vodka at ten in the morning," Tom said, chuckling as a vodka bottle appeared like magic on the table, "but who could resist a toast now?"

It was proposed by our co-host, novelist Sergei Alexeyev, whose most recent spy thriller sold 4 ½ million copies.

"To the hunt," Sergei beamed as Dmitri interpreted, "the bond that brings all men together regardless of nationality, regardless of custom. Long live the hunt!"

We all lifted our glasses and cheered this insightful toast. Alexeyev is a well-known Russian author who loves to retreat to the forest to relax and recharge his batteries. We were surprised and honored to share our camp with him.

"I've often thought there would be no wars if hunters and anglers, and not neurotic politicians, decided world affairs," Tom mused.

Can we hear an amen to that?

• Here you see the stark contrast between the male (left) and female (right) Capercaillie. (Denny Geurink photo)

We spent the next few days hunting black grouse in open farm fields, hiding in little huts the guides constructed from pieces of wood and straw.

The tetera, unlike the glukhar, carries on its mating rituals in the middle of a field next to the forest, rather than deep in the forest.

The guides set out taxidermy mounts as decoys and called to the birds to bring them close. It was a new experience for us, and one we thoroughly enjoyed.

Hazel grouse? Maybe a problem. We learned that the season on hazel grouse is open only in the fall. The season is closed in the spring. Males and females are indistinguishable and game biologists don't want people shooting hens during mating and nesting seasons. This was a disappointment to Tom, who needed the hazel grouse to fill in his World Slam of grouse.

• *J. D. McDonald, center, poses with a European Black Cock and a Capercaillie he collected for the Chicago Museum of Natural History. Tom Huggler from Outdoor Life is on the right, Denny on the left. (Dmitri Sikorski photo)*

• *J. D. McDonald (center) with Hazel Grouse and European Black Cock he collected for the Chicago Museum of Natural history. Flanking him is our guide Alexi Trapezikov, left, and famous Russian novelist, Sergei Alexeyev, right.. (Tom Huggler photo)*

When Alexi, who also was a local game warden, and Sergei, one of Russia's most prominent novelists, learned how disappointed Tom was, they made some phone calls. They apparently were good friends with one of the directors of the regional game department in St. Petersburg.

A couple of days later, a courier arrived at camp with a small legal document that proclaimed a special spring season for hazel grouse. The season would be open for one day, with a bag limit of one grouse.

The Russians had created a hazel grouse season just so Tom, an American, could take one of these birds home with him and complete his World Slam of grouse. It was one of the most remarkable moments in my outfitting career in Russia.

When talking with Tom later, he noted that one of the special memories he has of this trip, besides this generous gesture, was the warm hospitality of the Russian people he encountered. This is reflected in the opening paragraph of a story written when he returned home.

His writing:

"It is two o'clock in the morning, and I am sipping honeyed tea in the home of Yuri, my local guide, waiting for the rain to stop sliding down the window. Yuri's mother, a farm wife who appears to be about 80, my mother's age, enters the yellow pool of light that defines her kitchen.

"'Chea?,' she gestures with the teapot.

"I smile back, folding my hands under an ear to make a pillow. I wonder if Yuri's mother will go back to bed.

"'Nyet.' She grins broadly, as though her life's purpose -- to be routed in the middle of the night to play hostess to a visitor from America -- has now been achieved.

"We are unable to converse further, but I see the history of twentieth-century Russia in her tired, proud face. Imagine a life that began under the last czar. Picture the many upheavals: the Bolshevik Revolution, the Great Patriotic War, Stalin's purges, the dissolution of the Soviet Union, now the new democracy that brings a Cold War enemy to her kitchen on a rainy night in early May."

Tom was so impressed with his hunt and the warmth of the people he wrote to me: "This trip is up there with the best of any I've taken. The hunt was great. I'm going back!"

He went back that fall to hunt European woodcock and European quail. That's another story for another time.

Like A Chicken With A Big Beak

• *We quite often saw Capercaillie in the spring in the snow looking for food. In areas with large Capercaillie populations, the guides frequently take shotguns along on the hunt to shoot the birds for camp meat or let the hunters borrow their shotgun to shoot the bird for a take-home trophy.(Photo by Denny Geurink)*

CHAPTER 20

ENCOUNTER WITH A RUT-CRAZED BULL MOOSE

EVERYONE HAS HEARD THE stories about bellicose bull moose squaring off with approaching trains and 18-wheelers during the rut. The blind rage of a rutting bull is legendary. When a bull moose gets caught up in the rut, it becomes stupid and extremely aggressive. It now has a one-track mind. All it can think about is lovely cow moose. A lovesick bull will wallow in the mud, pee on itself, and moan like a drunk with a toothache. During its non-stop search, it will fight with anyone or anything that gets in its way.

That's what they say. Put me in the "they" crowd.

I've witnessed some weird rutting bull moose behavior first-hand while chasing these one-ton beasts near the Arctic Circle. I've also heard exciting "crazy moose" stories from my hunters.

When we shoot a moose a long distance from camp, on the first trip back to camp we generally bring the cape and antlers, along with a tenderloin for dinner. We leave the rest of the carcass in the bush to retrieve the next day. The meat is piled on the skin and covered with cheese cloth or a tarp. Then the guide pokes a stick in the ground beside the carcass and hangs a coat or shirt over the meat pile to ward off wolves and grizzly bears. The human scent on clothing usually discourages predators from the kill for a couple of days, but not always.

After the meat is secured for recovery the next day, the guides load cape and antlers onto pack frames and head back to camp.

This trek can get hairy. Besides being followed by grizzlies, several clients and their guides have been charged by other bulls You know the bulls are really cranked up on hormones if they can't tell the difference between a real bull and a guy carrying a moose rack. It's like the bulls are in a drug-induced stupor.

Generally, guide and hunter are able to scare off the bull before anyone gets hurt. The charging bull usually, but not always, comes to its senses when it gets close enough to see the men and hear them yelling. The bull's survival instinct suddenly trumps its lust.

My guides told me several stories about how they or their friends have been knocked down and seriously injured by a rut-crazed bull. They try not to shoot a testy bull if it's too small. They would rather scare it off, but sometimes they have to shoot it to protect themselves.

Guides consider a bull in rut just as dangerous as a bear. This opinion is backed up by scientists and researchers, who report that moose attack more people than do bears and wolves combined. According to Wikipedia, moose injure more people than any other wild mammal. Worldwide, only hippopotamuses injure more people.

On a hunt with one of my hunters and a guide named Ferda, the hunter had downed a giant bull. We had spent an hour or more caping it and getting ready for the trek back to camp.

We helped Ferda tie the rack and cape to his pack frame and hoist it onto his back. The antlers stuck at least two feet over his shoulders and head.

We made jokes about hoping another hunter wouldn't see us coming through the woods. From a distance, Ferda looked a lot like a moose slipping through the trees and tall grass. Only the giant rack over his head would be seen.

After walking maybe 15 minutes, we noticed a small bull heading our way across a large clearing. We didn't know if it had seen us or simply was walking in our direction. Ferda made a few lovesick bull sounds, then started laughing when the young bull began waving its head side to side. Then the bull made a noise best described as somewhere between a groan and a roar. It definitely had seen us.

We thought that, once the bull saw the size of the rack Ferda was carrying, it would turn tail back into the woods, and we would all laugh about the good joke we pulled on it. The rack was at least 65 inches wide, with massive paddles. The young bull's rack was barely 45 inches wide, but it wasn't in a joking mood.

The young bull lowered its head and started trotting toward us. Ferda still thought it was funny, but I couldn't see as much humor in the situation. The bull paused on the way in to whack its antlers against a small tree, paw in the mud and give out a few more "umphs." Ferda continued to call to the bull while my client and I looked for a big tree to climb

The young bull rolled its eyes back in their sockets, shook its head again and kept coming. As it closed to 30 yards, Ferda didn't think it was so funny anymore. He began yelling at the bull. It paid no attention to him. By now my bladder was weakening.

When the bull closed to 15 yards, Ferda began firing shots in the air from his SKS rifle. This stopped the animal. Its eyes rolled back to look forward, and it stared intently at us for at least 10 seconds, maybe more. I wasn't counting.

After taking a few more stiff-legged steps toward us, it realized three people were standing in front of it, not another bull. It slowly turned and headed back toward the woods. We breathed a giant sigh of relief. That was as close to a rut-crazed bull as any of us ever want to get.

This bull walked to within 10 yards of us before turning and leaving. That would have seemed like a mile to Michael Pilarski from Romeo, Michigan. On a September hunt, he had one of the closest calls a hunter can have with a rut-crazed bull without being killed or seriously injured.

Here's his story:

***

Two of the greatest moments in my hunting years happened on a Russian moose hunt with Denny. The wildest one started on Day Two of the hunt, about seven miles out of camp.

My guide and I were working up the side of a small mountain when we cut fresh moose tracks in the muddy snow. The guide pointed to the tracks, which seemed to indicate that a group of five to seven moose had passed through, most likely a good bull with some cows.

We followed the trail slowly and quietly. About one hundred yards farther up the mountain, the guide stepped on a small twig. It snapped loudly. We stopped to listen. After a slight pause and hearing nothing, we continued. In a few more steps, my ears picked up a small snap maybe 60 yards to the right. I stopped the guide with a quieting "wiss, wiss" sound. He looked at me. I pointed to my ear then to the direction of the snap. We both paused.

The action was about to begin. We heard a "whau, whau" sound in the brush. A bull moose had pinpointed us and was coming for a fight.

At 40 yards, we could see the beast rocking back and forth with its eyes rolling back in its head and its massive antlers swaying side to side. What a breath-taking sight!

At 30 yards, we decided this was not a shooter. Its spread probably was 54 to 58 inches. It would have been a trophy in many places, but not here. I eased up the barrel of my rifle and rested the butt of the stock on my knee, fascinated by the fearless challenge the bull was putting on. Then I realized it wasn't stopping! My heart really started pounding as we tried to back up. With my left hand on the guide's shoulder, holding him in front of me, I started glancing over my shoulder, looking for any kind of cover to run behind if the bull decided to charge. My heart really started to race when I realized I was screwed.

This mountain side was skinny re-growth, most of it tall pines three to five inches in diameter; the size and types of trees I would get hung up on or bounce off if I tried to run, but no problem for an 1,800-pound bull to plow over.

The bull closed to 10 feet, maybe less!

"Whau, whau, whau!," it groaned in lust.

I had a perfect shot at the bull's vitals, which were eye level with the guide's head. I remember thinking that the guide could walk under this huge beast and his head would just scrape the bull's belly.

I'm not sure if I froze with fear, shock, or a little of both. I was ready to dive out of the way.

The guide stretched out his left hand with his pre-World War II rifle over the nose of this monster. I thought, 'What is he doing?' Is he going to smack it on the nose?

BANG! He shot! My eyes must have been as huge as baseballs! The end of the barrel was just past the bull's nostrils and six inches over its head. Six inches! Is he crazy?

The beast stood still; its ears had to be ringing worse than mine. Then it shook its head and massive antlers. After a short pause, it cross-stepped slowly to change direction and slowly walked about 15 yards.

I was starting to come out of my state of shock and amazement when it started all over!

"Whau, whau!" It's eyes rolled back and it started posturing again to fight, swaying its massive antlers back and forth. Then it started to circle back at us.

The guide looked at me and gestured with his hands as if he were taking a picture. My camera! I grabbed it out of my pocket and looked down to advance the film. As I did, I

heard something galloping. I looked up. The bull was gone.

As soon as it got downwind it disappeared, leaving me without even a picture. That's when my heart finally dropped out of my throat and back into my chest. I was shaking like a leaf. My skin was cold and clammy, but my guide and I we were both still alive! I had gone nose to nose with a giant bull moose and lived to tell about it! I didn't get the picture on film, but it will forever be etched in my mind. I left that mountain side that day having had the most amazing encounter of my life!

The second most-amazing encounter happened just three days later when I called up two monster bulls that were ready to fight.

Yes, I shot the big one! With a 68-inch spread and scoring 497-6/8 in the Safari Club International (SCI) record book, it became the number one Yakutia moose of all time. With massive palms, it was everything I could dream of in a trophy moose.

Thanks for a great adventure.

Six Hunters ... Six Big Bulls

• *Six hunters in camp, and each shot a nice bull during the rut in late September. Some bulls were called in; others were located by hunters while walking the woods. They could hear bulls moaning, groaning and thrashing trees. This was in the late 1990s. We were the first hunters in this region; big bulls seemed to be everywhere. Bulls in rut become stupid, for want of a better term, and will charge anything they see as a threat to steal their cows. There are stories of moose charging oncoming, whistle-blowing trains.*

Largest Bull Taken

• *This rutting bull was shot in late September as it roamed the woods looking for cows. Rack width was 78-1/2 inches, the largest ever taken in any of our camps. Taken by Wayne Wilde from Iowa. Besides great width, the antlers also had massive palms and lots of points, factors you always look for.*

CHAPTER 21

BEAR CHARGES SNOWMOBILE

ONE OF THE MOST spine-tingling incidents during our two-plus decades in the bush occurred in the '90s on a spring hunt. The bears generally hibernate at lower elevations of the numerous mountain ranges scattered along the Kamchatka Peninsula. We use snowmobiles on spring hunts to transport clients from the camps to denning areas. Once in a denning area, the guides locate a high vantage point from where they can survey the snow-covered landscape with a spotting scope or binoculars to locate bears moving in the area. When a bear is spotted, the guide plans a stalk. The hunt is on.

Each guide has his own snowmobile with a big sled in tow. The guide drives the snowmobile while the hunter rides behind on the sled. This is the best way to get around. Putting guide and hunter together on a snowmobile just wouldn't work.

Most sleds have a seat or chair attached to it, along with a box or crate in which to haul extra gear, lunch, spare snowmobile parts, etc.

Quite often, on the way out to denning areas, the guide and hunter encounter bears wandering around searching for food. On this particular hunt, that's exactly what happened. The guide and hunter have asked me not to use their real names as they think someone might think they were careless or negligent. It could be embarrassing, maybe, but not negligent.

The guide, "Yuri", and the hunter, "Bill", were heading through the woods to the mountains when they rounded a corner on the trail and saw a nice bear in a small opening. The bear struggled in the deep snow, giving Bill time to rack a round in the chamber, jump off the sled, and get down on one knee for a shot. Unfortunately, his shot hit the bear's mouth.

The bear let out a blood-curdling roar as it shook its head from side to side. Bears are intelligent animals; this one quickly put two and two together. Its pain and displeasure had something to do with the two creatures on the loud thing. It immediately charged the men and their machine. Someone was going to pay for its missing teeth and sore mouth.

Yuri yelled frantically at Bill to get back on the sled so they could get out of Dodge. He wanted nothing to do with a charging, wounded bear in this heavy stand of woods. The bear was too close and infuriated to try to put down at short range. He wanted more distance between them and the bear before taking another shot.

Bill jumped aboard the sled. Yuri hit the throttle and sped away as fast as he could, just in time. The bear was almost on the sled.

Yuri was able to put a bit of distance between them and the charging brown fury. As the snowmobile and sled sped through the woods, the bear kept its focus on the whirlwind of blowing snow and loud noise that roared ahead of it. Spurred by anger and adrenaline, the bear moved surprising fast through the deep snow, staying hot on the snowmobile's tail.

Yuri was doing everything he could to shake the bear but was having a hard time maneuvering snowmobile and sled through the thickly-wooded bottomland. Meanwhile, Bill hung on tightly as the sled bucked and kicked through the snow. Yuri wove in and out of the trees, trying not to get the sled hooked on a root or branch. It wasn't easy. A snowmobile alone would have been no problem, but the extra weight and length of the long sled, twice as long as the snowmobile, made it difficult.

Just as Yuri was beginning to put distance between him and the bear, things went from bad to worse. He made a sharp turn to avoid smacking into a snag. The snowmobile missed the snag, but the sled didn't. It rammed into the snag at 30 miles an hour, tipped sideways and threw Bill against a tree. His rifle smacked the tree so hard the stock cracked. Bill glanced off the tree but didn't break an arm or leg. The momentum from the crash rolled Bill down a small hill and into a bush, bringing him some safety away from the path of travel.

As Bill lay in the snow, he saw his banged-up rifle 10 yards away. He knew he couldn't get to it in time to shoot the bear. He didn't know if the rifle still would shoot.

The bear barreled around the corner in a cloud of snow. It was panting hard, enraged and determined to put the hurt on the thing that busted up its mouth.

Bill froze in terror! He was certain this was the end. He started imagining details of how it would end and silently began making peace with his Maker.

As he was about to have a heart attack, Bill watched in total surprise as the bear ran past him. The enraged bruin was so focused on the fleeing snowmobile and sled it hadn't seen Bill roll off the sled into a bush nor noticed him as it ran past.

Now flushed with adrenaline of his own, Bill scrambled up the hill and retrieved his rifle. The stock was cracked, but the rifle looked like it still worked. He prepared for the bear to come back, knowing there would be a fight to the death in this patch of woods in the middle of Siberia.

While continuing to drive as fast as he could, Yuri looked back to see if Bill was still on the sled. He was terror-stricken when he saw the sled was empty. What happened? Why was the bear still chasing him?

The guide swung the snowmobile in a big circle and headed back for the trail he had just blazed through the woods. Dead or alive, Bill had to be along the trail.

With the sled now lighter and the bear starting to tire, Yuri was able to put nearly 125 yards between him and the bear, but the bear wasn't giving up.

After what seemed like an eternity to Bill, he heard the snowmobile coming down the trail into the patch of woods where he was crouched in the snow.

Yuri saw Bill and sped to him, shouting for him to get back on the sled. Bill jumped on, and away they went one more time. The bear was still coming after them!

Yuri drove the snowmobile out into a large field and cut the engine. Bill jumped off, sat in the snow, and brought his rifle up on one knee. Yuri jumped off beside him and threw his rifle to his shoulder.

When the charging bear closed to 80 yards, Yuri and Bill began shooting. The big bruin plowed to a stop in flying snow less than 20 yards from them. It made one last, blood-curdling roar and fell limp.

Yuri and Bill also fell limp. The sheer terror and adrenaline rush left them exhausted. They hugged and congratulated each other for surviving the nearly unbelievable ordeal.

This is not April in Paris, but ...
It <u>is</u> April in Siberia

• This bear has just come out of hibernation. It is headed to lower elevations and river bottoms looking for food. Bears at this time are extremely hungry. Probably shorter tempered than usual, too, due to hunger. (Photo by Bob Lyter)

CHAPTER 22

MORE TALES OF BEAR ATTACKS FROM SIBERIA

OVER THE YEARS I have come across dozens of dangerous bear encounter stories while in Russia. You read about some of them in Chapter 4. Here are more, not just stories of attacks on people but also on cows, goats, and cadavers! Yes, even cadavers!

One of the weirdest stories came from the Tomsk region of Siberia in 2011. It reveals just how dangerous and destructive bears can be when they get hungry, and also how cunning they can be.

This story is unusual because of the nature of their victims -- milk cows in small villages -- and a bit terrifying due to the manner in which the bears attacked the cows. They ganged up on the cows much as a pack of wolves does when they attack prey.

A pack of wolves is dangerous enough, but a pack of giant brown bears! This behavior is unusual for bears. They normally are solitary predators. While a sow and her cubs may work together, it is strange for bears not of the same family group to coordinate an attack.

This style of attack on cattle in the Tomsk area is, unfortunately, becoming more frequent, according to Konstantin Osadchi, head of the Department of Environmental Protection for the Tomsk region. Bear attacks on cattle in the region jumped from three reported attacks in 2010 to ten in 2011.

"Changes probably took place in the bears' minds; they are curious or have lost their fear of man," Osadchi said in a statement to *Interfax* news agency. "Previously, cases never happened where bears joined in groups to kill cattle. It is typical behavior of wolves, not bears."

According to the *Interfax* story, Osadchi said that some bears will go right into a barn to attack cows. He states that these attacks are usually made by young bears, about three years old. He speculates that conflicts over food between adults and young animals may be one of the causes of the bears' "pack" behavior.

Osadchi estimates the bear population in the Tomsk region may be as high as 10,000 bruins. He says the number of bears could increase even more in the next few years due to the huge forest fires that have been occurring nearby. The fires are expected to drive more bears out of the surrounding regions and into the Tomsk region.

According to local authorities, liberalizing the hunting regulations could help to control the burgeoning bruin population, but that may not happen because local villagers cannot afford to buy licenses and tags.

"Currently, permission for hunting costs just over $100 and an additional amount more per animal," Osadchi said. "The hunting of bears is very expensive and therefore unpopular with hunters."

This packing behavior of bears in remote Russia also occurred in the Olyotorsky region on the Kamchatka Peninsula in July, 2008. A pack of 25-30 bears surrounded a mining compound and killed and ate two workers. The bear pack continued to hang around the compound after the attack, looking for more people to eat. Understandably, the workers were so terrified they didn't dare leave their quarters.

Reports from the mining camp said the miners were trapped and so frightened they refused to go back to work until the bears were dealt with. Government officials in Petropavlovsk ordered a team of snipers to the area to

dispatch the bears after authorizing a special off-season hunt, because the regular season was closed.

At about the same time, authorities released a statement saying that villagers in nearby Khailino also were afraid to leave their homes after bears were seen rummaging through garbage cans near their homes.

Similar incidents happened in several villages of the Altai Region in 2010, according to a story Dmitri Sikorski told me a couple of years ago. Sikorski said it became so bad there local authorities had to issue a curfew in Yailu and Bele, telling residents to be in their homes by sunset each night. They warned that anyone who ignored the curfew was at risk of being killed and eaten by bears.

Both villages are located within the Altai Game Reserve, which is where most of the local residents worked. Older residents said they couldn't remember ever seeing so many bears patrolling the towns looking for something, or someone, to eat.

More than 15 bears were seen in the two villages in a two-week time span. Local authorities blamed the bruin invasion on poor berry and pine nut crops. The bears, trying to put on weight for hibernation, looked for anything edible. They broke into barns, back porches, and garbage cans. One evening they destroyed three chicken houses, and killed a milk goat and a calf.

Making the situation more dangerous was that the bears were not afraid of residents. Several residents tried firing warning shots in the air with their shotguns to run off the bears, but the bears kept coming. The locals had to kill three of the most aggressive bears to protect themselves and their livestock, even though killing the bears was forbidden by law in the reserves.

Members of the regional game department went to the villages to look into the legitimacy of killing bears that presented a threat to human lives. While they fussed over whether residents had the right to shoot aggressive bears within a nature reserve, the bears became more and more dangerous every day.

One bear brazenly walked into the village during the middle of the day and tried to break through the roof of a cattle barn. The frightened farm hands tried to chase off the bear, but it paid no attention to them or to their barking dogs. Firing warning shots in the air and shouting did nothing.

Conditions became so bad in Yaila and Bele that local villagers were forced to form a posse to patrol the streets, with orders to shoot and kill any bear that became too aggressive. Eight remote forest stations within the sanctuary also were besieged by bears.

Meanwhile, members of the regional game department debated among themselves on how best to handle the situation. They wondered whether they should feed the bears to keep them away from the villages, but some local ecology experts didn't want to begin feeding bears as a matter of principle.

"The sanctuary is to support Mother Nature's flora and fauna complex in its natural condition, not interfere with the natural processes," a spokesman said. He added that the present situation, with marauding bears in the region, was not extraordinary. Failure of the berry and pine nut crops, or the bears starving, is a natural phenomenon, usually happening only once in several decades.

One of the most dangerous bear behaviors created by a severe shortage of natural foods is a 'walker' bear, as the locals call it. These bears are still hungry in late fall due to the lack of natural foods. They delay going into hibernation until they can put on enough fat reserves to survive the long Siberian winter.

When natural foods are especially scarce, some of these 'walker" bears may not hibernate all winter. They keep roaming, looking for something to eat. These bears become especially dangerous when they begin hunting livestock and people because nothing else is available.

There were so many 'walker' bears roaming Sakhalin

Island during the winter of 2008, looking for livestock and people to eat, that officials dubbed it the Year of the Wild Bear. Conservation officials said there were more than 200 reported cases of close bear encounters that winter. Many more went unreported.

A similar situation occurred in the Kurily Isles that winter, with residents forced to kill about 40 bears that came into town and got dangerously close to people. One bear was shot in front of the mayor's house.

One of my interpreters jokingly told me this is how they enforce term limits in Siberia -- when a mayor's term is up, they send in a bear to eat him.

Even more bizarre bear behavior was reported in some remote villages of eastern Siberia recently. Bears began raiding cemeteries, pulling dead bodies out of their coffins and eating them.

According to the Russian newspaper *Moskovsky Komsomelets*, two women from Vezhnya Tchova, a small village near the Arctic Circle, were visiting their local cemetery when they came upon a large bear eating a corpse. From a distance it looked like a large man in a fur coat was leaning over the grave of a loved one to pay his respects, but when they walked closer they realized it was a bear devouring a corpse.

The shocked women screamed in panic, scaring the bear back into the woods. That's when they discovered the partially-eaten corpse and the dead man's clothes scattered around the scene.

While some bear experts blamed this bizarre behavior on a lack of natural foods, others said the bears had plenty of food and raided cemeteries out of laziness, treating the graveyards as big 'refrigerators' according to a report in the *Guardian,* a British newspaper.

"In Karelia, one bear learned to open a coffin," Masha Vorontsova, Director of the International Fund For Animal Welfare (IFAW), said in an interview

with the *Guardian*. "It then taught others. They are quick learners."

Many bear researchers and biologists have tried to figure out or explain why bears do what they do.

Timothy Treadwell was a self-proclaimed researcher who tried living with bears in Alaska's Katmai National Park. Treadwell, a former alcoholic and drug addict, had some strange ideas. He didn't think bears were inherently dangerous and often tried getting close to them to talk to them. He even tried to pet them. He and his girlfriend were killed and partially eaten by a bear in 2003.

Russia had its version of Treadwell -- Vitaly Nikolayenko -- who was killed and eaten by a bear shortly after Treadwell's death. The 66-year-old Nikolayenko was trying to live with bears on the Kamchatka Peninsula along the Tikhaya River when he was attacked and partially eaten by a bruin. A can of empty pepper spray and the tracks of a medium-sized bear were found next to what remained of his body.

Nikolayenko at least had a healthy fear of bears. Treadwell, on the other hand, after using a can of pepper spray to defend himself, said he felt sorry for spraying the bear and wouldn't do it again. This decision may have cost him his life.

These men did, however, prove one thing -- bears are dangerous and unpredictable. Trying to live with them, pet them, talk to them, and give them warm fuzzy names thinking that this will somehow 'civilize' them, is not a good idea. Bears are not social creatures with human attributes. They are wild animals to be left alone.

One person who certainly should have known enough to leave bears alone lived in the small village of Ozernovsky along the western coast of the Kamchatka Peninsula. Nadya Dolevskaya, a cook and the wife of Vacily Dolevskaya, our head guide at one of our camps, told me an incredible story about the interaction between this man and a bear in the 1950s.

Dolevskaya grew up in Ozernovsky and lives there with her husband and son. Ozernovsky is surrounded by wild, picturesque streams chock full of salmon and trout. Of course, any time you live near a river full of salmon and trout in Russia, you are going to be living near big, hungry brown bears. That is exactly the case in Ozernovsky. Many of the residents in this remote village have had close encounters with brown bears.

In the animal kingdom, legend has it that the elephant has a photographic memory; it never forgets. Dolevskaya would argue that an elephant has nothing over a brown bear in the memory department. The chilling story she told me was about a brown bear that never forgot the man who stole her six-month-old cubs.

"I was a young girl when it happened," Dolevskaya said. "The man's first name was Sergey. I don't remember his last name. I do, though, remember him as a crazy man who liked to eat bear meat, especially the meat of young bears. He was particularly fond of bears under one year old. He claimed that cub meat was a delicacy. He would go into the forest and look for young bear cubs. He would run the mother bear off, or kill her if need be, then take the cubs home and eat them.

"One day Sergey came upon a mother bear and her two young cubs. He shot and wounded the mother bear and ran her off. He then killed the two young cubs and took them back to his home in the village where he ate them, as he had done with young cubs many times before.

"One year later, Sergey was in the forest, in the same spot, looking for something to eat. After a day, he returned to the village. A few minutes later, people in the village remember seeing a bear enter the town. They were afraid of the bear and fled to their homes. The bear didn't follow them but walked through the village like it knew where it was going. It walked straight to the home of Sergey, the man who liked to eat young cubs.

"Sergey was working in his garden when the bear came

into his yard. The bear attacked and killed him and then went on its way.

Later, people in the village reasoned that the bear had seen the cub-snatcher in the forest and remembered Sergey as the man who took her cubs. She recognized either his face or his scent. Probably both. She then followed Sergey's scent back to the village and right to the man's home. There she attacked and killed him for stealing her cubs.

"None of the villagers were surprised by the attack, as they knew that some day the man would be killed by an angry mother bear. They were surprised, however, by the mother bear's great memory. She only attacked and killed the man who had taken her cubs. After she had killed this man, she left the village and did not attack anyone else."

CHAPTER 23

THEY'RE ALL HEART AND DETERMINATION

ONE OF THE THINGS I liked about taking clients on hunting or fishing trips was watching the excitement on their faces when they caught a big fish or bagged a nice animal. I was just as excited as if I had taken the critter myself. Many clients told me their trip was something they had dreamed about their entire life, and that I helped make that dream come true.

One of the things I was proudest of in my years of taking people on big game hunts to Russia was helping a quadriplegic guy take a record book brown bear in 2004.

Chris Whitley from Crestview, Florida, had been hit by a drunken driver when he was 17. Relegated to spending the rest of his life in a wheelchair did not dampen his enthusiasm for the outdoors. He adapted and continued his hunting passion.

When he called me about doing a brown bear hunt, he told me he was a quadriplegic and wondered if we could help him fulfill his dream of taking a big brown bear, given his limitations. He told me a heartwarming story of a guide who carried him on his back, up the side of a mountain, to shoot a mountain lion. I told him my guides would work just as hard and would figure out a way to help him make his dream come true.

They did. I was extremely proud of their efforts. They did such a good job of positioning Whitley along the bank of a salmon stream the bears were traversing that he was even able to pass up several bears before shooting a big brown in the nine-foot class.

As far as we know, he is the only quadriplegic in the world ever to shoot a big brown bear.

I've taken many older hunters in their 70s and 80s on these hunts as well. Their last big hurrah, they tell me. And I've also taken a lot of youngsters. These father/son and father/daughter hunts are especially rewarding. Creating a lifetime of memories for a kid and his or her dad is priceless.

While we have had a number of fathers and sons on these hunts, usually the son is in his 20s or older. We even took a 60-year-old son and his 81-year-old father on a hunt. The youngest brown bear hunter to go with us to Russia was 13-year-old Noel Hilty, of Fenton, Michigan. Our oldest hunter was 83-year-old Royce McNeill from Charlotte, North Carolina.

Noel's schoolteacher wanted him to do an independent study on Russia while he was gone from class for nearly two weeks. Earlier, I had suggested to Noel's father, Loren, that his son keep a daily diary on this trip. It's something I had my son, Corey, do when he was 13 and I took him on a fly-in fishing trip to Canada. It's always interesting to see a trip like this through the eyes of a youngster.

Noel did just that. Here are excerpts from his journal:

* * *

Mom, because I can't send a letter out, I am keeping a journal of everything I did. Thank you and to everyone that made it possible for me to have this experience. Your son, Noel.

1st Day

I am told by the guide that I'm the youngest hunter to book this hunt for brown bear. It gets dark here at 11:00, later than at home. We had flown here during the past 20 hours from Detroit to Chicago to Frankfurt, Germany, and then to Moscow, Russia. Also checked our rifles at customs. We checked into the hotel and on the evening of their Victory Day celebration, we took a walk down the main street of Moscow.

2nd Day

Today another flight took us to Petropavlovsk on the Kamchatka Peninsula on the east side of Russia. A helicopter picked us up and took us to camp. As soon as we got to camp, we asked if we could go hunting and were told yes. Behind the camp, large solid white hares ran from us and we also saw bear tracks within one-quarter mile from camp.

About three miles behind the camp, the guides spotted three bears on a hillside and my dad got a brown bear. Vodka was poured on the bear's head as a sign of respect to the bear and its family. For dinner we had squid salad, pasta with meatballs and pickled garlic greens.

3rd Day

Got up early and headed out. The night before was rainy and softened the snow. Saw one bear but it was small. The early part wasn't bad but by half day we got stuck next to a stream for 1-½ hours. While following a large bear track, we got stuck two more times and the last time was bad. Tonight my feet swelled and the cook put vodka on them. For dinner we had reindeer, squid, and biscuits with a cabbage center.

4th Day

Got an early start, cold, and conditions were perfect. Bear tracks were every quarter mile for 15 miles. On a plateau on Andiey (a volcano that's been extinct for millions of years) we came upon my bear. Its size was obvious and I was happy to get it. Also saw a wood grouse, which is on the Red List for extinction. Vodka was poured on my bear's head, same as my dad's.

While heading back to our cabin, we stopped at the guide's trapping cabin and then helped repair a suspension bridge to cross machines on. Harvested bark for tea-making (hard birch sap). Had a late lunch of cold soup containing meat, corn, and garlic. We have two guides, one interpreter, one cook, and Sergio who lives here 365/24/7.

5th Day
Rain in morning then turning to sun. The sun was strong and burned our faces. We volunteered to fix bridges today. And the dogs were missing today (Mishka and Tiga). American music and movies are big. One mile from camp, we built a bridge and tore out debris to prevent water and ice backup.

6th Day
Day started with rain and heavy winds. Later in the day we were told spring has started. Rivers were starting to swell. We were told that good hunting weather had been given to good people. Helicopter will try to pick us up tomorrow. Some dogs were missing two days. Sergio was worried because he lost dogs to river ice two years ago.

7th Day
Dogs returned overnight. Helicopter won't be able to pick us up because of the fog. Snowmobiles will take us to a utility road. Crossed a river on a cable car. On our way back to Petropavlovsk, we stopped at a small village that their only product is pies (meat, wild berry, potato). The women did not leave their cart unattended. Different shifts kept them open 365/24/7.

8th Day
We walked downtown and to Abachta Bay where a U.S Coast Guard ship had docked to help celebrate their Victory Day. English is spoken by many and prejudice is so far non-existent. For dinner we had fish soup.

9th Day

Because of fog others in group could not get out of camp. Tomorrow we fly out to Moscow for one day of tourist attractions. Small water and veggies in local diets. *Married With Children* is popular there (popular in U.S. 20 years ago). Found out I got the second-biggest bear in group (nine of us total) and only three inches shorter. The weather started to clear and we were hoping for them to come (other hunters). Went to dinner in a really nice restaurant. Got a call saying the others in group are coming. (Finally!) Met our interpreter and her son at hotel and went to Avacha Bay (a very great view). Went back to hotel and went to bed.

10th Day

Woke up at 7:00 a.m. Ate breakfast and proceeded to airport. Will chase sun in flight so after nine-hour flight will land only 1/2 hour after we took off. We almost got younger. Took a taxi to Red Square for sightseeing. Had great dinner at Russia style restaurant with music and great atmosphere.

11th Day

We only flew today. We had breakfast buffet at hotel. (Good food.) I miss my friends and family.

Loren, Noel's father, called to say that an official scorer for SCI had measured Noel's bear. The skull measured just under 26 inches, which will place it at right around 35th in the world record books. Not too shabby for a 13-year-old kid. The only problem he will have during the rest of his hunting career is figuring out how to top something he did when he was just 13years old!

•Thirteen-year-old Noel Hilty poses with his record book brown bear. Noel is believed to be the youngest American hunter, and possibly the youngest hunter ever, to take a Russian brown bear.
(Loren Hilty photo)

EIGHTY-THREE-YEAR-OLD MAN BAGS BIG BROWN BEAR

Our interpreter Masha and I had just gone back into the cook shack to drink a second cup of coffee when we heard a snowmobile rumbling back into camp.

We had just sent off the guys several minutes earlier after an early-morning breakfast. We had watched them load their gear on the sleds, put on their warm hats and jackets, and head down the trail.

"Somebody must have forgotten something," I said. We walked outside to see who was coming back.

Eighty-three-year-old Royce McNeill and his guide motored into camp.

"Forget something, Royce?," I shouted over the roar of the noisy snow machine.

"No, I didn't forget anything." McNeill smiled. "I just shot a bear about 200 yards from camp. The other guides are skinning it now."

"Are you serious? You shot a bear already? We didn't even hear the shot; of course, it's pretty windy and noisy today. You're not pulling my leg? You shot a bear already?"

"I sure did," McNeill said. "By the way, I have a bone to pick with you. This is the second hunt I've been on with you and I still haven't had a chance to be in the woods more than a couple hours. What kind of a hunt is this?"

"A pretty darned good one, I'd say!" I laughed as I gave McNeill a big hug. He had become a good friend over the past two years.

My first contact with McNeill had happened four years earlier. He had called me to set up a hunt when he was 79 years old. He was wound up, so I was surprised when he didn't show up at the airport when we took off for Russia.

When we got to Petropavlovsk, I phoned my wife to see if she had heard anything from McNeill. Something bad must have happened. She told me his wife called to say that McNeill was in the hospital. Apparently on the way to the airport, he had suffered a liver problem and was in bad shape.

When we returned from that trip, I called McNeill to see how he was doing. He told me his liver had given out and he was on the transplant list. "I'm planning to go to Russia with you next spring," he said in an upbeat voice. "What do we have to do to get ready?"

Over the course of the following year, we talked often and made plans for McNeill's second try for a Russian brown bear. We purchased airline tickets, filled out visa applications, bought bear tags, etc.

Then, about a week before the hunt, McNeill called me. "I have bad news," McNeill began. "I won't be able to make the hunt this spring. My wife just passed away."

"I'll be ok. I'm planning on going next spring."

"I'm really sorry to hear that, Royce," I said. "Don't worry about this hunt. I'll get everything I can transferred to next spring."

Two years in a row McNeill had had to cancel due to

serious issues. I was wondering if he would ever make it. He would be 81 by the following spring. He had a bad liver and wasn't getting any younger, but we talked a lot and got ready for attempt number three.

I was really looking forward to meeting McNeill after all the time we had spent on the phone talking and planning. I figured he was a pretty nice guy by how upbeat he was through all his troubles. He was an even nicer guy than I could have imagined.

That night at the dinner table, vodka appeared and toasting began.

"Royce has the camp record for quickest hunt ever," toasted Vasiliy Dolevskiy, head guide at our Kamchatka bear camp. "It took him 15 minutes and 34 seconds to shoot his bear. He's a master hunter."

Everyone raised their glasses and saluted the 83-year-old great-grandfather from North Carolina. A hunt of this magnitude is an accomplishment for any hunter, let alone a hunter of his age. Of course, the 34 seconds was tacked on just to illustrate how quickly McNeill had taken his big brown. It's not often a big game hunt can be measured in minutes and seconds.

The previous year he had tagged a bear after only a 45-minute hunt.

McNeill is one of the oldest and most successful hunters we took to Russia during our 20-plus years of hunting in the Land of the Bear. He also is one of the kindest, most modest, and gentlest human beings I have had the pleasure of working with.

"I've hunted bears with you two years in a row now, but I still haven't hunted more than an hour," McNeill said, referring to the short hunt he had experienced the previous spring. "I want to come back next year and try it again. This time I want to hunt two hours."

"I'll tell the guides to run you in circles until noon," I said, "then take you to the bears."

"You know I don't care about the size of the bear, or whether I even shoot a bear," he responded. "I just come

• *Eighty-three–year-old Royce McNeill with his record book brown bear. Royce is believed to be the oldest American hunter to take a Russian brown bear. (Denny Geurink photo)*

on these hunts to be in camp with you and all these fine people. It's all about the experience, about meeting new people, eating new foods, and learning new customs.

The older you get, the more you understand it's not about shooting something but about the experience. Shooting something is just a bonus."

McNeill wasn't blowing smoke when he said this. He is happy just to be able to enjoy an exciting big game hunt at his age. While most people his age have either passed on or are living in a rest home, McNeill is traveling around the world in search of adventure. It's not hard to understand why the experience is all that matters to him. He knows the true meaning of a hunt. Too many people go into an adventure like this with blinders on, focusing only on shooting something. They miss everything that is going on around them.

I have noticed over the years that guys like McNeill, who don't really care if they shoot something or not, are always the most successful and seem to shoot the biggest bears. The guy who goes into a hunt all anal, with blinders on, concerned only with shooting the biggest bear in camp, usually has the hardest hunt and winds up with the smallest bear. I think it has something to do with "the bear gods smiling on the people who know that a real hunt is the experience" as the Eveny people tell me.

"I just hope I can still feed myself when I'm your age," I joked with McNeill, "let alone travel all over the world chasing bears and moose. My hat is off to you. I look forward to sharing another camp with you next spring."

Author's note: McNeill came back the following spring and shot the biggest bear of his life, a bruin that squared over nine feet and made the record book.

It took him only half a day to get this bear. So he wound up taking three Russian brown bears in less than a full day of hunting. God Bless you, Royce! You deserved your success!

EPILOGUE

AS A YOUNGSTER GROWING up in rural Michigan I could never have imagined that a big chunk of my life would be defined by what would happen in, of all places, Russia! Whenever I am introduced at a sport show, banquet, or some other function where I am a guest speaker, it's always, "Denny was one of the first Americans to hunt and fish in Russia." Even when one of my friends introduces me to one of their friends, it's the same; it always comes around to Russia.

Writing this book brought back memories of my time in the Land of the Bear. I found myself shaking my head as I dug through my old notes. It's difficult to believe I actually hunted with the KGB in the old Soviet Union ... or hung out with Apollo astronaut Jim McDivitt, and four-star general and spy plane pilot Earl O'Loughlin ... or went to horse races in Moscow with a colonel in the Russian army ... or slept in a tent in Siberia surrounded by bears and wolves.

When I contacted former clients to discuss this project, to make sure I had my facts in order regarding their expeditions, it often came down to them shaking their heads and saying, "I can't believe I actually went to Russia and did that!"

It's been a wild ride. Witnessing first-hand the transformation of a country from an oppressive, secretive culture to an open, freewheeling society has been fascinating. While a lot has changed in Russia over the past two-plus decades, a lot has remained the same. The biggest changes have occurred in major cities like Moscow and St Petersburg. They have been transformed from old, run-down islands of decay to modern, bustling hubs of tourism and culture. The number of restaurants, night clubs, and high-end hotels that have sprung up to meet the demand of foreign visitors is incredible. Here's a country that once closed its doors to the outside world but has now become one of the world's hottest tourist destinations. Where once you couldn't find a restaurant in Moscow, now it seems there is one on every corner.

When you leave the big cities and get out in rural areas, the changes are less evident and not as dramatic.

When you get out into the really remote areas in Siberia, not much has changed. People here are still living in log cabins and scratching out a living from the land ... and they're still getting eaten by bears.

There's a lot of ballyhoo in our media about Russia's brand of democracy. To be sure, it is different from ours, but it's still in its infancy and is evolving. You have to realize this is a country that was under the rule of a dictator, czar, or communist boss since its inception. Democracy is as foreign to the Russian people as communism is to us.

Many of their political leaders don't like it. When Russians first threw off the yoke of communism, they didn't know how to act. Think of the Russians in the early 1990s as teenagers, growing up under very strict parents, who suddenly turned 21 and were kicked out of the house. As I mentioned earlier, it was somewhat like our Wild West in the mid to late 1800s. Nobody knew who was in charge; nobody really cared.

That's what made our early expeditions so mind blowing. To watch the total rebirth of a country first-hand has been very special to me. While the transformation is still underway, Russia is a whole lot different and a whole lot more stable than it was two-plus decades ago.

Of course, the big attraction for me and the thousand or so clients I have taken with me to Russia is the plethora of wild game animals found in Russia. Besides boasting huge regions of trackless wilderness, the fact that the common, ordinary Russian citizen was not allowed to own a gun under the communist system (they didn't want an armed populace that could overthrow the government, which it surely would have) meant there was very little hunting taking place. This translates into a large, harvestable population of game.

We felt really good about the money we pumped into the local economy by way of hiring local guides, cooks and interpreters; buying food locally; staying in local hotels, etc., plus giving the meat to the villagers. Many years we pumped more than half a million dollars into the economy.

We also are proud of the fact that we helped reduce poaching and contributed to sound management of game populations by making the animals a recognized valuable and renewable resource. Scientists have proven that if managed properly, game animals are an extremely renewable food source like grain, fruit or vegetable products. We helped demonstrate this.

Like any hunting or fishing trip, the harvesting of game is just the icing on the cake. The experience itself, and the people with whom you enjoy the experience, are the most important part of the trip. Visiting new places, seeing new sights, meeting new people, eating new foods, these are the things that count.

That's what I take away from my many years in the Siberian wilderness. I feel privileged to have been in the right place at the right time on history's time line.

Back in the Saddle Again...

Denny admitted that he was a failure at retirement and his palms still itched when thinking of hunting Russian brown bears and moose. He said he missed the business and traveling to Russia and the friends he had there. So after much deliberation, he bought back the business he sold in 2011 and is once again going great guns.

Go to his website – **www.dgoa.com** -- to learn more about his hunts, pricing, what's included and what's not.

The "On Target" Series of Outdoor Books
from Target Communications Outdoor Books

UNDERSTANDING WINNING ARCHERY, Hall of Fame Commemorative Edition, by Al Henderson, coach of the 1976 U.S. Olympic Archery Team. Mental control means better shooting results, easier archery gear set-up and tuning, more-productive practices, and winning archer – target, field and hunting.
122 pages. ISBN: 0-913305-20-0. $12.95

TAKING TROPHY WHITETAILS, by Bob Fratzke with Glenn Helgeland. In-depth, detailed information on year-round scouting, and its huge payoff, scrape hunting, rut hunting,, late-season hunting, camo, use of scents, mock scrapes and licking branches.
140 pages. ISBN: 0-913305-02-2. $10.95

TO HECK WITH GRAVY wild game cookbook, by Glenn & Judy Helgeland. Great meals from quick, easy recipes; don't be tied to the kitchen. Includes 209 recipes – roasts, steaks, marinades, soups/stews, ground meat, fish, birds. Plus field dressing, meat handling/processing tips, spice charts, low sodium diet tips.
120 pages. ISBN: 0-913305-05-7. $12.95

TASTY JERKY RECIPES, by Glenn & Judy Helgeland. Spicy, mild, sweet and no-sodium recipes for three meat cut thicknesses and tendernesses; gives three different tastes for each recipe.
$2.00 plus stamped, self-addressed #10 return envelope

TUNING YOUR COMPOUND BOW (5th Edition), by Larry Wise. If you shoot a compound bow, this book belongs in your tackle box! Round wheel, single cam and super cam set-up and tuning chapters, making/serving/repairing strings and cables, pre-use bow preparation, draw stroke, power stroke, shooting from the valley, fine tuning, test shooting, tuning fast-flight cable systems, building and tuning aluminum and carbon arrows. Includes a chapter on asymmetrical (hybrid) cams, an extensive chapter on 3D, tuning and shooting for bowhunting, and updated cam materials on all cam systems.
146 pages. ISBN: 0-913305-19-7. $13.95

TUNING & SILENCING YOUR BOWHUNTING SHOOTING SYSTEM
(3rd Edition), by Larry Wise. Problem-solving info on fitting bow (compound, recurve, longbow) to your body style and shooting form; broadhead effects on arrow flight; noise reduction throughout entire system; aiming/shooting strategy; proper practice; plus much of the compound set-up and tuning info in Tuning Your Compound Bow.
170 pages. ISBN: 0-913305-16-2. $13.95

BECOME THE ARROW (The Art of Modern Barebow Shooting), by famed archery trick shot Byron Ferguson with Glenn Helgeland. Details the 'become the arrow' philosophy; explains how to visualize arrow flight path and sight picture; shooting form practice and mental exercises; tuning for barebow shooting, bowhunting details and more.
Book -- 112 pages. ISBN: 0-913305-09-X. $13.95
Video (VHS 45 minutes). UPC 8-29493-12467-9. $19.95

THE WILD PANTRY wild game cookbook, by Glenn & Judy Helgeland. 200-plus recipes (steaks, roasts, goulash, stews, Mexican, jerky, sausages (patties, links, summer, etc.); mostly venison, but upland birds, fish, waterfowl, too. You will enjoy the stories and anecdotes about wonderful (and some not-so-wonderful) wild game cooking experiences and meals.
156 pages. ISBN: 0913305-13-8. $12.95

CORE ARCHERY, by Larry Wise. Learn proper back tension and much more. This is a systematic set of shooting form steps built around the proper use of your skeleton. Throughout each form step, the governing theme is to maintain skeleton and minimize muscle effort for maximum efficiency. If you do this, your form will be energy efficient, fatigue resistant and highly repeatable.
128 pages. ISBN: 0-913305-18-9. $13.95

NEW! THE BEAR HUNTING OBSESSION OF A DRIVEN MAN, by Bill Wiesner Jr. and Glenn Helgeland. Ten hunting how-to chapters and 10 memoir chapters. How-to chapters include black bear natural history; distribution, population & record book entry totals (by state and province); hunting gear (rifle, slug gun, handgun, muzzleloader, bow, crossbow), camo, and other items; hunting from ground blinds; hunting styles (D-I-Y, guided, hounds, spot-and-stalk); scouting; baiting and scents; new twists (food plots, calling, decoying); the shot (before, during, after); care of hide for taxidermy; care of meat (processing, freezing, recipes).
172 pages. ISBN: 978-0-913305-11-9. $19.95

NEW! IN THE LAND OF THE BEAR, by Denny Geurink. Danger and adventure hunting brown bears and moose in Russia's forbidding Siberia. Geurink was the first American guide/outfitter in Siberia, spending spring and fall for nearly 25 years in a strange land among a foreign culture, guiding clients to huge brown bear (largest and most aggressive in the world, and more of them than anywhere else) and huge-antlered moose. An inside look at the excitement (hunting with the KGB, etc.), mystery, danger and adventure of hunting and traveling in Russia in the last decade of the Twentieth Century and first two decades of this century, a time of Russian political and cultural turmoil. Chapters on the Siberian people, their culture, their food, and the dangers brown bears pose in the daily lives of rural people. In addition to hair-raising adventure stories of bear-hunter interaction, there is historical perspective of what was happening politically in Russia at that time, how it affected hunting opportunities, and presents inside info about how the people lived, worked, survived ... and what they thought of Americans.
294 pages. ISBN #: 978-0-913305-17-1 $21.95